HITLER'S MASTER OF THE
DARK ARTS

HITLER'S MASTER OF THE
DARK ARTS

Himmler's Black Knights
and the Occult Origins of the SS

Bill Yenne

ZENITH PRESS

First published in 2010 by Zenith Press, an imprint of MBI Publishing Company, 400 First Avenue North, Suite 300, Minneapolis, MN 55401 USA

Zenith Press titles are also available at discounts in bulk quantity for industrial or sales-promotional use. For details write to Special Sales Manager at MBI Publishing Company, 400 First Avenue North, Suite 300, Minneapolis, MN 55401 USA.

To find out more about our books, join us online at www.zenithpress.com.

Layout by Diana Boger
Cover design by Simon Larkin

Printed in China

LIBRARY OF CONGRESS CATALOGING-IN-PUBLICATION DATA
Yenne, Bill, 1949
    Hitler's master of the dark arts: Himmler's black knights and the occult origins of the SS / Bill Yenne.
        p. cm.
    Includes bibliographical references and index
    ISBN 978-0-7603-3778-3 (hbk. w/jkt)
    1. Himmler, Heinrich, 1900-1945. 2. Nationalsozialistische Deutsche Arbeiter-Partei. Schutzstaffel—History. 3. Nazis — Biography. 4. Cults — Political aspects—Germany—History—20th century. 5. Paganism—Political aspects—Germany—History—20th century. 6. Occultism—Political aspects—Germany—History—20th century. 7. Knights and knighthood—Political aspects—Germany—History—20th century. 8. Germany—Politics and government—1933-1945. 9. Political culture—Germany—History—20th century. 10. Germany—History, Military—20th century. I. Title.
    DD247.H46Y46 2010
    943.086—dc22   2010009820

CREDITS
On the cover: *U.S. National Archives*
On the back cover: Himmler inspects Slavic Red Army prisoners, somewhere on the Eastern Front, circa 1941. *U.S. National Archives*

This man, Hitler's evil spirit, cold, calculating and ambitious, was undoubtedly the most purposeful and most unscrupulous figure in the Third Reich.

—General der Infanterie Friedrich Hossbach (longtime military adjutant to Adolf Hitler), from *Zwischen Wehrmacht und Hitler*, 1949

He [Himmler] seemed like a man from another planet.

—General Heinz Guderian (chief of staff of the German army and the architect of blitzkrieg tactics)

I had never been able to look Heinrich Himmler straight in the eye. His eyes were always hooded, blinking behind his pince-nez. Now, however, when I could see them gazing at me from the photograph and I thought I could detect one thing in them—malice.

—Alfred Rosenberg (Reich minister for the East and a key architect of Nazi ideology)

This Germanic Reich needs the Order of the SS. It needs it

Contents

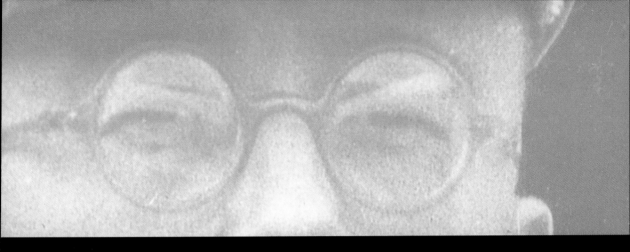

Introduction

THE NAZIS WERE an evil cult.

Few people will argue with this notion in the metaphorical sense. The political movement that seized control of one of the world's largest industrialized nations in the 1930s and carried the world into its most destructive war can certainly be characterized as being evil. But can the Nazis really be characterized as a cult?

Webster's dictionary, which we always consult on matters of semantics, tells us that a cult is a system of religious rituals that involves an obsessive devotion to a person, principle, or ideal. The Nazi Party, or the *Nationalsozialistische Deutsche Arbeiterpartei* (National Socialist German Workers' Party), began not explicitly as a religion, but as a political party. However, this party did indeed morph into a personality cult devoted excessively to one person, Adolf Hitler. But can the Nazis really be characterized as a cult in the sense of their being a religious movement?

In fact, the doctrinal underpinnings of the Nazi cult were very much drawn from a mystical dogma that had its own roots in ancient spiritual beliefs. This dogma had been forming in the late nineteenth and early twentieth centuries from a swirling mass of ideas, concepts, and metaphysical currents that were flowing through Europe in those days. Guided by the Viennese prophets Guido von List and Jörg Lanz von Liebenfels (both of whom had added "von" to their names for an air of nobility), the creed preceded the Nazis. It had originated, these so-called prophets said, long, long ago, in the misty distant past, in a cold and icy place that some would later call Thule. Paraphrasing and borrowing loosely from ancient Scandinavian scriptures, these prophets told

Heinrich Luitpold Himmler, Reichsführer SS (1900–1945)
U.S. National Archives

1

of gods and of heroic supermen, who were gods themselves and who were the progenitors of a superrace. This idea, which became an ideal, infused a generation with the belief that their race had its roots among the god-men.

At the same time that this mystical dogma was congealing, a pseudoscientific culture filled with strange theories and half-proven half-truths emerged to provide what some would argue to be a concrete foundation upon which this supernatural dogma could rest.

What happened next in those turbulent times after the first world war was a fusion of this pagan mystical nostalgia with a nationalist nostalgia.

Into the political maelstrom that was the Germany of the early 1920s came the Nazis, who spoke nostalgically of a golden political and military past that had been stripped from the nation and from the Germanic people by their defeat in World War I. Within the movement that congealed into the Nazi Party, there was the need to sanctify the uniqueness of the Germanic people and their transcendent superiority above all others. What better dogma than the belief in the Germanic people being descended from a race of god-men?

Adolf Hitler, a 1941 portrait in charcoal by Conrad Hommel.
U.S. Army art collection

Into the Nazi Party came the silver-tongued orator who would make it all happen politically—Adolf Hitler.

And into the Nazi Party, there soon came the man who truly believed in the complex notion of the Germanic peoples as the chosen people, as the descendants of the god-men. This man was Heinrich Himmler.

In the decade after Hitler brought the Nazis to power politically, Himmler crafted a state religion, complete with the trappings of creed and ritual, which elevated one race to superhuman status. Over time, Himmler became so obsessed with the ideal of Germanic superiority that he created a mechanism by which Germany and all of the land that it conquered in World War II would be cleansed of races that he considered inferior, people whom he considered so subordinate as to be unworthy of life itself.

As we look back today on the Third Reich of the 1930s, we are looking into a dream world on the threshold of becoming the nightmare world of the 1940s—the nightmare of World War II and of the Holocaust. Nazi Germany was like a scene from a fantasy film. Adolf Hitler was the evil emperor, ruling his kingdom with an iron fist from a dark and stony castle. In the shadows behind the emperor's throne, whispering in the ear of the ruler, is the evil shaman, the evil sorcerer, the perpetrator and guardian of the canon law upon which the empire is based—Heinrich Himmler.

Before them stand fierce, helmeted warriors—the black knights of Himmler's *Schutzstaffel* (SS), a special class of warriors defined by race and blood. They were handpicked as the most racially Germanic of Germans. In Himmler's mind, they were Germany's tangible link with the primordial warriors, who were both supermen and gods, and with a future ruling class that would last for a thousand years. Even today, the image of an SS storm trooper in full regalia causes chills. They were the ruthless true believers, inspired by that witch's brew that Himmler stirred in his caldron, using a recipe that was cribbed from a conglomeration of arcane sources and the doctrines of the prophets List and Lanz.

Hitler was the charismatic madman who brought Nazism to power. Himmler was the ruthless figure in the shadows, the man who took the philosophies that were at the roots of Nazism and methodically shaped and codified them. Himmler is the man whom General Heinrich Hossbach described as "Hitler's evil spirit, cold, calculating and ambitious . . . undoubtedly the most purposeful and most unscrupulous figure in the Third Reich."

CHAPTER 1

Darkest Beginnings

———

HEINRICH I, KING OF THE GERMANS, was born in Memleben in Saxony in the year 876, a turbulent time often referred to as the Dark Ages. It was an age of wars, of dark, cold castles, of blazing bonfires and stark banners.

The son of Otto, duke of Saxony, and his wife, Hedwiga, a descendant of Charlemagne, Heinrich had been destined for greatness. He succeeded his father as duke in 912, and four years later he was crowned the first king of the Germans. As the originator of the medieval German state, Heinrich remained on the throne until his death in 936, but his memory would live on in the chronicles of German national identity.

Heinrich Himmler, born over a millennium later just 250 miles south of Memleben in Munich, capital of the German state of Bavaria, fancied himself a reincarnation of Heinrich I. He considered himself to have been reborn in 1900, called again to be an important, even majestic, figure in the chronicles of German national identity.

At the dawn of a century that many felt would be a golden age of technological promise, this Heinrich played a pivotal role in plunging the promising century into what most historians agree was a true dark age. This Heinrich would help to re-create a medieval world of dark, cold castles, of blazing bonfires and stark banners—and the greatest and bloodiest war the world had yet seen.

4

Charlemagne (left) defeated the Saxons and resettled Franks in their lands. A millennium later, Himmler resettled Völksdeutsche peasants in the lands of Slavic peasants in the conquered Ukraine. Otto I (right), son of Heinrich I, ruled the Holy Roman Empire. They were memorialized on SS Feldpost postage stamps issued in occupied Flanders. The languages on the stamp are Flemish and German. *Collection of Kris Simoens, used by permission*

COMING INTO THE WORLD on October 7, 1900, Heinrich Luitpold Himmler was not of noble birth, although his father had once tutored Prince Heinrich of the house of Wittelsbach, Bavaria's royal family, and the sixteen-year-old prince became the young Himmler's godfather and name-sake. Heinrich was the middle child of schoolteacher Joseph Gebhard Himmler and Anna Maria Himmler, née Heyder, the daughter of a Regensberg merchant. His older brother, Gebhard Ludwig, was born July 29, 1898, and his younger brother, Ernst Hermann, was born two days before Christmas in December 1905.

When the boys were young, Joseph took a job as headmaster at the Wittelsbacher Gymnasium in Landshut, about fifty miles northeast of Munich. Heinrich Himmler grew up here, in a comfortable and secure middle-class home, an environment where there was ample opportunity for daydreaming. Heinrich's daydreams turned to the glorious days of old, to the days of castles and banners and of Heinrich I.

Known as the Fowler, or *der Vogler,* because he was netting small birds when informed he had been picked to be king, Heinrich I was a true leader, a man who inspired his subjects—or at least the nobility among them—to elevate him to the throne. The twentieth-century Heinrich Luitpold Himmler inspired through inducing an unprecedented measure of mortal dread.

Heinrich I was a father figure of German national identity, and he was the father of Otto I, known as Otto the Great, who in 962 was crowned emperor of what would be called the Holy Roman Empire. As emperor, Otto was the first ruler of a church-sanctioned empire that included much of what is now Germany and Austria, as well as adjacent lands and even parts of Italy.

In Heinrich Himmler's mind, the historical origins of the German identity stretched back into distant, murky mythology. Himmler imagined the mystical time before the church wielded both political and ecclesiastical power in northern Europe, a place where ancient Nordic warrior princes walked among the gods and iron weapons were forged in the fires that belched from the center of the earth. Most boys outgrow such fantasy worlds, but some remain within their fabricated universe, living in a comfortable place away from the disappointments of reality. Such was the case with the reborn Heinrich.

Known until his twenties as Heini, the young Himmler grew up in a nice home just down the hill from Landshut's most imposing landmark, the thirteenth-century Burg Trusnitz. Staring each day at this old stone castle that overlooked a bend in the Isar River, Himmler probably imagined himself living near the Rhine, the mother river of Germanic folklore, as part of the seminal legends of Germany. He probably fantasized about the *Nibelungenlied,* the ancient German epic whose central character, Siegfried, was the greatest German warrior of them all.

Like his interest in Heinrich I, Himmler's interest in artifacts of the past was not that of the archeologist. He cared not for what could be learned from the past but, rather, for what he could draw from his fantasy world and read into the past.

Though he was raised as a Catholic and attended mass regularly until his midtwenties, Himmler was an early convert to the pagan creed of Heinrich I's ancestors. It certainly suited his sensibilities to rhapsodize less about Jesus Christ delivering the Sermon on the Mount than about Wotan, the chief deity of Nordic paganism, seated in his rugged mountaintop abode. Called Ygg or Odin in Old Norse, Wotan in Old High German, and many other names across the mythology of ancient northern Europe, this god of gods holds the portfolios of wisdom, war, and death—as well as of victory and deception. In this ancient world, at the beginning of time itself, Wotan reigned with his earth-goddess wife, Jörd, and they beget a son, Thor (in German, Donar or Donner). With his fiery red hair and beard, Thor became an enduring figure in Norse mythology. The powerful god of thunder, Thor wielded an enormous hammer called a *mjöllnir,* and he was the hero of many tales preserved in the ancient Nordic scriptures known as the Eddas.

Wotan and Thor, as well as their mythic extended families, became part of the ancient folklore in Germany and Austria, and in the region from Britain to Scandinavia. Like the Greek and Roman gods and goddesses, they remained as integral parts of the literature and culture of Europe long after the arrival of Christianity. Indeed, like those of Greek and Roman deities, their names remain alive in popular culture to this day (and in the days of the week: Wednesday and Thursday).

The image of Wotan seated, with his pair of wolves beside him, on his golden throne at Asgard has been a part of Nordic folklore for millennia. Donald MacKenzie, writing in 1912 in *Teutonic Myth and Legend,* describes the great city of the gods as standing on "a holy island in the midst of

Heinrich I receives word in 919 that he is to be the first king of Germany. The painting is by Willy Pogany, a popular book illustrator in the late nineteenth century. *Author's collection*

a dark broad river flowing from the thunder vapors that rise through the great World tree from Hvergelmer, 'the roaring cauldron,' the mother of waters. The river is ever troubled with eddies and fierce currents, and above it hover darkly thick banks of kindling mist called 'Black Terror Gleam,' from which leap everlastingly tongues of [lightning] filling the air and darting like white froth from whirling billows."

Such imagery, with its hammers, thunder, and ferocity, could easily have been drawn from the sorts of twenty-first-century fantasy films and video games that attract young boys today. It certainly inspired the impressionable imagination of the young Himmler. He saw Asgard's "dark and lofty wall" in the walls of Burg Trusnitz, where he had acted out his own naive pagan fantasies as a child.

The slight boy with the primeval imagination was a soft child, a poor athlete, and a mediocre student who overcompensated for his shortcomings through cunning. At school, Himmler spied on fellow students for his father, the principal. In fact, his deviousness apparently astonished even the elder Himmler. In an interview with the *Berlin Kurier,* reprinted in the *New York Times* in June 1947, a former classmate, Hans Hirthammer, recalled that the strict headmaster referred to his deceitful son as a "born criminal." Hirthammer added that the boy "delighted in dreaming up ingenious punishments."

Hard of spirit, but delicate of body, Himmler resented his physical weaknesses and his poor eyesight. His early diaries, now in the collection of the Hoover Institution at Stanford University, reveal a young man obsessed with bodybuilding and physical fitness. He was ashamed of his inability, despite his efforts, to bulk up his slender frame. A psychologist might be tempted to suggest that his delight in concocting punishments flowed from the disgrace he felt about his lack of physical prowess.

Shortly before Himmler turned fourteen, the German Empire found itself at war. The Holy Roman Empire, known as the *Reich* (German for "empire"), had outlived its glory days, fragmented, and ceased to exist as Napoleon Bonaparte rose to power at the turn of the sixteenth century. However, by the 1860s, one German state, Prussia, had emerged as one of the most powerful states in Europe. After inflicting a humiliating defeat on France in the Franco-Prussian

War of 1870–1871, Prussia became the nucleus for a new pan-German empire. Prussia's King Wilhelm I was crowned as emperor, or *kaiser,* of a new German empire, and the Second Reich was born.

In 1914, after four decades as the preeminent military power on the European continent, Germany went to war, imagining an easy replay of the Franco-Prussian War in the west and an easy defeat of the bumbling armies of Russia in the east. Allied with Germany was the Austro-Hungarian Empire, a kingdom 25 percent larger than the Second Reich. Though a multiethnic empire, Austro-Hungary was German at its core and at its court in German-speaking Vienna.

The war, then known as the Great War or the World War, and now known as World War I, began in August 1914. Like toppling dominoes, the nations of Europe virtually stumbled over one another with declarations and counter-declarations of war. It began easily, amid pompous pronouncements and unfurled colors, and everyone predicted a quick resolution.

As the war began, Heinrich Himmler followed the progress of German armies intently, fantasizing about being a heroic warrior himself. When he saw troops marching near Landshut, he confided in his diary that he longed to "join in." When his brother Gebhard enlisted in 1915, he was deeply jealous. Himmler also watched as his noble namesake, Prince Heinrich, went off to war and imagined him fighting bravely, which he actually did. However, exactly one month after Heinrich Himmler turned sixteen, his prince died a hero's death, shot down by a sniper in Transylvania.

The duplicitous boy with the soft hands reached his late teens as the war reached its climax. By 1918, the enthusiastic days of banners and glory had been superseded on German streets by the harsh reality of wounded veterans, food shortages, and bad news from the front. Nevertheless, the middle son of the stern schoolmaster still hung on to dreams of glory.

Seeing his middle son yearning for the military life, the elder Himmler pulled some strings with his friends in the Bavarian court in June 1917, and got young Heini on the list for future army-officer candidate school. In the meantime, the young Himmler had apparently joined the 11th Bavarian Infantry Regiment as an enlisted man. He had entertained thoughts of joining the kaiser's navy, but they did not accept recruits who wore glasses. Though he was on the roster of the 11th Regiment, he never served anywhere near the front. His later claims to have led troops in battle were fabricated. He saw no combat and had not completed officer training before the war ended on November 11, 1918.

For Germany, it was a crushing defeat. In losing World War I, the Second Reich imploded. With the failure of the bold spring and summer 1918 offensives crafted by Field Marshal Erich Ludendorff, it was apparent within Germany that defeat was imminent, and social order began to disintegrate. Once the most powerful monarch on the continent of Europe, Kaiser Wilhelm II saw his authority weakened by discontent within the ranks by 1918 and abdicated on November 9—after three decades on the throne as the second and last modern German emperor.

Meanwhile, the Austro-Hungarian Empire also ceased to exist. Austrian emperor Franz Josef I, who had reigned for sixty-eight years, died in 1916, but his grandnephew Karl abdicated within days of Kaiser Wilhelm, as the last of the empire's non-German dominions slipped away. While the Second Reich imploded, the Austro-Hungarian Empire disintegrated. The land ruled from Vienna at the end of 1918 was about 12 percent the size of the empire that was ruled from that city in 1914.

In both countries, especially in Germany, there was a power vacuum into which flowed idealogues from across the political spectrum. On both ends of the spectrum, extremist political parties, some with their own private armies, cropped up. Indeed, numerous alternative parties had been growing in popularity during the latter months of the war, as Germany lost the battlefield initiative and as the kaiser's government grew visibly weaker. Many of these political movements shared an opposition to the war and the monarchy, especially when it became apparent that the war was not winnable. And all shared a dissatisfaction with the postwar status quo after the November armistice.

On the far left, socialists and communists, inspired by the success of the 1917 Bolshevik Revolution in Russia, attempted to seize power. In fact, a socialist government led by the charismatic Kurt Eisner ruled in Bavaria for a few months during the winter of 1918–1919.

Burg Landshut mit Blick auf Cues.

April 17ͭ ͤ ͤ 18ͭ ͤ 1906.

On the right were the nationalists who were nostalgic for the glory days of German military and political power. After decades of being subjects of the most powerful and well-ordered nation in Europe, the nationalists felt the emptiness of disorder and of the remnants of their reich collapsing around them. Many nationalists blamed wartime industrial strikes arranged by communists and socialists for Germany's loss of the war and, therein, the loss of its honor as a nation. Their perception that the communists and socialists had stabbed Germany in the back infuriated the nationalists.

Heinrich Himmler grew up in Landshut on the Isar River, just down the hill from the thirteenth-century Burg Trusnitz. He spent his childhood staring up at this stone castle and imagining a bygone era of ancient heroes, knights, and glory. *Author's collection*

In June 1919, the wartime allies who had defeated Germany in World War I handed German extremists of all stripes a gift upon which they could agree. The Treaty of Versailles, which officially concluded World War I, was so harsh in its humiliating treatment of Germany that it was vilified by both the right and left within Germany. Indeed, the treaty demanded that Germany accept sole responsibility for the war. While Germany had been the principal combatant among the Central Powers, plenty of nations on both sides had a share in the blame for the war having started. Because Germany had been so obviously singled out, the treaty provided the extremist rabble-rousers with a convenient lightning rod to use in their public diatribes.

After a winter of discontent, a conference held in the city of Weimar in August 1919 finally settled on a democratic constitution to replace the German monarchy. Though the Weimar Republic brought some structure to the postwar political void in Germany, it was a compromise that essentially pleased no one. The extremist political parties on both right and left merely added disaffection with the Weimar Republic to their long lists of grievances.

Also on this list was the economic collapse that Germany suffered after the end of the war. It is impossible to exaggerate the impact of this economic crisis. Unemployment and hyperinflation reached staggering levels that have few, if any, comparisons in the history of modern industrialized nations. These conditions crippled and eventually doomed the Weimar Republic.

Heinrich Himmler, meanwhile, was down on the farm. During the summer of 1919, as the Weimar government was formed and as dissatisfaction over Versailles swept the land, he had left the city to work as a farm laborer. Like many a city boy with a summer job on a farm, Himmler was overwhelmed with the rustic charm of rural life. He even joined and became a leader in a short-lived back-to-the-land organization called the *Artamanen Gesellschaft* (Artaman League), which boasted two thousand members in 1924. Himmler and the Artamanen were not alone, nor were the Artamanen the first to want to turn urban wage slaves into jolly peasants. Throughout the late nineteenth century, German intellectuals with too much time on their hands had embraced a romantic notion of the peasantry being a link to the pure, agrarian roots of the German national identity. This idea became the foundation of what had come to be known as the *Völkische*—literally translated as "folkish" or "folksy"— movement. At its simplest, the Völkisch idea was a reaction to the cultural alienation of the post-industrial world. The movement embodied a nostalgia, which appealed to both right and left, for the quaintness of an agrarian past and the village life of simpler, happier times.

Part and parcel with the Völkisch movement was the *Blut und Boden* (blood and soil) ideology in which one's "blood" (ethnicity) is intertwined with one's "soil" (traditional homeland). A corollary to this concept is that those who cultivate the soil of their forefathers have a stronger connection with their ancestral ethnic identity that city dwellers.

The Völkisch movement gained considerable popularity as a subcurrent of Germanic culture and self-identity in both Germany and Austria in the late nineteenth century. (In this, it was not unlike the back-to-the-land movement in the United States of the 1960s, which saw numbers of American college students dropping out and going off—usually for no more than a few warm summer months—to rural agricultural communes.) For Himmler, his own brief stint on the farm ended ignominiously when he suffered a bout with salmonella poisoning.

In September 1919, during the last month of his teenage years, Himmler moved, along with his parents, to Igolstadt, where his father had taken another job as a school principal. A month later, he entered the Universität München (University of Munich), planning to study agriculture.

At the university, he traded in his glasses for a pince-nez, which he thought made him look more important and more grown up. He also went out for fencing, the traditionally favored sport of the German military caste. Indeed, flaunting a dueling scar on one's face had been the premier status symbol among the Prussian elite. However, potential opponents found Himmler a demeaning competitor because he was so small and so frail. Reportedly, he did not earn his scar for three years. At the same time, he turned out to be a poor candidate for college fraternity life because his weak stomach made it hard for him to drink beer.

It was a time when much of Germany had lost its stomach for militarism, but there were still those who yearned for the days when Germany was Europe's superpower. For them, there were opportunities not only in the traditional arts such as fencing, but also in the private militias that sprang up around the political parties.

Like the Second Reich itself, the wartime Imperial German Army had ceased to exist in 1918, and reconstituting it was forbidden by the Treaty of Versailles.

Having come close to losing to the German army, the Allies did *not* want it back. The treaty did, however, allow the Weimar Republic to stand up a glorified national police force, a weak entity known as the *Reichswehr*. This entity could hardly absorb the millions of unemployed veterans who drifted about Germany looking for work and for meaning in their lives. Many of those nostalgic for military life eschewed the feeble Reichswehr to join a number of paramilitary *freikorps* (free corps), militias that sprang up across Germany in the service of the vast left-to-right spread of political ideologies. Among these was the *Reichskreigsflagge,* the nationalist freikorps that Heinrich Himmler would later join.

Among the myriad of nationalist political parties from which to choose, Himmler would later join that which evolved from the *Deutsche Arbeiterpartei* (DAP, or German Workers' Party). The DAP was created in Munich in January 1919 by locksmith Anton Drexler, a former member of the Fatherland Party, and journalist Karl Harrer. In the beginning, the party was just one of many gaggles of malcontents, but over time it would evolve into a monster.

Among the DAP's early members were economist Gottfried Feder and playwright Dietrich Eckart, though it attracted a number of war veterans to its fold. One such veteran was Rudolf Hess, the Egypt-born son of a German merchant. Hess had served with the 7th Bavarian Field Artillery Regiment and briefly as a fighter pilot during the war. He had been awarded the Iron Cross, second class, and came to the DAP having also been a member of the *Eiserne Faust* (Iron Fist) freikorps.

The DAP also attracted a few men who were still in uniform. One in particular was a thirty-year-old Austrian who had earned an Iron Cross, first class, while serving as a corporal with the 16th Bavarian Reserve Regiment. Having joined the postwar Reichswehr, he was assigned to infiltrate and spy on the DAP. However, he instead liked what he saw and officially joined the DAP on September 12, 1919. He was a man with big ideas and a big mouth, and his remarkable gift for oratory caught the attention of the party founders. They recognized that this man would be an extraordinary spokesman for their fledgling political organization.

The man's name was Adolf Hitler.

CHAPTER 2

The Court of the Godfather

T HE MUNICH OF HEINRICH HIMMLER'S university years was a turbulent place, not unlike American college campuses in the late 1960s. In Germany in 1920, as in the United States in 1968, the political turmoil on the streets spilled onto the country's campuses. Political organizations with extreme views and zealous adherents came and went, morphed into alternate incarnations, merged and fractured. Disagreements often turned violent. Demonstrations and counter-demonstrations were common student activities, though, as in the 1960s in the United States, those who stirred up the crowds were often not students.

As on the American campuses of the 1960s, advocates across the spectrum of political beliefs rubbed shoulders on the postwar German and Austrian streets with proponents of a cultural revolution. Just as there were political tides that surged against the post-imperial establishment, there was a cultural tsunami whose 1960s analog would be termed a "counterculture," and whose 1980s analog would be called the "New Age" movement.

In Germany and Austria in the 1920s, there was a resurgence of interest in a broad range of exotic mythological dogmas. As in the 1960s, astrology and numerology became a fashionable coffee-house diversion. However, the postwar Austro-German counterculture was merely a flowering of an under-current that had been rippling through the salons of the educated middle class throughout the latter nineteenth century. During this Germanic "New Age,"

Guido Karl Anton List (1848–1919), who called himself Guido von List, was the godfather of Völkisch Germanic mysticism in the early twentieth century. He was also the creator of the Armanen Futharkh runic system, which he claimed to have received in a vision. Born in Vienna, he had followers throughout Germany as well as Austria. *Author's collection*

there had been a growing interest in mysticism and alternative theologies, from Rosicrucianism to Kaballah, from Buddhism to ancient Egyptian beliefs—and especially the old paganism of Nordic gods and heroes. Indeed, the latter had been current in German pop culture since the 1870s, when composer Richard Wagner had popularized the tales in his grandiose operatic cycle *Der Ring des Nibelungen (The Ring of the Nibelung)*. This mammoth work, which became a favorite of the Völkisch movement, consisted of four operas: *Das Rheingold (The Rhine Gold), Die Walküre (The Valkyrie), Siegfried,* and *Götterdämmerung (Twilight of the Gods),* the stories of which read like an encyclopedia of Germanic pagan lore. Wagner borrowed from the Eddas and Nibelunglied to craft a four-part tale that includes the great hero Siegfried, as well as Rhine maidens, who guard the hidden gold from which the titular ring was crafted; ugly dwarves; the valkyries (the women warriors of Germanic legend); the primeval earth goddess Erda; and Wotan himself.

While the prewar Germanic New Age had broadly embraced the popular utopian Völkische movement, after the war, the Völkisch ideals were especially resonant among the nationalists. It was not so much that they were keen to get dirt under their fingernails planting beets or cabbage, as it was that they were attracted to the idealistic Völkisch association with German ethnicity. Identification with one's ethnicity is neither uncommon nor inherently negative. The Irish flags that one sees on bumper stickers in Boston around St. Patrick's Day, or the Mexican flags seen on bumper stickers in Los Angeles, are examples of the same Völkisch idea. At its "blut und boden" extreme, however, the Völkische concept can be extrapolated as implying ethnic or racial superiority.

Meanwhile, the dark side of any counterculture contains characters who emerge to exploit an interest that a group may have in a particular doctrine. In the United States of the 1960s, as middle-class children dabbled in esoteric doctrines from witchcraft to Tibetan Tantraism, lifestyle gurus such as Timothy Leary and Richard Alpert used ancient religious doctrine to fashion a widely popular cult religion around psychedelic drugs. While Leary and Alpert had used correlations to mystical aspects of Hinduism and Buddhism to legitimize their psychedelic precepts, many of the prophets in the German counterculture of the 1920s embraced aspects of the ancient roots of Germanic paganism. While Leary quoted liberally from the Bhagavad Gita, the seminal text of Hinduism, Völkisch gurus delved into the ancient myths and lore from the Eddas and the Nibelunglied, as well as tales of the ancient Nordic pantheon.

The Timothy Leary of the Austro-German counterculture at the turn of the century was a man who called himself Guido von List. He was born Guido Karl Anton List in Vienna on October 5, 1848, fifty-two years and two days before the birth of Heinrich Himmler. Similar to Himmler's claim of being a reborn royal, List later added the aristocratic "von" to his name to pump up his prestige. To legitimize such a claim to aristocracy, he insisted that he was descended from Burckhardt von List, a twelfth-century knight who is mentioned in *Germania Topo-Chrono-Stemmato-Graphica* by Gabriel Bucelinuss, published in Nuremberg (Nürnberg in German) in the seventeenth century.

Like Heinrich Himmler, Guido List was born into comfortable middle-class circumstances that permitted him opportunities for daydreaming and for his imagination to create an alternate universe. Guido's father, Karl Anton List, was a well-to-do leather merchant. Just as Himmler's fantasies were fueled by his views of the cold stone walls of Burg Trusnitz, the fires of List's later obsession for Nordic paganism were stoked by a field trip to the catacombs beneath the city of Vienna at the age of fourteen. Within these damp and musty cellars, specifically beneath the old city post office, his tour group came to an old altar, which he decided, or was told, had actually originated as a shrine for the worship of Wotan.

"We climbed down, and everything I saw and felt excited me with a kind of power that today I am no longer able to experience," List wrote in his 1891 book *Deutsch-Mythologische Landschaftsbilder.* "At that point my excitement was raised to fever pitch, and before this altar I proclaimed out loud this ceremonial vow: 'Whenever I get big, I will build a Temple to Wotan!' I was, of course, laughed at, as a few members of the party said that a child did not belong in such a place." But List had found his personal connection with the hallowed being he believed presided over the very roots of the Germanic identity.

Like Himmler, List was one of those excitable boys who did not discard the nineteenth-century equivalent of *Dungeons and Dragons* fantasies as he became a man. Though he dutifully went into his father's leather business, List also freelanced as a writer, initially penning articles mainly for outdoors and mountaineering publications such as the *Neue Deutsche Alpenzeitung,* the German alpine newspaper. As an avid outdoorsman, List readily adopted the Völkische rural romanticism, preferring field and stream to the noise and bustle of modern city life. After his father died in 1877, List turned to journalism full time and began writing more and more about metaphysics and mysticism, including spirits and sprites that he imagined inhabiting the natural world. (It was in the following year that he began occasionally inserting the "von" into his name, although he would not use it consistently until after the turn of the century.) List's mystical writings were increasingly focused on Völkische themes and on the origins of the German identity, which he traced back to Wotan himself. He came to believe in a primeval cult of priests called *Armanen,* whose powers flowed directly from Wotan. His source for the term "Armanen" was a recent translation of the book *De Origine et Situ Germanorum (The Origin and Situation of the Germans),* written by the Roman historian Gaius Cornelius Tacitus in about AD 98. In the book, Tacitus describes Germanic tribes living beyond the boundaries of the Roman Empire, calling them Irminones. From "Irminones," List derived "Armanen" as the name of the primeval priestly cult of the Germans.

In his spare time, List also devoted his energy to writing a novel entitled *Carnuntum,* after the ancient Roman military base located near Vienna and which List liked to visit. In this book, which was not published until 1887, he explored a culture clash between the Romans and his romantically idealistic interpretation of the Völkische Germanic civilization. Having read Tacitus, he was especially proud of the Irminones, the Germans who lived beyond the fringes of Roman civilization.

Like Heinrich Himmler, Guido List had been raised Catholic, but he came to regard Christianity, especially Roman Catholicism, as a perpetuation of the Roman occupation of northern Europe, and the Christian God as a pretender to Wotan's rightful throne.

Though he nurtured a fondness for the simple Völkische life of the mountains and rural villages, List found plenty of time to rub shoulders in the circles of Viennese literati, including fellow poets and authors who were riding the crest of the romantic revival of metaphysics and mysticism that characterized the late nineteenth-century New Age movement. List was right at home among these people, especially after the success of *Carnuntum,* and later works gave him a prominent place in fashionable Völkische circles. Among his other popular works that perpetuated his enthusiasm for Wotanism and Nordic paganism were *Götterdämmerung (Twilight of the Gods,* 1893), *Walkürenweihe (Valkyries' Initiation,* 1895), and *Der Unbesiegbare (The Invincible,* 1898). In these, he imagined a Völkische utopia while borrowing from Richard Wagner's celebration of the sacred works of Nordic paganism.

It was in the 1880s that List also became interested in the writings of Madame Helena Blavatsky, who, coincidentally, used the term "New Age" in her books. The daughter of a Tsarist military officer, she had been born in 1831 in Ukraine as Elena Petrovna Gan. Because the family traced its origins to German nobility, her name is also seen translated as Helena von Hahn. Like Himmler and List, she grew up with plenty of opportunity to exercise an active imagination. In her case, she became convinced—or at least she successfully convinced others—that she had psychic abilities. However, her youth ended abruptly at age sixteen when she was forced to wed a middle-aged Russian politician named Nikifor Vassilievich

Blavatsky, in Armenia. She skipped town after three months of a reportedly unconsummated marriage and spent the next decade traveling the world from Egypt to Mexico, on her father's dime. During this time, she spent two years living in Tibet, where she was greatly influenced by the same aspects of Buddhist mysticism that would enjoy a revival in Western salons and campuses in the 1960s. In 1873, she arrived in New York, where she made her mark on society. Like List and the gurus of the 1960s, she was soon able to take the mystic beliefs she had come in contact with and adapt them into a sort of cottage industry.

A popular parlor diversion of the Victorian upper middle class was the seance, in which groups of people gathered in darkened rooms to communicate with spirits. These sessions were led by a medium, or spiritualist, who allegedly had the ability to call forth the spirits from "beyond." (This practice, a popular drawing room diversion around the turn of the twentieth century, would be revived and repackaged in the 1980s under the name "channeling.") With her lifelong "psychic gifts" and what she had learned in her travels, Madame Blavatsky became a popular medium on the New York seance scene. Though she was widely criticized as a fraud and a plagiarist, she also had many loyal devotees who supported her and the ideas that she espoused.

In 1875, she started the Theosophical Society, a spiritualist organization that centered on her quasireligion called Theosophy, a word that blends the terms "theology" and "philosophy." Having attracted many important and well-heeled followers to Theosophy, she penned a best-selling book, *Isis Unveiled: A Master Key to the Mysteries of Ancient and Modern Science and Theology.* Published in 1877, the book referenced religious works from the Bible to the Egyptian Book of the Dead, and quoted philosophers and religious figures from Plato to Siddhartha Gautama, the Buddha.

In 1884, during a visit to Germany, she established a German branch of the Theosophical Society under the direction of a German Colonial Office bureaucrat named Wilhelm Hübbe-Schleiden. This gave Theosophy a prominent profile among the myriad of movements, schools of thought, and pseudoreligions that were then bubbling in the meeting places of the Austro-Germanic New Age. By this time, List was paying attention. One tenant of Theosophy in particular resonated with List: Blavatsky's notion of a hierarchy of primordial races of humanity—a hierarchy that Nordic people were at the apogee of.

The idea that humankind had evolved through multiple evolutionary threads was not new to science—the English naturalist Charles Darwin had summarized evolution in his 1859 book *On the Origin of Species*—but neither was the idea that some forms of life are inherently superior to others. Obviously this conceit had driven the institution of slavery for hundreds of years. As nineteenth-century anthropologists studied the differences between human races, it became popular in some quarters to suggest that one race of people was superior to another and that this could be demonstrated scientifically. The French aristocrat and novelist Arthur de Gobineau published *An Essay on the Inequality of the Human Races* several years before Darwin published his book, and it became quite influential in conveying the idea that white people were superior. Meanwhile, in Japan, the same doctrine of superiority was being applied to "pure blooded" Japanese.

Among the various distinct races of humans delineated by early anthropologists was the so-called Aryan race. Today, the Aryan race is usually defined as white northern Europeans, but the term was originally applied more broadly, to the hundreds of ethnicities who speak any of the hundreds of Indo-European languages and dialects. These include the major languages of Europe, as well as those of Iran, northern India, and parts of Central Asia. Those who insist on the term being defined as white northern Europeans would be disappointed to know that the word "Aryan" itself is derived from the term *arya,* implying nobility, which dates back centuries to India and ancient Hindu and Zoroastrian scriptures.

The Aryan race was referred to as the "master race." Initially, "master" may have been applied in the benign scientific sense, as in the phrase "master key," to imply the Indo-European ethnicity was the *source* from which other races may have evolved. However, nineteenth-century ethnocentrists were only too willing to translate "master race" as "superior race." Since, to them, the Aryan race was superior, it naturally followed that Aryans were the master race.

Originally, anthropologists believed that the Aryan race, like the Indo-European linguistic group, originated somewhere in Central Asia. This concept went along with the idea, expressed by medieval Arabic geographers, that there was a *Jabal al-Alsinah,* or "Mountain of Tongues," located somewhere in the Caucasus Mountains.

However, in the late nineteenth century, the theories of Gustaf Kossinna began to gain some traction, especially in Germany, playing into the hands of Guido von List and other Nordic chauvinists. Born in 1858 in Lithuania, Kossinna was an avid student of Indo-European cultural theory and a professor of archaeology at the University of Berlin. Based on his own excavations of neolithic sites, he placed the origin of a particular form of neolithic Indo-European pottery called "corded ware" in northern Germany, extrapolating that the Aryan race and culture originated there. Specifically, he located this point of origin in the north German state of Schleswig Holstein, near the Danish border.

Archeological theories, even if flawed or suspicious, carried a great deal of weight because they were based on things that laymen could actually see and touch. Kossinna could point to his excavations and easily assert that concrete artifacts do not lie. Conversely, the artifacts can say whatever the archeologist or his disciples interpret them to say. Later in the twentieth century, archeology would play a key role in Heinrich Himmler's theories and justification for the primacy of the Aryan race. However, as when he was a child in Landshut, Heinrich's interest in the artifacts of the past was not that of the archeologist. He cared not for what could be learned from the past, but rather for what he could draw from his fantasy world and read *into* the past.

Another nineteenth-century author whose works perpetuated the myth of Aryan superiority was Houston Stewart Chamberlain. He was an upper-class Englishmen who first became enraptured with Völkisch Nordic culture in the 1860s when, as a teenager, he was sent to the spas of Germany to take a "cure" for his frail health. He remained in Germany and became a rabid proponent of Aryan superiority, authoring the influential (in Völkisch circles) *Die Grundlagen des Neunzehnten Jahrhunderts (The Foundations of the Nineteenth Century),* published in 1899. He became a German citizen, a fan of the darker themes of Wagnerian opera, and even married Richard Wagner's daughter, Eva. Among Chamberlain's more unique Aryan theories was that Jesus Christ was part of a Nordic colony in the Middle East that was in conflict with the Jews.

While intellectuals theorized, Madame Blavatsky had gone a step further by turning the idea of racial hierarchy into a quasireligious dogma, placing the Aryans atop a hierarchy of races within the doctrine of Theosophy. The *non*-Aryans, and hence, the secondary and lesser races within her hierarchy, included such people as Africans, Asians, Australian Aborigines, and Semites. The latter group included the Jews, who had long been the object of distrust, hatred, and ethnic enmity throughout Europe.

Jews had been blamed for a variety of misdeeds, ranging from the crucifixion of the Jew who started Christianity to the lending of money. In the case of the latter, it was evidently overlooked by anti-Semites that Jews went into banking because of laws precluding them from real estate ownership and other vocational options that were open to non-Jews. Since well before they were famously persecuted in the Spanish Inquisition of the fifteenth century, Jews had been the target of violence. Though overt state sponsorship of Jewish persecution had faded by the nineteenth century in Western Europe, thousands of Jews in the Russian empire were killed and many more displaced in officially sanctioned pogroms. But while Jews had been disliked and blamed for various societal ills for centuries, what had begun to congeal by the early twentieth century—thanks to men such as Gobineau and Chamberlain—was a "scientific" justification for the belief that Jews were inferior.

List blended his own Völkische and metaphysical beliefs with the theories of Aryan superiority and a Germanic origin of the Aryan race into a doctrine of Germanic racial and ethnic superiority. This he called Armanism, after the Armanen, the ancient priests who he imagined were endowed with their powers by Wotan himself. This doctrine would later be the groundwork for Himmler's secret society of initiates.

In the course of his studies of pagan Nordic lore, List also became especially interested in runes, the ancient alphabets that had originated in northern Europe prior to the adoption of the Latin alphabet around the eighth century. Like

New Age devotees of the late twentieth century, List and others attached special significance to these old alphabets, believing them to embody magical powers. List also liked the fact the use of runes predated the arrival of Christianity in northern Europe. He imagined that the runes had their roots in the earliest forms of Wotan worship, even though the earliest known runes were more or less contemporary with the Bible's New Testament. Like the idea of an ancient Armanen priesthood, runes became a foundation stone of List's Armanen liturgy, providing a vital link between the present and the mystical past.

There are a number of well-known northern European runic alphabets, some dating back to around the first century. Those in Scandinavia are known as *futhark,* or, in Anglo-Saxon, *futhorc.* In Scandinavia and northern Germany, there was originally a twenty-four-character runic alphabet called the Elder Futhark, which was used only by the literate, of whom there was an exclusive few. Again, we find the idea of a select group of initiates with inside information. Later, after the eighth century, a simplified, sixteen-character runic alphabet, called the Younger Futhark, came into use as literacy became more widespread and as the marauding Vikings spread Nordic culture more widely. Even after the acceptance of the Latin alphabet, runic alphabets continued in limited use for several hundred years.

Despite his attraction to the oldness of runes, List created his own, a *new,* twentieth-century runic alphabet, which he called the Armanen Futharkh. List claimed these runes were not fabricated by him, but revealed to him, through his "inner eye." He claimed that the Armanen Futharkh came to him in 1902 during a period of temporary blindness caused by cataract surgery. His insistence that they were from a mysterious time and place gave them an air of legitimacy that they would not have enjoyed if List had admitted that he simply made them up. Just as Himmler was preoccupied with what he could read into archeology, List was interested what he could draw from his fantasy world and read into the Futharks of old, rather than in the Futharks themselves.

There were eighteen runes on List's list, sixteen of them based on those of the Younger Futhark, and two others borrowed from the Anglo-Saxon Futhorc. As List explained, the number eighteen was significant because that is the number of projections of light that can be made using the facets of a hexagonal crystal. In tying his Armanen Runes to crystal structure, he anticipated the crystal-healing movement that was briefly popular during the New Age movement of the 1980s. List eventually summarized his runic theory in his book *Das Geheimnis der Runen (The Secret of the Runes),* which was published in 1908, the same year he turned sixty.

Even before the rune book was published, List was considered an elder statesman of the Völkische New Age movement. With this recognition came calls for the creation of a Guido von List *Gesellschaft,* or Guido von List Society. When the society was officially formed at a ceremony in March 1908, the members included fellow mystics and authors, as well as prominent business leaders such as Friedrich Wannieck and Vienna's mayor, Karl Lueger. By this time, List had devotees throughout the Austro-German New Age circles, and the Guido von List Gesellschaft attracted members from Berlin to Hamburg to Munich.

In 1908, List had made the important transition from a lone theoretician to the centerpiece of a movement—or, perhaps we should say, a cult. Within this cult, List created as inner circle *inside* his circle, a select brotherhood of initiates. They were known, not unexpectedly, as the *Hoher Armanen Orden* ("Higher Armanen Order").

The idea of a formalized circle of chosen elite within the already select organization was hardly new. All major religions have both clerical and lay orders entrusted with certain specified knowledge and responsibilities. Such inner orders also existed in the ancient world and are mentioned by classical historians such as Heredotus, Plutarch, and Pliny the Elder. In modern society, there are also numerous nonreligious fraternal orders and service clubs, ranging from the Masons to the Rotary Club—all with members-only knowledge and the proverbial secret handshake.

Among the lay orders of Christendom were numerous well-known military orders that had secret wisdom, some of which was purported to be mystical. Of special interest to those interested in closed societies with mysterious, secret knowledge are some of the societies that were organized at the time of the Crusades, Europe's "holy wars" against the Muslims holding

Guido von List's Armanen Futharkh Runes

Fa, the first rune of the Armanen Futharkh, is based on the Fe rune of the Younger Futhark and of the Feoh rune Anglo-Saxon Futhorc. It means wealth and corresponds to the Gothic f, or Faihu.

Ur is related to the Younger Futhark rune Ur, meaning "rain," and the Elder Futhark rune Uruz, meaning "wild ox." It corresponds to the Gothic Urus, the letter u.

Thurs is related to the Elder Futhark Thurisaz rune and the Younger Futhark Thurs rune, both meaning "giant." It is similar in shape to the rune Thorn (or Dorn), which means "thorn," in the Anglo-Saxon Futhorc. The rune is identified with the digraph for the phoneme th.

Os is from the Younger Futhark and possibly derived from "Aesir," the plural term for the part of the Nordic pantheon to which both Wotan and Thor belong. In an old Icelandic rune poem, it is stated that Óss is prince of Asgard and lord of Valhalla, identifying him, thus, as Wotan. The rune is identified with the letter a.

Rit, interpreted as meaning "journey" or "ride," is a similarly shaped variant of the Elder Futhark rune Raido, the Younger Futhark rune Reid (or Raeid), and the Anglo-Saxon rune Rad. The runes are all identified with the Gothic letter r, which is called Raida.

Ka is the same as the Younger Futhark rune Kaun, meaning "ulcer." It is considered an equivalent if the Elder Futhark rune Kaunan, meaning "torch," although the shape is different. The Anglo-Saxon rune Cen is an inverted Kaun. These runes are all identified with the Gothic letter k, which is called Kusma.

Hagal is derivative of the Younger Futhark rune Hagal or Hagall, meaning "hail." The runes for "hail" in the Elder Futhark and Anglo-Saxon Futhorc are Hagalaz and Haegl, respectively, and both are dissimilar in shape to Hagal and Hagall. The runes Hagal and Hagall are identified with the letter h. List and his disciples considered Hagal to be the mother rune in his Futharkh and saw it as representative of a hexagonal crystal. The Anglo-Saxon rune Ior, is similar in shape to List's Hagal, but it means "eel."

Nauth is associated with the Younger Futhark rune Naud (or Naudhr), meaning "need." It is similar in shape to the Anglo-Saxon rune Nyd, meaning "need" or "distress," and associated with the letter n.

Is is derived from the Younger Futhark rune Isa, meaning "ice." It is the same as the Elder Futhark Isaz and the Anglo-Saxon Futhorc Is, both meaning "ice." The runes are associated with the Gothic letter i, called Eis, the German word for "ice."

Ar is a variant of the Younger Futhark rune Ar, meaning "year" or "harvest," and is associated with the Elder Futhark rune Jeran (or Jeraz), which has the same meaning, but is shaped differently. The rune is identified with the letter j.

Sig, the eleventh rune, was adopted by Himmler's SS. It is derived from, and is similar to, the Anglo-Saxon Futhorc rune Sigel, the Younger Futhark rune Sol, and the Elder Futhark rune Sôwilô, all of which mean "sun." However, List changed the meaning of his Sig to "victory," after the German word "sieg," which means "victory." In all four runic alphabets, the rune is identified with the letter s.

Tyr is named for the god Tyr, the deity associated with individual heroism. In some ancient legends, he is said to be a son of Wotan. List's rune Tyr is the same as the Younger Futhark rune of the same name, the Elder Futhark Tiwaz, and the Anglo-Saxon Futhorc rune Tir (or Tiw). The rune is identified with the letter t.

Bar is derived from the Younger Futhark rune Bjarken, and it is associated with the similarly shaped Elder Futhark rune Berkanan and the Anglo-Saxon Futhorc rune Beorc. All of these runes mean "birch" or "birch tree" and are associated with the letter b.

Laf is derived from the Younger Futhark rune Logr, meaning "water." It is also similar in appearance to the Anglo-Saxon Futhorc Lagu, meaning "sea" or "lake," and the Elder Futhark rune Laguz (or Laukaz), meaning "lake." It is analogous to the Gothic letter l, called Lagus.

Man is an inverted Armanen rune Yr. Literally meaning "man," it is the equivalent of the Younger Futhark rune Madr, and associated with the dissimilarly shaped Elder Futhark rune Mannaz and Anglo-Saxon Futhorc rune Man, both of which mean "man." All four runes are identified with the letter m.

Yr is an inverted Armanen rune Man. It is derived from the Younger Futhark rune Yr, meaning "yew," and it is an inverted form of the Elder Futhark rune Algiz and Anglo-Saxon rune Eolh, both of which refer to "elk."

Eh is associated with the dissimilar Younger Futhark rune Eh, meaning "horse."

Gibor, the eighteenth rune, has no equivalent among other runic systems, although some have associated it with the somewhat similar Elder Futhark rune Eihwaz and the Anglo-Saxon Futhorc rune Eoh, both of which mean "yew." However, it is much closer in shape to the old Germanic *Wolfsangel* (wolf's hook), a Viking-era magical symbol associated with the Yggdrasil, or ancient Nordic World Tree.

Author's collection

Jerusalem. Notable among these many groups were the Knights Templar and the Teutonic Knights.

The Knights Templar are perhaps the best known, having figured in countless twentieth-century thriller novels, as well as in countless conspiracy theories about lost or hidden wisdom. The order was initially formed early in the twelfth century on the Temple Mount in Jerusalem by French knights who had participated in the First Crusade. Officially sanctioned by the Catholic Church, their mission was to protect pilgrims visiting the holy sites. According to legend, they found and possessed the Holy Grail, the cup from which Jesus Christ drank at the Last Supper and which later held his holy blood, spilled during the Crucifixion. Financed by wealthy patrons in Europe, the Knights Templar grew in power and head count, creating an elaborate financial and banking infrastructure stretching from Jerusalem to Europe. After two centuries, the powerful order came under the suspicion of the church and later was officially persecuted by the church. They were disbanded early in the fourteenth century, but the legend lived on.

The Teutonic Knights, a Germanic order, was of particular interest within the early twentieth-century Austro-German counterculture. Formed late in the twelfth century, the Teutonic Knights were also a well-financed organization. Though they were initially Crusaders, most of their battles were fought against the Slavic people on the southern and eastern rim of the Baltic Sea. Here, they formed a substantial fiefdom, which encompassed much of East Prussia and the modern Baltic states and which reached its greatest extent early in the fifteenth century. The Slavs, like the Jews, would later have a place on the hit list of Heinrich Himmler's secret knighthood.

Himmler, as we shall see, was quite enthralled with Guido von List's idea of the Armanen Orden and the notion of perpetuating a select brotherhood. However, it was the idea of the glorious armed orders, such as the Templars and the Teutonic Knights, that most fired his imagination as he dreamed of an elite corps of exceptional Aryan warriors. With Guido von List's pre-World War I Hoher Armanen Orden, though, the emphasis was strictly on the mystical. They were out for the sort of romps in the countryside with candles and torches and ancient stone edifices that one finds when modern New Age groups greet the sunrise at Stonehenge and like places.

Like many in New Age circles then and now, List and his order picked solstices and equinoxes as times for key events. In June 1911, for example, List and his followers organized a solstice field trip designed to recapture the same sort of goosebumps-down-the-back sensation that List felt in the underground catacombs beneath Vienna when he was a teenager. The elder patriarch led his followers to experience the power and presence of Wotan at subterranean grottos beneath ancient buildings in and around Vienna, as well as at the ruins of Carnuntum. He called these damp, musty shrines by the collective name "Ostara," after the Germanic goddess of rebirth. Known as *Eostre* in Old English, this name is thought to be the origin of the term "Easter," the Christian holiday celebrating the resurrection of Jesus Christ, which is itself superimposed on the pagan celebration of the rebirth of the earth after the winter. The term "Ostara" is still used in reference to modern Wiccan celebrations of the spring equinox.

Also of interest to the early twentieth-century pagans was the observance of *Walpurgisnacht* (Walpurgis Night) on the night of April 30 and May 1 and the festivals celebrating the arrival of spring. The holiday is named for St. Walpurga, an eighth-century English saint who traveled in Germany, because her feast day falls on May 1, but the commemoration predates the arrival of Christianity. In Germany, Walpurgisnacht was traditionally the night when the witches danced with the gods on the highest of the Harz Mountains. Celebrations, often accompanied dramatically by bonfires, are still held throughout northern Europe.

-----Theozoology -----
or the Science of the Sodomite Apelings and the Divine Electron. An introduction to the most ancient and most modern philosophy and a justification of the monarchy and the nobility. With 45 Illustrations.

Dr. Jörg Lanz von Liebenfels

The cover page of an English translation of Jörg Lanz von Liebenfels's bizarre 1905 book, *Theozoologie oder die Kunde von den Sodoms-Äfflingen und dem Götter-Elektron (Theozoology or the Account of the Sodomite Apelings and the Divine Electron).* Lanz concocted a pseudoscience called "Theozoology," writing that Aryans, whom he called *theozoa,* or Gottmenschen (god-men), were actually descended from the gods. Everyone else was descended from sea monsters, hybrid beasts, or "apelings." *Author's collection*

The influence of the Hoher Armanen Orden was such that it became the catalyst for other Völkisch secret societies to materialize out of the dark, polished woodwork in the castles and manor houses of rich, Nordic-centric Germans with time on their hands. One such society was *Germanenorden* (Germanic Order), which was originally formed in 1912 in Berlin. Among its founders was Theodor Fritsch, the author of some especially inflammatory anti-Jewish literature and an outspoken opponent of industrialization, the ills of which he blamed on Jewish businessmen. Like those belonging to List's Armanen Orden, the members of the Germanenorden (a name that, uncannily or deliberately, rhymes with Armanen Orden) worshiped Wotan, rapaciously devoured ancient Germanic literature, staged elaborate solstice rituals, and considered the Aryan race superior. Mainly, they all seemed to admire Guido von List as an esteemed prophet, the godfather of the ideals they cherished.

The popularity of the List Society and the Hoher Armanen Orden was directly attributable to the charisma of Guido von List, but unlike many other cult leaders, before and since, he was not so much the leader of the society that bore his name as its figurehead. While List himself had no aptitude for organization, he was surrounded by others who actually ran the society. Among these was the man who had emerged as, for want of a better term, List's eager understudy, Adolf Josef Lanz.

Like Heinrich Himmler, Lanz was the son of a schoolmaster. Born in Vienna in 1874, he grew up middle class and comfortable. At the age of nineteen, he became a monk of the Cistercian order, took the name "Jörg," and entered the 760-year-old Austrian monastery at Heiligenkreuz (Holy Cross). While here, Lanz proved to be quite diligent in his studies, becoming quite a knowledgeable biblical scholar and an expert in the Latin Vulgate.

Like Guido von List, Lanz received an epiphany about the ancient, mythical roots of the Nordic or Germanic identity while he was meditating on ancient stones that had been touched by his ethnic ancestors. This scrutiny came about in 1894, when he was reflecting upon a thirteenth-century carving that had been unearthed at the monastery. It showed a nobleman standing above a small creature with a long tail and an apparently human head. Lanz interpreted this creature as a subhuman beast. This view was not particularly unusual, insofar as religious buildings all across Europe had been encrusted with gargoyles and grotesques for centuries. However, for Lanz, this one specific image was full of deep meaning. He interpreted it as representing the age-old conflict between *human* goodness and *subhuman* evil.

While pondering this grand struggle, Lanz apparently wandered a trifle from the straight and narrow himself. In 1899, he was asked to leave the Cistercians and Heiligenkreuz for having submitted to the temptation of what is described in the official paperwork as "carnal love" (with whom and under what circumstances is not known). Released from his vows, Lanz was back on the streets of the secular world, looking for meaning in his life. This he found in Theosophy and in the flourishing Austro-German New Age movement—especially in the teachings of Guido von List, whom he first met in the early 1890s.

In List, Lanz saw a man who, like himself, had grown up middle class, but who was, in fact, more special than his mundane origins suggested. Like List, Lanz imagined himself as possessing long-forgotten roots in nobility. Like List, he cast about for a good excuse to be able to insert the aristocratic "von" into his name. He found a fifteenth-century Hans Lanz, who had married a noblewoman, gained title to her property, and later ennobled himself as Lanz von Liebenfels. Though a direct relation to the man was tenuous at best, Adolf Josef "Jörg" Lanz renamed himself as Jörg Lanz von Liebenfels in 1903. He also began bragging, erroneously, that his schoolmaster father was actually a titled baron who had once used the Liebenfels name himself. There are stories that he also changed his birthdate in order to misdirect astrologers.

In the first years of the twentieth century, Lanz was counterintuitively dividing his time between conventional religious scholarship and his growing preoccupation with the counterreligious aspects of the Austro-German New Age movement. On one hand, he was invited to contribute a chapter to *Zur Theologie der Gotischen Bibel,* a scholarly study, involving Jewish as well as Christian scholars, of theology in the Gothic Bible. At the same time, he was drifting in and out of several New Age groups that were part of the Viennese intellectual scene.

Burg Werfenstein, seen on the left, was an old hilltop castle overlooking the Danube near Vienna. Jörg Lanz von Liebenfels used the castle for solstice celebrations. In 1907, atop Burg Werfenstein, he became the first Ariosophist to hoist a flag emblazoned with a swastika. *Author's collection*

Werfenstein-Wörth

Like Guido von List, Lanz became convinced of the racial superiority of the Aryan race. Remembering the "beast" carved in stone at Heiligenkreuz, he incorporated this notion into his own ideas about human goodness versus subhuman evil. He decided that it was the Aryan race that embodied *human* goodness, while the other races in the pseudoscientific hierarchy were contaminated with *subhuman* evil.

When looking around the streets of turn-of-the-century Vienna for "other races" upon which to fixate, Lanz saw few Africans or Asians. However, it was not hard to see a substantial number of Jews—especially when they accounted for nearly ten percent of the city's population. For List and others, Jews were definitely a race that was outside the Völkisch mainstream, but Lanz went a step further. He decided that they were not merely inferior, but they were also the physical embodiment of the subhuman evil he had seen in the carving at the monastery.

It has never been fully explained why, if Jews and semites were so substandard, List, Lanz, and their fellow Völkisch counterculturists moved in circles where the ancient Jewish mysticism of Kaballah was so widely studied and so thoroughly appreciated. Also a paradox was how, if Asians were inferior, the mystical scriptures of Buddhism, Hinduism, and Taoism could be so widely revered.

Arthur de Gobineau and his fellow pseudoscientists had racial chauvinists from Helena Blavatsky to Guido von List to justify their superiority complex, but Jörg Lanz wanted more. He wanted to believe that non-Aryans were not merely inferior humans, but nonhumans. In the absence of a pseudoscientific theory upon which to anchor his beliefs, he set out to formulate one. Whereas Madame Blavatsky created Theosophy from a fusion of theology and philosophy, Lanz called upon Theosophy and zoology, naming his radical new pseudoscience Theozoology. His doctrine was summarized in his strange 1905 book *Theozoologie oder die Kunde von den Sodoms-Äfflingen und dem Götter-Elektron (Theozoology or the Account of the Sodomite Apelings and the Divine Electron)*. Lanz wrote that Aryans, whom he called *theozoa* or *Gottmenschen* ("god men"), were actually descended from the gods, and that other races, which he dubbed *anthropozoa,* were descended from beasts, or "apelings." He insisted that "sodomy" between the gods and apelings had resulted in the sorry state of humanity, and something should be done about it.

If this book seems a long stretch from his work on *Zur Theologie der Gotischen* Bibel, it should be pointed out that nearly every line in the weird work contains a biblical reference, primarily to the Old Testament. Nearly every other line contains a reference to sex—generally violent or illicit sex. Indeed, the defrocked Cistercian (who was bounced from the monastery for dabbling in "carnal love") spent an inordinate amount of time in *Theozoologie* discussing the sexual practices of apes, humans, and subhumans—as well as sea monsters and "sodomite hobgoblins"—in lurid detail.

As for the "godly" electrons in his book title, Lanz was also one of many in the early twentieth century who shared the belief that newly discovered invisible electronic rays, such as x-rays, were somehow connected with otherworldly mysticism. The supposed connection between electronics to mysticism would crop up again during the heyday of Heinrich Himmler.

In *Theozoologie*, Lanz also embraced aspects of a yet more radical pseudoscientific theory that was making the rounds of universities and think tanks in the late nineteenth century. Social Darwinism was so named not because it had anything to do with Charles Darwin, but because it embraced a mirror image of one of his basic tenets. Darwin coined the term "survival of the fittest" to describe the natural selection that was ongoing in nature. Social Darwinists described natural selection in human society and advocated sidelining those in society who were considered less productive. At their extreme, Social Darwinists advocated eugenics, the selective breeding of humans to perpetuate desirable traits. Eugenics would also crop up again during the heyday of Heinrich Himmler.

Lanz eagerly accepted eugenics, but he went beyond merely proposing animal husbandry to refine the bloodline his "superior" race. He embraced the notion that people with hereditary defects or mental illness should be sterilized so as not to pass on any undesirable characteristics, and he also advocated he sterilization of lesser, *anthropozoa,* races, especially the Jews. He also proposed that the sick, weak, and infirm in society should be not just sterilized, but also *euthanized.* These were more ideas from the pseudoscientific fringe that Heinrich Himmler would later enthusiastically bring into the mainstream.

To go along with the aristocratic "von" and his fabricated title, Jörg Lanz von Liebenfels had also bought himself a castle. Situated on a picturesque hilltop overlooking the Danube, about seventy miles west of Vienna, Burg Werfenstein was actually more of a ruin than a castle, but this suited Lanz's craving for an old stone edifice.

Always ready to mimic his hero, Guido von List, Lanz also created his own secret society, which he headquartered at Burg Werfenstein. Using Latin, with which he was quite familiar as a biblical scholar, Lanz named his society *Ordo Novi Templi,* or "Order of the New Templars." The name suggested a connection with the Knights Templar, which Lanz obviously intended, but the dogma was straight out of Lanz's view of Aryan supremacy. Also, based on a reading of *Theozoology,* one can imagine that the rituals and festivities the New Templars held amid the bonfires and banging drums at the castle probably involved orgies.

According to Lanz's across-the-river neighbor, Franz Herndl, quoted in the periodical *Die Trutzberg,* Lanz and his cronies celebrated the winter solstice in 1907 by running up a banner over Bad Werfenstein. As a heraldic centerpiece for his flag, Lanz chose a bright red runic symbol. Rather than waiting for a vision or creating something out of his own imagination, as Guido von List did with his runes, Lanz picked a pre-existing emblem. He chose an ancient rune that had been widely used by many cultures around the world, a symbol known in Sanskrit as a swastika.

In 1905, among his other activities, the busy Jörg Lanz started a magazine. Apparently, the magazine was quite popular, for it reached a peak circulation of around 100,000 and ran for nearly one hundred issues before it ceased publication in the turning-point war year of 1917. Much of what is known about Lanz and the activities of the New Templars comes from articles published in the magazine. We learn that, among other things, he decided that Burg Werfenstein had played a role in the ancient Nibelunglied legends popularized by Richard Wagner.

Coincidentally, or perhaps intentionally, Lanz named his publication *Ostara,* for the same goddess that was the namesake of Guido von List's Wotanist theme parks. The magazine was subtitled *Briefbücherei der Blonden und Mannesrechtler* (or *Newsletter of the Blonde and Masculist),* "Mannesrechtler" being a term for an antifeminist philosophy that was current in early twentieth-century Europe. Essentially, it was a magazine for blonde men who were proud to be blonde and manly. It was also aimed at an audience who were anxious about the age-old struggle between good and evil—or, in Lanz's view, between Aryans and everyone else.

Another significance of the name was that List and Lanz imagined the creation of "Ostara," the long-discussed Völkische utopia. They not only advocated, but also predicted a purely Aryan nation-state within Austria and Germany.

Among the thousands of subscribers to *Ostara* was a struggling Viennese art student and German army corporal named Adolf Hitler.

CHAPTER 3

Almost
Hocus-Pocus

G UIDO VON LIST died in Germany in that terrible, turbulent spring of 1919, as
Jörg Lanz von Liebenfels continued crafting his strange beliefs into dogma,
and as Heinrich Himmler was heading down a Völkisch country lane to
the farm.

World War I was a wake-up call for List and Lanz. As Himmler had thrilled
to the sight of flags and to the sound of marching boots in the heady days of
1914–1915, the old Wotanist and his understudy had confidently spun the
war—in those thrilling early years—as a great struggle in which Germanic
legions would naturally triumph.

Neither List nor Lanz was touched directly by the conflict. When the war
started, List was sixty-six, and Lanz had just turned forty, so neither served in
uniform. However, by the dark days of 1917–1918, civilians were feeling the
pinch indirectly. Wartime restrictions on paper availability probably played
a role in Lanz's ceasing publication of *Ostara* in 1917. Severe food scarcity
devolved into food riots and affected everyone. The shortages certainly played a
role in List's failing health.

Shortly after the war ended, one of List's financial backers, Eberhard
von Brockhusen, invited the old man to come visit him at his home near Berlin.
Brockhusen also headed the orthodox wing of the Germanenorden, which had
split during the war. List made the trip, but only as far as the German capital.

The fatigued old guru could not go on. Hacking and wheezing, his lungs failing, he checked into a *gasthäus* near the station, and a doctor was called. After a bad night, List coughed himself to death. The cause may have been pneumonia or perhaps the residual effects of the global influenza pandemic that had killed millions around the world in 1918.

Lanz spent the war years in denial of his mentor's death, editing *Ostara,* partying at Burg Werfenstein, and designing quasireligious rituals and vestments for his New Templar acolytes. Even as the Austro-German empires were collapsing violently around them, the New Templars in both countries carried on glibly. It was during the war that Lanz had repackaged his Theozoology doctrine, renaming it Ariosophy and defining it more simply as Aryan mysticism, rather than as the decidedly hard-to-digest fusion of theology and zoology. "Ariosophy" came to be used as a general term describing a dogmatic belief in Aryan superiority.

In the months after the war, as List prepared to leave Austria for Germany, Jörg Lanz found his way to Budapest. Hungary, free from centuries of rule by various monarchies, including that of the Austrians, was redefining itself as an independent republic. Here, Lanz expanded the reach of the New Templars and fell in with anti-Bolshevik and anti-semitic activists fighting to keep Hungary from going communist. Whereas the prewar coffee houses in Vienna had buzzed with abstract philosophical debate, revolution was in the air now, and talk was now backed by the threat of armed confrontation. Such was also the case in Munich, where the various freikorps and other assorted armed groups surged in the political fringes and scuffled in the streets. Against this backdrop, Heinrich Himmler was negotiating his course through the university.

Though he voted for nationalists in student elections, Himmler's political persona was still in its formative stage. He had but a passing awareness of Guido von List at this point, and his fascination with Völkisch themes was still that of a romantic environmentalist. His views about Jews were still ambivalent. Indeed, he associated with Jewish fellow students at the university, and in his diary, he confessed a fondness for Jewish cabaret singer named Inge Barco, whom he had met in a bar.

Adolf Hitler is here surrounded by an enraptured crowd of adoring fans. They liked his message, but they loved the way he delivered it. As Dr. Karl Alexander von Müller, a history professor at the Universität München, wrote, "Hitler had turned them inside out, as one turns a glove inside out, with a few sentences. It had almost something of hocus-pocus, or magic about it."
Author's collection

This unconsummated fascination was par for the course. Himmler was far from being a lady's man. While in school, he admitted to have fallen in love with Maria Loritz, the daughter of a family friend and distant relative. However, Maja, as she was known, did not return his affections—even when Himmler offered her a ride on his newly acquired motorcycle. While the Wotanists were engaging in frequent orgiastic rituals in the countryside, Himmler's diary suggests that he may not have had his first sexual encounter until his mid-twenties.

Himmler graduated from the Universität München on August 5, 1922. The young credentialed agriculturist took a job as an agricultural assistant at a fertilizer company called

Stickstoff-Land GmbH, located in the town of Schleissheim. It was a short commute from Munich, but Himmler may have lived in the town for a while. Though he had toyed with the idea of traveling abroad and had even confided in his diary that he might like to live in Russia or Peru, he stayed put in Bavaria.

During his school years and immediately after, Himmler was exposed to the various Völkisch New Age factions that frequented the coffee houses and beer halls around Munich. One such group that piqued his interest in archeology and the ancient origins of the Aryan race was the *Thule Gesellschaft* (Thule Society). It had originated in Berlin as the *Studiengruppe fur Germanisches Altertum* (Study Group for German Antiquity), and a leading figure in the group was a crippled World War I veteran named Walther Nauhaus, who was also an important member of the Germanenorden. Around the time that Nauhaus moved to Munich, in 1917, the cumbersome and academic-sounding name was changed to the more manageable Thule Gesellschaft.

It has been suggested that Nauhaus's Thule group may have been used as a front for the nationalistic Germanenorden to help avoid its members being bothered by Bolsheviks, but the group did have a unique doctrine. The essential premise of the Thule Society was that the original source of the secret wisdom of the Aryan race was a remote Nordic never-never land called Thule. It was located somewhere in the far north, making it sort of an arctic Atlantis. For the Thule Gesellschaft, the Thule of the distant past was home to a primeval group of superbeings who were similar to—or arguably identical to—Guido von List's Wotanist/Armanen priests. This concept made sense to the Ariosophists because, after all, the Eddas described Wotan and the other founding figures of Nordic mythology as living in such a place.

Stories of this mythical place called Thule were not new. They had been around for more than two millennia, and the legend had been embellished, re-embellished, and over-embellished many times. Any study of the mythology of the Eddas is indebted to twelfth-century Icelandic historian Snorri Sturluson, who wrote the Prose Edda, or Younger Edda. It was Sturluson's theory that the gods of Nordic mythology were actually human warriors or monarchs, around whose burial sites cults developed. In turn, these cults evolved the legends of

Adolf Hitler and his entourage of tough young Aryan followers pose for the camera in Munich in the early 1920s. By this time, the silver-tongued orator had established himself as the Führer of the Nationalsozialistische Deutsche Arbeiterpartei (National Socialist German Workers' Party), best known as the Nazi Party.
Author's collection

the great heros to the point that, in the telling and retelling of the sagas, the heroes became deified. Hence, Guido von List and the Thuleans were right, their heroes *were* gods—and vice versa.

As for the origins of the place called Thule, the Greek explorer Pytheas is said to have written about such a place toward the end of the fourth century BC. There are many mentions in medieval literature of Thule or "Ultima Thule" being located in the distant north, beyond the edges of the known world. The Austro-German New Age was also aware that the Greeks had written of a place called Hyperborea, located in the distant north and inhabited by a powerful race of people. The name "Hyperborea" means "above the northern lights," or aurora borealis, and the legend states that the sun never set in this place. This description suggests that someone may have actually ventured north of the Arctic Circle and based the Hyperborea legend on fact.

Thule had been mentioned by numerous writers, from Pliny the Elder to Edgar Allan Poe. Like the mythical lands of Atlantis, Lemuria, or Hyperborea, Thule was mentioned so often in literature that it often seemed like a real place. The exact location has never been determined, although it has been suggested that the stories may be based on reports by mariners who visited Iceland, Greenland, or the islands off the windswept north coast of Scotland.

Heinrich Himmler, seen here in the center, wearing glasses, was literally the standard-bearer for the Nazis during the November 1923 Beer Hall Putsch in Munich. He and his companions are behind barricades at the offices of the Military District for Bavaria, the former Bavarian war ministry. The flag itself was the old Imperial German battle flag. *Author's collection*

The name was so entrenched in popular lore that it was borrowed by the Danish explorers Knud Rasmussen and Peter Freuchen as a name for a trading-post settlement they established on the northwest coast of Greenland in 1910—a town that still exists.

When Heinrich Himmler first became aware of the Thule Gesellschaft, he would have come in contact with Walther Nauhaus's energetic new partner, a globetrotting merchant seaman turned astrologer and mystic hobbyist named Adam Alfred Rudolf Glauer. A Freemason and Germanenorden member, Glauer also dabbled in Theosophy, as had so many members of the German counterculture. Having traveled widely in the Middle East, he had also experimented with spiritualist doctrines, from Jewish Kabbalah to Islamic Sufism, from Egyptian mysticism to Rosacrucianism. His own fictionalized life story, entitled *Der Talisman des Rosenkreuzers (The Rosicrucian Talisman),* was published in 1925.

Like both List and Lanz, Glauer had abandoned his birth name for a pseudonym with the aristocratic "von." As Rudolf Freiherr von Sebottendorff, he was a ubiquitous New Age man-about-town in Munich in the early postwar years. Sebottendorff was an avid follower of Lanz von Liebenfels and student of runes, especially those of Guido von List's Armanen Futharkh.

Another Thule Society member of note was the Bavarian playwright Dietrich Eckart, the enthusiastic Ariosophist who was also an early member of the Deutsche Arbeiterpartei (DAP). In addition to his politics, Eckart studied Hindu and western metaphysics, and thought of himself as a philosopher in the mold of Arthur Schopenhauer. He had gone so far as to develop a doctrine of a higher human—Aryan, of course—genius that was based on the theories of Lanz von Liebenfels.

As corded-ware had made ancient Aryans real for Gustaf Kossinna, the thought that Thule was a real place must have greatly stirred the amateur archeologist in Heinrich Himmler. Indeed, the idea of the Aryan race having originated in a far away icy land became a vividly real part of Himmler's beliefs.

Like Eckart, Dr. Alfred Rosenberg was a DAP member who also joined the Thule Society. An Estonian engineer and an enthusiastic Ariosophist, he had lived in Russia during the 1917 Revolution and had developed a strong dislike for Bolsheviks, as well as for Jews. Rosenberg was a follower of Houston Stewart Chamberlain's more extreme Aryan superiority ideas and of Gustaf Kossinna's thesis that the Aryan race had originated in northern Europe. He was also a member of the Lübeck-based *Nordische Gesellschaft* (Nordic Society), a Völkisch organization with members throughout Scandinavia and the Baltic rim.

Rosenberg believed not only that the Aryan race was the master race of all Indo-European races, but also that the Wotanist religion of the Aryan race was the *master religion* of the Indo-European races. As such, he believed that Wotanism not only predated, but also influenced Zoroastrianism, the ancient religion of the Persians, and Hinduism, two creeds that are generally ranked as the two oldest of the world's major religions.

Rosenberg was also one of the first of the future Nazi racial theorists to use the term *untermensch* ("under man," or "subhuman") to describe both Slavs and Jews. In this, he was borrowing a concept widely discussed in Völkisch circles around the turn of the century and expounded upon at length by Jörg Lanz von Liebenfels in his bizarre *Theozoology*. The word "untermensch" may have originated with Lothrop Stoddard, the American author of *The Revolt Against Civilization: The Menace of the Under-man,* published in 1922. Or it may have been coined as the flip side of the term *über-mensch* ("over-man" or "superman"), which features in the 1883 work *Also Sprach Zarathustra (Thus Spoke Zoroaster)* by the gloomy German philosopher Friedrich Nietzsche, the prophet of nihilism. Like Nietzsche, Rosenberg had an interest in Zoroaster (Zarathustra), the Persian prophet who lived sometime before the tenth century BC and who had founded Zoroastrianism.

Rosenberg's belief that Aryan paganism was the mother creed of both Hinduism and Zoroastrianism was an idea that was very much a part of the academic premise of Hans Friedrich Karl Günther, a cultural anthropologist and self-styled racial theorist who bounced around to the faculties of universities in Jena, Berlin, and his native Freiburg during the 1920s and 1930s. Like Chamberlain and Kossinna, Günther gave academic credence to the Völkisch believers in Aryan superiority. His writings included *The Knight, Death and the Devil: The Heroic Idea* (1919)—based on the famous apocalyptic woodcut of the same name by Albrecht Dürer—and *The Racial Elements of European History* (1927). These books interwove Völkisch paganism with a form of biological nationalism. Among the neopagans and Ariosophists who seized upon Günther's works with great enthusiasm was Heinrich Himmler.

A heroic illustration of Nazi Sturmabteilung (SA) "brown shirts" attacking communist agitators, thus defending the Nazi Party and the nation from what they perceived as the sickness of Bolshevism. *Author's collection*

Like participants in the American counterculture of the 1920s and 1960s, Himmler also developed a keen interest in Hindu scriptures. Even in later years, like Timothy Leary, he carried a copy of the Bhagavad Gita with him as he traveled. Perhaps he enjoyed the war stories as much as the philosophical content. The central character, Krishna, is a deified warrior-hero who would have been right at home with Thor or Siegfried, the fighting heroes the Eddas.

While Günther had bought into the Kossinna's "confirmation" that the superior Aryan race had originated in northern Europe, he also believed the race

Right: The first post–World War I issue of Jörg Lanz von Liebenfels's Ariosophist magazine, *Ostara*, published in 1922 and reissued in 1930. *Author's collection*

Far right: There is no mistaking the degenerate "apeling" on the cover of this 1923 issue of *Ostara*. Jörg Lanz von Liebenfels filled the pages of his magazines with diatribes against subhuman creatures, whom he feared were everywhere.

Author's collection

was part of the greater Indo-European family. As part of this idea, he wrote that the Aryans had migrated across Asia, through Persia, and into India, where they were responsible for the great theological literature of Hinduism, specifically the Vedas. Like Kossinna, he pointed to archeological evidence, citing similarities in Hindu and Nordic runes, burial mounds, and so on.

During the early 1920s, as Himmler wound up his college career and entered the work force, he found an opportunity for the military experience that had eluded him during World War I. At the suggestion of his friend Ernst Röhm, he joined the freikorps militia originally known as *Reichsflagge,* but recently renamed as *Reichskreigsflagge* (Nation-War-Flag).

Röhm was a veteran who had served as an officer in a Bavarian infantry unit during World War I. Discharged as a captain, Röhm was active in brokering weapons for various underground nationalist groups in Munich. Himmler had met Röhm early in 1922 at a beer hall political meeting in Munich, and the two became friends.

Röhm and Himmler were an odd pair. Thirteen years older than Himmler, Röhm was a large, beefy former officer, while Himmler was a small, slender man who had only yearned for military life. Himmler looked up to Röhm, treating him with the deference of an enlisted man for an officer. Though Röhm was openly gay, there is no indication that their relationship was ever physical.

It was Röhm who introduced Himmler to Adolf Hitler.

When World War I had ended, Hitler was in a hospital recovering from injuries suffered in a poison gas attack he endured just a few weeks before the armistice. Psychologists who have analyzed Hitler ad nauseam through the years have deduced that the depression borne of this experience was the origin of the anger Hitler manifested in later years. Others have suggested that he had always had a few screws loose. In any case, Hitler had returned to Munich—his adopted home—rather than returning to his native Austria. He had remained in military service, though he had exchanged his Imperial German Army uniform for that of the newly formed Reichswehr.

In July 1919, two months after the death of Guido von List and three months before Heinrich Himmler entered the university, Hitler got an assignment that changed his life and the course of twentieth-century history. The Reichswehr ordered him to spy on Anton Drexler's Deutsche Arbeiterpartei. Among the right-wing and left-wing organizations screaming for attention around Munich in the summer of 1919, the DAP was still a relatively tiny organization, with just fifty-four members. Hitler was captivated by Drexler and his message, especially the DAP hatred for the Bolsheviks and the part about how the Jewish industrialists were to blame for Germany's embarrassing defeat in World War I. Such individuals were considered to have greedily stabbed the Reich in the back. Furthermore, they were lumped together in the mind of the Völkisch nationalists with the Weimar Republic's government as the "November criminals," who sold out the Reich by agreeing to the November 1918 armistice.

Instead of infiltrating the DAP, Adolf Hitler joined, becoming member number fifty-five. It was a match made in heaven—or hell, as we see in historic hindsight. Just as Hitler fell in love with a doctrine that was so congruent with his own beliefs, Drexler was mesmerized by Hitler's uncanny personal presence and his gift for oratory.

Drexler knew that the key to running an organization was membership, and when you have just fifty members, you have plenty of work to do. A skilled orator can attract members, and Hitler did not disappoint Drexler. The party grew in number, as well as in prominence. Soon, prominent men such as World War I flying ace Hermann Göring joined. Even the popular and prestigious General Erich von Ludendorff, arguably Germany's greatest World War I commander, supported the cause.

By the winter of 1919, the DAP "workers" party had expanded the scope of its appeal by adding terms to its name to appeal to both nationalists and socialists—though the socialists to whom they appealed were socialist only insofar as they despised *Jewish* capitalists. In February 1920, the DAP became the *Nationalsozialistische Deutsche Arbeiterpartei*

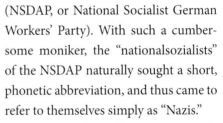

(NSDAP, or National Socialist German Workers' Party). With such a cumbersome moniker, the "nationalsozialists" of the NSDAP naturally sought a short, phonetic abbreviation, and thus came to refer to themselves simply as "Nazis."

Heinrich Himmler was probably attending Nazi Party events with Ernst Röhm while he was still in the university, and he had certainly been acquainted with Adolf Hitler before he formally joined the NSDAP in August 1923.

Within the Nazi Party, Himmler soon found a number of members of the Thule Society. The Ariosophists gladly embraced a supportive myth, and the idea of the Aryan race rising from a distant, ice-bound land seemed as stirringly real as anything for the Nazis, just as it did for Himmler.

A saluting Hitler is the centerpiece of this Heinrich Hoffman photo of a 1928 Nazi Party rally in Nuremburg. Hermann Göring is in the foreground on the left.

U.S. National Archives

Hitler had already superseded Drexler as the central figure of the NSDAP even before he officially became party chairman in July 1921. By the time that Himmler met him, Hitler had progressed within party leadership to the all-new post of *Führer,* meaning simply that he was *the* leader. Under a policy known as the *Führerprinzip,* or leader principal, the Führer became the party dictator, the exclusive determiner of party policy. As his deputy Führer, he chose Rudolf Hess.

Himmler's mentor, Ernst Röhm, had been named to head the NSDAP's paramilitary security apparatus, their inhouse freikorps. As noted earlier, the Munich of the postwar years was a tough and violent place, where the police were outnumbered and the streets were ruled by street gangs. In the sea of chaos, where assassinations were rampant, extremist groups on both political extremes needed private armies to defend themselves against one another. The NSDAP freikorps took its name, *Sturmabteilung,* from the shock troops or "storm troopers" that had been used during World War I to infiltrate enemy lines or the spearhead infantry assaults by the German army. Abbreviated as SA, the Sturmabteilung outfitted its members in military-style uniforms that included brown shirts. For this reason, the SA thugs were also referred to as brownshirts. In the service of the NSDAP, the brownshirts were used to break up fights at meetings, to intimidate rival organizations, and to beat up Bolsheviks.

By the fall of 1923, the NSDAP had grown from fifty-five members to around 20,000, not just in Munich, but across Germany. The party's newspaper, the *Völkischer Beobachter (People's Observer),* a decades-old suburban weekly taken over by the Nazis, grew rapidly in circulation. Among the key staff members at the paper during the early 1920s were Thule Society stalwarts Dietrich Eckart, Alfred Rosenberg, and Rudolf Freiherr von Sebottendorff.

A megalomaniac like Hitler is nothing without grandiose dreams, and in Hitler's case, he looked at the weak leadership within the government of Germany's Weimar Republic and thought he could fill the void. He promised his members a restoration of Germany's national pride, and all the things that Guido von List and Jörg Lanz von Liebenfels had imagined in their Aryan utopia.

By the fall of 1923, the time seemed right for Hitler's scheme. The situation was so turbulent that the Bavarian *ministerpräsident* (state governor), Eugen von

Knilling, declared martial law. He brought in his predecessor, Gustav Ritter von Kahr, a well-known, right-wing political leader, as *Staatskomissar,* or state commissioner. Kahr was the senior part of a triumvirate that also included police chief Colonel Hans Ritter von Seisser and Reichswehr general Otto von Lossow, and the three ran Bavaria as a virtual dictatorship.

With Kahr—a man Hitler assumed to be sympathetic to his cause—in power in Bavaria, Hitler decided to stage a coup against the November criminals, the German national government. He hoped that by getting the ball rolling in Munich, his coup—called a *putsch* in German—would spread all the way to Berlin.

On the evening of November 8, 1923, there was a huge meeting at the Bürgerbräukeller on Rosenheimerstrasse, the immense beer hall operated by the Bürgerliches Bräuhaus brewing company. There were around 3,000 people present. Gustav Ritter von Kahr was scheduled to address them, and he was expected to back Hitler's scheme. Both Seisser and Lossow were also present. However, the night turned dark for Hitler when Kahr and the others withdrew their anticipated support. Hitler then entered the vast room, surrounded by an entourage of armed henchmen, and took the triumvirate into a side room, where he unsuccessfully harangued and threatened them to change their minds. He returned to the stage to greet a crowd that began to jeer. Firing a pistol round into the ceiling to get their attention, he began to speak.

Present in the room was Dr. Karl Alexander von Müller, a history professor at the Universität München. In the description in his 1966 book *Im Wandel einer Zeit (In the Change of Time),* Müller recalls that the speech was "an oratorical masterpiece, which any actor might well envy. He began quietly, without any pathos. . . . I cannot remember in my entire life such a change in the attitude of a crowd in a few minutes, almost a few seconds. There were certainly many who were not converted yet. But the sense of the majority had fully reversed itself. Hitler had turned them inside out, as one turns a glove inside out, with a few sentences. It had almost something of hocus-pocus, or magic about it. Loud approval roared forth, no further opposition was to be heard."

Heinrich Himmler missed the show at the Bürgerbräukeller. He and Röhm had been at another beer hall, that of the well-known Löwenbrau brewery, with a contingent of Reichskreigsflagge goons. Himmler was probably feeling rather self-important, for Röhm had entrusted him to carry the unit's colors, an old imperial German battle flag. When they heard what was going on with Hitler, Röhm, Himmler, and the others moved out to join them. En route, they were intercepted by messengers carrying orders from Hitler, redirecting them to seize the offices of the Military District for Bavaria, in the former Bavarian war ministry. This they did, succeeding quite easily.

The following morning, buoyed by the response he received at the Bürgerbräukeller, Hitler set out to lead a large number of his followers, including Dietrich Eckart and Rudolf Hess, on massive march to the Munich city hall, hoping the Reichswehr would join with the Nazis to march on Berlin. The idea was patterned on the March on Rome, in which Fascist leader Benito Mussolini had seized power in Italy in October 1922.

Hitler was confident—indeed, overconfident. But why not? He had even earned the support of General Ludendorff, who would march at the head of the throng.

As they marched, the destination was changed to the former war ministry, but the marchers made it only as far as the Odeonsplatz, where they ran into a cordon of state police. The Bavarian government had regrouped overnight and was keen to prevent the putsch from succeeding. When feeling threatened, nervous men with guns are a prescription for disaster. Shots rang out, and the march dissolved into a disorganized herd scrambling for safety. The old soldier Ludendorff was among a handful who remained steadfast, facing down the police. Hitler and most of his followers ran. Ludendorff never forgave Hitler for his cowardice. When the dust settled, sixteen marchers and four police lay dead in the street. Among the wounded was World War I pilot Hermann Göring.

Heinrich Himmler missed the showdown in the Odeonsplatz, but got his own taste of the action when the police launched an armed attack to recapture the ministry building. Not wanting to inflame tensions, the police made few arrests. After ordering the insurgents to stack their weapons, the police let most simply walk away. Röhm, however, was taken into custody. So too were Hitler,

Ludendorff, and a number of others. Ludendorff was acquitted. Röhm had his fifteen-month sentence suspended, but was kicked out of the Reichswehr. Dietrich Eckart was jailed, though briefly; he died of a heart attack a month later. Convicted of treason, Hitler was sentenced to five years, although he would be released after just one. Göring, among others, escaped to Austria to avoid prosecution until a general amnesty for the putsch participants was enacted in 1927. The NSDAP was officially banned, and the *Völkischer Beobachter* was ordered to cease publication. Naturally, the Nazis did not go away, but merely slithered underground to weather the storm.

For Hitler, his incarceration at the minimum-security facility in Landsberg worked to his advantage. Assisted by both Röhm and Hess, he used the time to finish his book, which was dedicated to Dietrich Eckart. Entitled *Mein Kampf (My Struggle),* the book begins autobiographically, but goes on to outline Hitler's views of the world as it was and as he thought it should be.

In *Mein Kampf,* Hitler displayed a great deal of Völkisch nostalgia. The book conveyed a spiritual reverence for the Germanic national identity and its sacred roots in the distant and heroic past of Nordic mythology. In a diatribe that seems cribbed from the Armanenism of List, the Ariosophy of Lanz, and from ideas Hitler gleaned from reading *Ostara,* Hitler embraced the by then well-established doctrine of Aryan superiority. He describes the Jews as the worst of the worst in society, linking them with the perceived evils of both the industrialists and the Bolsheviks. He also lavished his wrath on the Slavic peoples, whom he despised.

Hitler blended the core philosophy of the Völkisch New Age with the political anger at Bolshevism then current on the right side of the German street and with the animosity toward Versailles that was found on both sides. He also outlined his vision for a greater Germany and a crying need for *Lebensraum* (living space), to accommodate an exploding German population outside the crowded borders of 1920s Germany. Where exactly was this living space to be?

Floating around Völkisch ideology since the mid-nineteenth century was a concept called *Drang Nach Osten* (eastward urge), which idealized a notion that it was the manifest destiny of ethnic Germans to occupy the homelands of the Slavic and Baltic people to the east. Thanks in part to the empire build-ing of the Teutonic Knights, there had been Germanic settlement in the east since the Middle Ages, but it was only after the late eighteenth century that a modern political Drang Nach Osten got its start. It began when Poland was dismantled as a nation state by the Congress of Vienna after Napoleon's final defeat at Waterloo in 1815. The country's land was partitioned between Austria, Prussia, and Russia. A century later, the Treaty of Versailles took away land from various countries, but mainly Germany, to re-create Poland. The Völkisch and nationalistic among the Germans, who were used to there not being a Poland, greatly resented this. So in *Mein Kampf,* Hitler proposed an eastward campaign of Drang Nach Osten to gain the Lebensraum that he felt was needed by the German people. He predicted the Germans' attempted occupation of the Soviet Union, which he would undertake seventeen years later.

When the word got out that Heinrich Himmler had carried the flag for the Beer Hall Putsch, that he had literally been the standard-bearer, he became a celebrity among the Nazis. For perhaps the first time in his life, the girls took notice of young Himmler. The putsch had been a tranformative moment both for Germany and for Heinrich Himmler.

It was almost like hocus-pocus.

CHAPTER 4

A Call to Duty

LTHOUGH THE BEER HALL PUTSCH had worked to Heinrich Himmler's advantage, after it, he was at loose ends. The political party to which he had devoted his attention was now out of business, and to make matters worse, he was also out of a job. According to the municipal archives in Schleissheim, he had quit or been laid off at Stickstoff-Land GmbH three months before the putsch. Now his resumé was being turned down all over town. He might have had trouble getting work because of his image as standard-bearer for a failed insurrection. The girls liked the bad boy on the motorcycle, but potential employers did not.

However, his ongoing unemployment may also have been a result of the dire economic collapse of the Weimar Republic. During 1923, Germany watched the value of its currency spiral out of control. Back in 1922, it had taken almost 300 reichsmarks to buy one American dollar. By February 1923, it took 20,000 reichsmarks, and in July 1923, the month that Himmler had joined the NSDAP, the number was around four million. By the time of the Beer Hall Putsch, hyperinflation had pushed it to four *billion.*

Like many who have tasted politics, Himmler savored the tang. After the NSDAP was banned, Ernst Röhm and many other Nazis moved to the *Nationalsozialistische Freiheitsbewegung* (NSFB, or National Socialist Freedom Movement). Himmler followed. Having no alternative, he sought paying work in a political campaign. In the months leading up to the May 1924 Bavarian elections, Himmler became a tireless campaign worker, racing about the countryside on his motorcycle, giving speeches, and carrying election propaganda for NSFB candidates, including Röhm. Himmler was in his element, relishing

Heinrich Himmler, the Reichsführer SS, is seen here on the left (in helmet and glasses). Saluting next to him is Kurt Daluege (1897–1946), who was his first and only serious rival for power within the SS. Himmler won, sidelining Daluege to posts far from the seat of power in Berlin. *U.S. National Archives*

the opportunity to carry the Völkisch message to the Völkisch heartland of rustic Bavaria.

As he put solitary miles on his BMW, Himmler had many hours to enjoy the scenery and wax romantically about the credo of Blut und Boden, blood and soil. On his metal steed in these remote lanes and medieval villages, he might have imagined himself as Heinrich I, a noble peasant king, a man of the earth, a man of the purist Aryan blood, riding through the villages and lanes of his domain on a mighty warhorse.

While not exactly mighty, the electoral success of the National Socialist and Völkisch parties in the election May 1924 election was significant. The NSFB alone won thirty-two seats in the *Reichstag*, the national parliament. This victory greatly buoyed the spirits of the closet Nazis. Having failed six months earlier to overthrow the German government, they now had "former" members seated in the Reichstag, as well as the Bavarian state legislature. Among the newly elected officials were General Erich Ludendorff and Ernst Röhm.

Adolf Hitler walked out of Landsberg prison on December 20, 1924. The following day, a *New York Times* headline read "Hitler Tamed By Prison," and the corresponding report explained that he had abandoned politics. Two months later, on February 27, 1925, the NSDAP was reconstituted, and Hitler resumed the post of Führer. The NSFB and some other smaller, like-minded parties happily folded themselves into the new NSDAP. Other National Socialist parties continued to exist independently of the NSDAP, mainly in northern Germany.

Like the *New York Times,* the conventional wisdom in Germany also optimistically held that Hitler's political career was over. It was hard to imagine that he could make a comeback, but he was determined to continue his rise to power all the way to the top. He renounced, at least for the near term, the sort of violence that had gotten him in trouble. To put a more civil face on the party, he forbade the SA from engaging in street fights with communists and other factions. He had learned an important political lesson. What he had failed to do in the street, he would now do by ballot box, smoke-filled room, and the sheer magnetism of his remarkable "hocus-pocus" charisma.

Given a job within the party, Himmler now found himself back in Landshut, staring up at thirteenth-century Burg Trusnitz, the stone edifice of his youth, and drawing a salary from the NSDAP. His job in 1925, as it had been the year before, was to function as a community organizer in the rural heartland of the Völkisch dream. Before long, the slender young man on the motorcycle was named as deputy regional NSDAP leader for Upper Bavaria and Swabia.

Despite having a rising career within the NSDAP hierarchy, he had decided to make a life for himself in the countryside. While rambling beneath the oaks and chestnut trees, traveling from village to village, Himmler became so enthralled with getting back to the earth that he decided he would buy a farm.

It was also during this time that Himmler met the blonde-haired, blue-eyed woman he would marry. There are at least two versions of the story. Heinz Höhne, writing in *The Order of the Death's Head: The Story of Hitler's SS,* tells that Himmler met her in Bad Reichenhall, Bavaria, in 1926 when he dashed into a hotel lobby to get out of the rain. Roger Manvell and Heinrich Fränkel, in their biography *Heinrich Himmler: The Sinister Life of the Head of the SS and Gestapo,* say that he met her on a visit to Berlin in 1927. They tell that she was Polish, and that her name was Margarete Concerzowo. On the other hand, Höhne cites a 1966 interview he did with a relative who wished to remain anonymous. From this interview, Höhne learned that Himmler's wife's maiden name was

Margarete Boden, although she had previously been married to man named Siegroth. Höhne's source said that she was the daughter of a German landowner in Goncarzewo (a.k.a., Goncarzewy), then in West Prussia, now in Poland. In either case, she was a trained nurse, had an interest in homeopathy and folk remedies, and operated a small clinic or nursing home in Berlin.

Though Himmler's family was displeased that he was marrying a divorced woman seven years older than he, he wed Margarete (or Marga, for short), on July 3, 1928. Some sources have suggested that he entered the bed that night still a virgin, but there is no way of knowing.

As Himmler might have observed, though, this was actually not his first marriage. His first wedding had occurred 1,022 years earlier in 906, when, in his previous life as Heinrich I, he had married a woman named Hatheburg, whose Saxon father was Count Edwin of Merseburg. This marriage lasted just three years before ending in divorce—or possibly annulment, as Hatheburg had been married previously. Heinrich then promptly wed a noble teenager named Mathilde. Renowned for her beauty, she was the daughter of Count Dietrich of Westphalia, who was a descendent of the Saxon hero Widukind. Heinrich had one son with Hatheburg, and two daughters and three sons with Mathilde. Among the latter was Otto I, Heinrich's successor and the first Holy Roman emperor. Heinrich Himmler was no doubt pleased to lay claim to such a majestic and most Aryan pedigree through his belief in reincarnation.

In 1928, Margarete Himmler sold her business, and her new husband bought them a farm near Waldtrudering, on the edge of Munich. Heinrich, the boy with an active imagination, had grown into Heinrich the husband and community organizer. But despite his living in the all-too-real world, he still inhabited a fantasyland. Like the flower children of the 1960s who raced off to rural communes, Himmler still imagined himself as a peasant, getting his hands dirty in the soil of rural Bavaria and getting in touch with his Völkisch side.

His views on the familiar theme of Blut und Boden, blood and soil, were influenced by the works of a South American, albeit ethnic German, author who would later play a key role in carrying out Himmler's bizarre racial policies. Born in Buenos Aires, Argentina, in 1895, Ricardo Walther Oscar Darré was the son of an expatriate German import-export executive who spent most of his youth studying abroad, in both England and Germany. Like Himmler, Darré had developed an interest in German farm life while still in his teens. Both he and Himmler had been members of the back-to-the-land Artamanen Gesellschaft (Artaman League).

Unlike Himmler, though, Darré was old enough for military service during World War I. As *Richard* Walther Darré, he served in the Imperial German Army and was wounded, though not severely, several times. Afer the war, as Himmler became a farm worker in southern Germany, Darré was a farm worker in eastern Germany, in Pomerania. As Himmler had studied agriculture in Munich, Darré studied the same at the University of Halle, where he finally earned his doctorate in 1929. In the meantime, he had joined the NSDAP and published his book, *Das Bauerntum als Lebensquell der Nordischen Rasse (Peasantry as the Life-Source of the Nordic Race).* The book naturally appealed to Himmler, who was then in the wings with Hitler, waiting for their moment in the lights of the national stage. In her 1985 biography *Blood and Soil: Richard Walther Darré and Hitler's "Green Party,"* Anna Bramwell wrote that Darré "defined the German peasantry as a homogeneous racial group of Nordic antecedents, who formed the cultural and racial core of the German nation. . . . Since the Nordic birth-rate was lower than that of other races, the Nordic race was under a long-term threat of extinction." The idea that the Aryan race might die out played into Himmler's determination to help save it, just as the belief in the idealized German peasantry as the wellspring of the race fed his Völkisch obsession. As the Nazi party grew in strength, Darré rose with the tide, becoming a tool in the effort to move the real peasantry under the party's big tent.

As for Himmler, he made an initial effort at becoming if not a real farmer, then at least a weekend peasant. A small home was built at the Himmlers' Waldtrudering farm, and Himmler himself built the chicken house, imagining that one day his flock would evolve into a large egg business. It never happened. Heinrich's dream became Margarete's nightmare. She did wind up as a farmer and would spend the coming few years tending a handful of chickens, as he went off to tend a growing number of Nazis.

The only daughter of Heinrich and Margarete, named Gudrun, was born on August 8, 1929. She would see little of her father as she grew up. Half a year earlier, on January 6, he had been called from his rustic idyll to head the palace guard of the NSDAP, the *Schutzstaffel*, or "Protection Squad," best known by its initials. The SS had been created in 1925, evolving out of Hitler's personal bodyguard, the *Stosstruppe* (Shock Troop), formerly *Stabswache* (Staff Guard). Whereas the storm troopers of the Sturmabteilung (SA) had acted as a sort of freikorps to guard the party and its functions, the SS was created as a more elite and specialized unit to guard the Führer. Soon, however, its mandate expanded.

While Hitler was in prison and out of the picture, Ernst Röhm had spent 1924 building the SA into an army. When his 2,000-man SA was formally banned at the same time as the NSDAP itself, Röhm simply changed the name. Using the front name *Frontbann,* Röhm proceeded to build a freikorps of about 30,000 paramilitaries *outside* the shell of the Nazi Party.

When Hitler reestablished the Nazi Party, it would have been natural to assume that it would reabsorb its former freikorps, but Röhm had refused to let it be. With this refusal, the NSDAP and Röhm formally parted ways on April 30, 1925. Hitler smiled a benevolent smile that belied an "I'll-get-you-in-due-time" sneer, and thanked his former underling for his valuable service. At that point, a conciliatory Röhm told Hitler that they were still friends, and that if he were needed, all Hitler had to do was call, and he would answer.

Röhm did not remain in Germany. Shortly thereafter, he was asked by the government of Bolivia, of all places, to come to South America and whip some Germanic discipline into its armed forces. He took the job.

As reported in the September 4, 1930, issue of the *Müchener Post,* Hitler decided that he needed a new freikorps, but one comprised of "men who enlisted unconditionally, ready to march against their own brothers. Rather a mere twenty men to a city (on condition that one could count on them absolutely) than an unreliable mass [such as Röhm's army]."

Such was the mandate that Hitler had in mind for his SS.

As would usually be the case with his ideas, the Führer left it to others to put this plan into motion. The first commander of the SS was Julius Schreck, who had previously been Hitler's chauffeur and head of his *Stosstruppe* bodyguard. He set about building the SS with tight-knit groups throughout Germany. He kept it elite. Men had to be physically fit party members, between the ages of twenty-three and thirty-five, and have two sponsors. He kept it small. Even Berlin had a contingent of only twenty men. Reportedly, the quality over quantity plan worked well. Communist rabble-rousers quickly learned the hard way that it was not a good idea to disrupt a Nazi Party event.

It was at this time that Hitler and his henchmen began organizing the NSDAP's operational apparatus beyond their Bavarian birthplace and on a national scale. It is clear that they imagined this organization not just as a political-party apparatus, but also as a template for one day *ruling* Germany. The interest that the Nazis took in the medieval roots of the German nation are evident in the terminology used for positions within the party. In the early twentieth century, as now, the German states forming the basic building block of German political geography were known as *lander.* However, the Nazis returned to the distant days of the early Middle Ages, when the basic building block was the smaller *gau,* roughly equivalent to an American county. With meticulous detail, the Nazis established an NSDAP leader, called a *gauleiter,* for each of these small districts across the country.

In April 1926, a year after the SS was formed, Schreck handed off command to Joseph Berchtold, another former SA man who had headed the security detail at the Bürgerbräukeller during the putsch. Berchtold was the first to be given the important sounding title of "Reichsführer SS," or national leader of the SS.

The all-black SS uniform came later. The party had earlier made a windfall purchase of brown shirts originally manufactured for the Imperial German Army's colonial troops in Deutsch-Ostafrika, Germany's African colony in what are now parts of Burundi, Rwanda, and Tanzania. When the Treaty of Versailles stripped Germany of colonies, the unneeded shirts were appropriated by the SA. While the brownshirts of the SA had also sported brown ties, the brownshirts of the SS wore black ones.

By 1926, Hitler was also ready to reconstitute the SA. The Frontbann had continued to exist, although it was essentially leaderless since Ernst Röhm was no longer involved. To head the newly reformed SA, the Führer picked Franz Pfeffer von Salomon, who had been an officer during World War I and now commanded a freikorps in northern Germany, an area into which Hitler was keen to extend NSDAP influence. Salomon, similarly, was keen to extend the influence of the SA over the SS.

Because the SA had less restrictive membership requirements than the SS, it quickly grew larger. Calls were made to have the SA absorb the small, elite SS, but Berchtold insisted that the SS should maintain a chain of command outside the SA—and even outside the main party apparatus—making it directly answerable only to Adolf Hitler himself.

Early in 1927, fed up with having to bicker with party and SA bureaucrats, Berchtold resigned, and his second in command, Erhard Heiden, became Reichsführer SS. He agreed with his predecessors that the SS should, by all means, remain as an elite corps, describing it as "perhaps super-efficient, but certainly arrogant." Even more than his predecessors, he believed in strict discipline for the SS, ordering its members to maintain an imposing presence at meetings, but to keep silent. This silence, of course, made the tall, physically fit guards even more striking. However, under Heiden's watch, the SS declined in both overall importance and in head count—from around a thousand members, it withered by more than two thirds. One person whom Heiden *did* bring on board was the young, unassuming gauleiter from Landshut.

In 1928, Heinrich Himmler looked like a clerk. (Arguably, he looked like a clerk all his adult life.) Perhaps Heiden made Himmler his deputy because he did not perceive him as a threat. Shortly after Himmler was hired, however, it came to Hitler's attention that Heiden had used a *Jewish* tailor for some alterations to his uniform. One wonders how this information may have reached the Führer. Could the source have been the "born criminal" who had once spied on fellow students for his father, the malevolent schoolmaster?

However he found out about Heiden's tailor, naturally, Hitler couldn't abide a Reichsführer SS who wore a suit tailored by a such an untermenschen creature. Heiden was out, and Himmler was in.

The young clerk took to his new job as Reichsführer SS with unprecedented diligence, immediately crafting an ambitious plan to reverse the decline in size and prestige suffered by the SS under his predecessors. Although he relaxed the minimum height requirement for SS to 173 centimeters (five feet, eight inches)—how tall, does one suppose, was the slight Heinrich Himmler?—he also introduced more stringent requirements. Under Himmler, Ariosophist criteria was brought to bear in the selection process. Schreck had required SS candidates to have young, well-toned bodies, but Himmler insisted that they also have Aryan pedigrees. In other elite paramilitary organizations throughout history, there had been a requirement of noble blood, the idea being that the aristocracy should have a place among a select corps. With Himmler, one needed not be the son of a duke or prince. One could be the son of a butcher, baker, or candlestick maker—so long as the butcher, baker or candlestick maker was a pure Aryan who traced his blood line only into the Nordic past that Himmler imagined stretched all the way back to the Armanen.

Despite the strict requirements, Himmler built the SS back to about a thousand men by the end of 1929 and doubled that number a few months later. Even Franz Pfeffer von Salomon, heading the much larger SA, took notice. The SA had the reputation of taking anyone who could wield a baton in anger. It was filled with men whose questionable backgrounds included a variety of petty and serious crimes and even, heaven forbid, tainted blood. However, the SA also included men who qualified for the SS, and many of them were jumping ship to the more elite unit. Salomon complained to the Führer. Hitler responded by ordering Himmler to stop poaching from the SA, but he also ordered Salomon to refer qualified candidates to the SS rather than admitting them to SA membership. Nevertheless, the SS remained technically a subsidiary of the SA. By sheer numbers, the SA was still clearly the muscle of the Nazi Party. The SA was especially powerful in Berlin and the big cities of the north, while the SS remained a more Bavaria-centric organization. At the end of 1930, it boasted a membership of nearly 100,000, while the SS had fewer than 3,000. But it was only a matter of time before the rising SS would come out on top.

The NSDAP itself, still headquartered at its "Brown House" in Munich, had the image of being a Bavaria-centric party. However, the appointment of Dr. Paul Joseph Goebbels as the Nazi gauleiter for Berlin raised the party's profile on the national scene. Goebbels, who had earned his PhD studying romantic Völkisch literature at the University of Heidelberg, was easily the second best orator in the Nazi party. He was also a tireless promoter and shrewd propagandist.

An SS officer candidate's guidebook, marked "Class 2, Booklet 6, 1942." *Photo by Kris Simoens, used by permission*

Recognizing the importance of the party's profile in Berlin and his need for personal control, Hitler had gone so far as to transfer a Berlin SA leader named Kurt Daluege to the SS in 1930. He also allowed Daleuge—for a time—to run SS operations in the German capital autonomously, without Himmler's operational control. Hitler himself was still ruling the NSDAP by finesse and by playing factions against one another. If he could see a day in the future when the SS would be his loyal analog to the Praetorian guard that had served as bodyguards to Roman emperors, he knew that day had not yet come. Instead, he could see that the immense army of the SA was for now the preeminent power, and that to control the party, he needed to control the SA.

The biggest SA thorn in Hitler's side was Walther Stennes, head of the SA in Berlin. Stennes was among those who disagreed with Hitler's ballot-box approach to seizing power. Many members had joined the SA for the reason many men joined any postwar freikorps (or any postmodern street gang): to get tough. They imagined that control of the German government would ultimately be decided by an armed clash with the communists. They saw the SA as the tip of the Nazi spear in this battle, and they were itching for a fight.

In August 1930, with a special election coming, Stennes even pushed Goebbels to allocate three Berlin-constituency Reichstag seats to the SA, threatening to pull the SA out of the party if his demands were not met. Salomon had made similar demands of Hitler, who had told him to shove it, but Stennes was ready to shove back. When push did come to shove, and the contention boiled over into a brawl, the SS came to the aid of Goebbels. SA fists had flown against SS fists.

Hitler then invoked the Führer principle and took over both organizations directly. Salomon, weary of the bickering, was only too willing to step aside. But Hitler had no interest in the hands-on management of freikorps. Ernst Röhm had offered to help if Hitler called, and now Hitler was calling.

Meanwhile, the times favored Hitler's approach to politics. The economy, especially inflation and unemployment, was going from bad to worse, and recruitment to the National Socialist and Völkisch message was snowballing. In the 1928 national election, the NSDAP alone won just 12 seats in the Reichstag and less than 3 percent of the overall vote. However, when the government collapsed and the September 1930 special election was held, the NSDAP won 107 seats in the Reichstag and over 18 percent of the vote, becoming the second largest party in German government after the Social Democrats.

In November 1930, Hitler formally made the SS independent of the SA, declaring that no SA commander could issue orders to an SS man. Himmler instituted a formal, military rank system within the SS and was finally able to change the uniforms. Out went the brown shirts, and in came the black.

When Röhm returned to resume his role in the SA, he walked Hitler's line assiduously. Early in 1931, he reorganized the SA hierarchy, making its regional units answerable to NSDAP gauleiters at every level. Stennes was bounced from the organization in April.

At the very moment that his old pal Röhm was appearing to curb the SA and bring it to heel for the Führer, Heinrich Himmler was at the threshold of recreating the SS as much more than just a freikorps or a palace guard. In his grand vision, the SS would become an order of Black Knights that would embody the purist Ariosophic ideals. He imagined their destiny was to be the greatest Nordic warrior caste since the Armanen elite had held their swords aloft to salute Wotan himself.

CHAPTER 5

The Old Crooked Cross

———

THE FLAG THAT HEINRICH HIMMLER had held so proudly in November 1923 was the red, black, and white standard of the Second Reich. He held it in defiance of the Weimar Republic and with nostalgia for the glorious past. Both reasons resonated strongly with many like-minded German nationalists in the turbulent days of the postwar political scene.

Hitler, too, was thinking of flags, but his idea was to go back to the future. He wanted to take the Nazi ideal forward by making a break with the recent past and going back into the remote corners of prehistory. Like Himmler, he saw the Nazi Party as more than a party. He imagined it deserving of an emblem that embodied simplicity and recognizability. He wanted a graphic symbol, a logo, to unify the iconography of this party that was more than just a party. In the case of an organization that would claim a link with primeval priests and heroes, the symbol must be ancient.

The study of ancient Nordic runes had been an integral part of Völkisch New Age literature. Guido von List had understood the importance of runes and had made them an integral part of his doctrine. Jörg Lanz von Liebenfels also was a student of ancient symbols, and he was probably the first member of the Völkisch New Age to use the symbol that became the icon of Nazism. Known in German as the *Hakenkreuz,* meaning "crooked cross," or "hooked cross," the emblem is best known by the Sanskrit term *swastika,* meaning "well-being" or "auspicious."

Known in German as the *Hakenkreuz*, meaning "crooked cross" or "hooked cross," this symbol is best known by the Sanskrit term "swastika," meaning "well-being" or "auspicious." Though it had been used globally for centuries, by such diverse peoples as the Buddhists in India and the Navajo in Arizona, the Nazis seized it and made it their ubiquitous emblem. As Hitler wrote in *Mein Kampf,* "An effective insignia can in hundreds of thousands of cases give the first impetus toward interest in a movement."

Author's collection

From a runic perspective, the hakenkreuz can be seen as two Sig, or Sigel, runes superimposed on one another at a ninety-degree angle.

Though it was not exactly unique, the swastika certainly qualified as primeval. Indeed, it had been used by ancient, albeit unrelated, cultures all over the world. It still is. It is often used to represent the sun, and often it implies, as in the Sanskrit word, good fortune. The author Joseph Campbell, best known for his popular works on comparative religion and mythology, has noted that the swastika had been depicted in human artifacts since at least 10,000 BC, when one was carved into a mammoth tusk by a paleolithic person near what is now Kiev in Ukraine. Since then, it has appeared often in decorative arts, from carvings to textiles, and in religious art around the world.

Archaeologists and anthropologists still argue whether it was passed around the world hand to hand, or whether the shape just occurred naturally to many people, as part of what the psychologist Carl Jung called the collective unconscious. Some have suggested that it is a geometric form that occurred naturally in basket weaving. Astronomer Carl Sagan notes that jets of gas from spinning comets can pinwheel into the hooked-arm shape of a swastika. In his book *Comet,* Sagan published a Chinese illustration of such a comet from the Han Dynasty period (circa 150 BC).

Archaeologists have found swastikas on Bronze Age pottery, and its use in Hinduism and Buddhism long predates the birth of Christianity and the use of the Christian cross as a symbol. Oriented both clockwise and counterclockwise, the swastika has also been found in numerous pre-Christian sites across Europe, from Ireland to the Balkans. It was used in ancient Greece, where it was known as the gammadion. In the regions of northern Europe that List and Lanz imagined as the origin of the Aryan race, swastikas were associated with the hammer of Thor. Swastikas later appeared on Christian churches, in association with secret societies such as the Teutonic Knights, and even in Jewish Kabalistic literature. It was also widely used as an official symbol in Finland and Estonia in the nineteenth and early twentieth centuries.

The archeologist Heinrich Schliemann, when excavating the site of ancient Troy in the 1860s, found swastikas in the ruins. Linking these with others that had been unearthed in Greece and northern Europe, he hypothesized ancient Indo-Europeans, migrating between India and Europe, shared a common religion, or at least a common religious symbol.

And then Madame Blavatsky had used a swastika in the Theosophical Society's seal, along with an ancient Egyptian ankh, the Star of David, and the ancient Ouroboros, a symbol of eternity that depicts a dragon eating its own tail.

Though the Ariosophists would make a big deal of the swastika's presence throughout the geography of Indo-European culture—from India and Tibet to northern Europe—swastikas were also widely used in pre-Columbian North America, especially among the Navajo. Indeed, because of the Navajo, swastikas appeared as an emblem on Arizona state-highway signage until the 1940s.

While it was certainly a religious symbol in certain contexts, the swastika was also used as a decorative symbol from architectural motifs to nineteenth-century greeting cards. By the late nineteenth and early twentieth century, it was widely used in advertising and packaging. For example, in the United States alone, the swastika could be found promoting or selling American Biscuit Company Snow Flake biscuits, Buffum Tool Company products, Crane Valve Company products, Duplex adding machines, Federal Milling flour, Good Luck canning jars, Iron City produce, IVW Brown Estate California eating fruit, KRIT automobiles, the Miller Brothers Wild West Rodeo, Pacific Coast matzos, Peoria Corporation grain alcohol, Standard Quality cigars, Swastika surf boards, and United States Playing Card cards and chips, as well as a popular soft drink called Coca-Cola.

When he first flew his swastika flag in 1907, Jörg Lanz von Liebenfels was probably the first to use the symbol in the context of Aryan superiority, unless you count its use by Madame Blavatsky in her literature and in talismans that she created.

The Germanenorden used various runes, and in 1916, they began using a swastika in ceremonial decoration and superimposed on a cross in their newsletter. The Thule Society, which was probably a spin-off of the Germanenorden, was using the swastika by 1918. Rudolf Freiherr von Sebottendorff of the Thule Society also used the rune called Ar to symbolize a rising eagle and hence the rebirth of Germany.

In 1919, Friedrich Krohn, a dentist from Starnberg, a longtime Völkisch researcher, and a member of both the Germanenorden and Thule Society, may have been the first to suggest the swastika become a symbol of the Nazi Party. Other sources suggest that Hitler himself may have fixated on swastikas that he probably saw at the Benedictine Abbey in Lambach-am-Traum, Austria, when he lived in the town with his parents in around 1898. Coincidentally, Jörg Lanz von Liebenfels spent some time studying manuscripts in the same abbey at about the same time, although only a few conspiracy theorists have suggested that he met Hitler, who would have been only nine or ten years old. Lanz also often used swastikas in his magazine *Ostara,* which Hitler read when he was a struggling art student in Vienna.

In *Mein Kampf,* Hitler devoted several pages to his version of the story of how the NSDAP developed its flag. He wrote that the flag "had to be equally a symbol of our own struggle" and " highly effective as a poster," adding that "anyone who has to concern himself much with the masses will recognize these apparent trifles to be very important matters. An effective insignia can in hundreds of thousands of cases give the first impetus toward interest in a movement."

Apparently the swastika figured into the majority of the flag designs that were proposed to Hitler. However, Hitler complains in *Mein Kampf* that "I was obliged to reject without exception the numerous designs which poured in from the circles of the young movement, and which for the most part had drawn the swastika into the old [German Imperial] flag. I myself—as Führer—did not want to come out publicly at once with my own design, since after all it was possible that another should produce one just as good or perhaps even better."

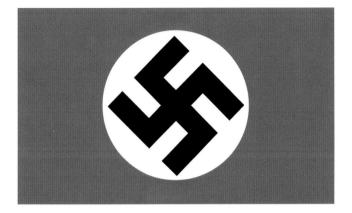

The German national flag (1933–1945) originated as the Nazi Party flag. Adolf Hitler himself claimed to have designed it, writing in *Mein Kampf,* "I myself . . . after innumerable attempts, had laid down a final form; a flag with a red background, a white disk, and a black swastika in the middle. After long trials I also found a definite proportion between the size of the flag and the size of the white disk, as well as the shape and thickness of the swastika." *Author's collection*

He finally confirms that the basic design came from Friedrich Krohn, observing that "actually, a dentist from Starnberg did deliver a design that was not bad at all, and, incidentally, was quite close to my own, having only the one fault that a swastika with curved legs was composed into a white disk."

At last, writes Hitler, "I myself, meanwhile, after innumerable attempts, had laid down a final form; a flag with a red background, a white disk, and a black swastika in the middle. After long trials I also found a definite proportion between the size of the flag and the size of the white disk, as well as the shape and thickness of the swastika."

In discussing the colors, the former art student went on to thoughtfully explain that "white is not a stirring color. It is suitable for chaste virgins' clubs, but not for world-changing movements in a revolutionary epoch," while black "contained nothing . . . that could in any way be interpreted as a picture of the will of our movement."

Ruling out blue because of its presence on the Bavarian state flag, Hitler came to a combination of black, white, and red, the colors of the old imperial flag, which he calls "the most brilliant harmony in existence." He continued, "As National Socialists, we see our program in our flag. In red we see the social ideal of the movement, in white the nationalistic ideal in the swastika the mission of

Adopted in 1932, the logo of Heinrich Himmler's SS was actually a pair of Sig runes from the Armanen Futharkh of Guido von List. The corresponding runes in earlier runic systems mean "sun," but List's Sig rune means "victory." The Sig rune is also the rune for the letter s. Therefore, by using a pair of Sigs, the SS logo literally reads "SS," *and* it screams "Victory, Victory!"

The flag of the Schutzstaffel showed the SS logo in white against a black background. The flag and innovative logo were designed by SS Sturmführer Walther Heck, a graphic designer who worked for the firm of Ferdinand Hoffstatter in Bonn, a manufacturer of emblems and insignias. The logo was also later referred to as "lightning bolts."

This rendering of the SS runic logo is from a typesetting font, circa 1933. The logo was so ubiquitous that it was actually typeset in place of a double s. Typewriters made in Germany during the Third Reich era had a key that typed the logo.

Author's collection

the struggle for the victory of the Aryan man, and, by the same token, the victory of the idea of creative work, which as such always has been and always will be anti-Semitic."

Hitler then goes on to say that "in midsummer of 1920 the new flag came before the public for the first time. It was excellently suited to our new movement. It was young and new, like the movement itself. No one had seen it before; it had the effect of a burning torch. We ourselves experienced an almost childlike joy when a faithful woman party comrade for the first time executed the design and delivered the flag."

Thereafter, the swastika became ubiquitous within the party, appearing on everything from posters to tie tacks, in addition to flags by the hundred and the armbands of both SA and SS members. The official emblem of the party was an eagle, its wings spread, atop a swastika inside a circle. In most applications, the swastika was tipped at a forty-five-degree angle, so its perimeter was that of a diamond, rather than a square.

"And a symbol it really is!" Hitler gushed when describing the Nazi flag. "Not only that the unique colors, which all of us so passionately love and which

The symbol known as the Wolfsangel (Wolf's Hook) has long been used in Germanic heraldry. Without the crossbar, the vertical variant seen here is similar to the Eoh rune in the Anglo-Saxon Futhorc and the Eihwaz rune in the Elder Futhark. The vertical Wolfsangel is associated with the Donnerkeil (thunderbolt) in heraldry.

The horizontal form of the Wolfsangel, also used in Germanic heraldry, has been used to symbolize werewolves. Among other Third Reich uses, it was the insignia of the Number 2 SS Panzer Division Das Reich and the Number 34 SS Freiwilliger Grenadier Division Landstorm Nederland.

The Totenkopf, or death's head, was also part of the SS iconography. Death's head emblems of one sort or another have been used off and on throughout history as a military insignia. As such, they serve the dual purpose of frightening the enemy and reminding the wearer that—if necessary—he is to give up his life for his corps. The SS used their Totenkopf for diverse applications, such as on banners and insignia, but most prominently on the uniform caps of SS officers.

Author's collection

once won so much honor for the German people, attest our veneration for the past; they were also the best embodiment of the movement's will."

Meanwhile, Heinrich Himmler was contemplating the vestments and trappings that would underscore the status of the SS as the elite within the movement. For the design of its insignia, the SS turned in to the rune Sig from Guido von List's Armanen Futharkh. This rune was derived from the Elder Futhark rune signifying the sun. At its origins, perhaps in the second century, the rune was the four-stroke shape of a Greek Sigma (Σ) and was called *Sól* in Old Norse, *Sôwilô* in Old German, and *Sigel* in Anglo-Saxon. After about the fifth century, in the Younger Futhark, the old rune was simplified by the removal of the bottom stroke, rendering a rune similar in appearance to a letter *S*.

In his 1915 book *Runic and Heroic Poems,* Bruce Dickins includes a couple poems that summarize the "character" of the rune Sig. In an Old Norse rune poem, the author writes that "Sól [the sun] is the light of the world; I bow to the divine decree." In another poem from Iceland, the ancient writer states that "Sól is the shield of the clouds and shining ray and destroyer of ice."

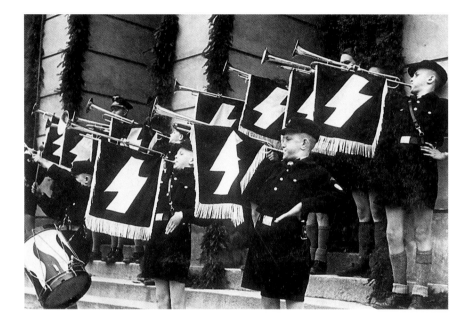

The Hitlerjugend (Hitler Youth) organization, specifically the Deutsches Jungvolk section for boys from age ten to fourteen, used a single Sig rune in their insignia. As with the SS, it was used against a dark background. *U.S. National Archives*

Such metaphors must certainly have gotten Heinrich Himmler's juices flowing. Also to Himmler's mystic pleasure had to have been List's having shortened "Sigel" to "Sig," implying the German word *Seig*, thus transforming the meaning from "sun" to "victory."

The person specifically responsible for turning the rune Sig into the SS logo was SS-*Sturmführer* (sergeant) Walther Heck, a graphic designer who worked for the firm of Ferdinand Hoffstatter, a manufacturer of emblems and insignias, in Bonn. Heck's clever design, rolled out in 1932, involved a pair of Sigs. Because the rune Sig looks like the letter *S*, especially a Gothic letter *S*, the SS logo was "SS" rendered in a pair of runes that literally screamed "Victory, victory!" The logo later was referred to as "lightning bolts," because of its appearance. Again, Himmler would have been pleased.

The Nazis were so impressed with the logo that in contemporary literature, when the term "SS" appeared in a narrative, it was often typeset using runes rather than letters, regardless of what typeface was used for the other text on the page. On many German typewriters manufactured in the 1930s and 1940s, there was even a single key that typed the pair of Sigs logo. Many documents typed with such machines still exist, and there are still probably a few such typewriters around.

The runic insignia was also used, of course, on SS uniforms, unit badges, and other materials. The most prominent use of the emblem was on flags and banners.

A flag with a single Sig was also later used by the *Hitlerjugend* (Hitler Youth Organization), but not as its primary insignia. The Hitlerjugend also used the Armanen Rune Tyr, borrowed directly from the Younger Futhark Tyr, which looks like an arrow pointing straight up. The rune is named for the Norse god of solo combat, who is identified as Wotan's son in some ancient literature. (Fantasy author J. R. R. Tolkien—an avid rune scholar himself—used the rune Sig, with its Anglo-Saxon name, "Sigel," to identify an imaginary place called Sigelwara Land. This land first figured in an essay of the same name that was published in 1932, the same year that Himmler turned to the rune Sig for the SS.)

The use of the runes as an SS symbol was preceded by Julius Schreck's adoption of the Totenkopf, or death's head, as an SS insignia. Resembling a skull and crossbones or Jolly Roger, this image was used as the insignia of several eighteenth-century pirates, and it survives as the familiar symbol on pirate flags in modern pop culture. Of course, the display of a human skull to threaten death goes back to the dawn of human conflict. Himmler probably imagined the ancient warriors of the antediluvian Armanenist past being decked out in death's heads.

As an official military insignia, the Totenkopf was used often throughout history. For example, in the early eighteenth century, Hussars fighting in the Prussian army of Frederick the Great used it. During the Napoleonic Wars, it appeared on the uniform of the troops of the duke of Braunschweig-Lüneburg and remained in use by units from Braunschweig through World War I. After the war, it cropped up on the uniforms of various freikorps. For many military units, the death's head was adopted to symbolize the willingness of the wearer to die for the unit or the cause. Such was the case with the SS, who pledged their lives to the objectives of the Third Reich.

While pirates and other early users of the Totenkopf depicted the skull straight on, the SS turned it slightly to the right. It was used on various banners and insignia, but most prominently on the uniform caps of SS officers, directly beneath the eagle-and-swastika insignia of the NSDAP and of the Third Reich.

Symbols are important not in themselves, but for that which the minds of the masses can and do read into them. Both Hitler and Himmler understood this as well or better than anyone. The age-old meaning of the death's head needed no explanation. The swastika came into the Nazi fold with many meanings, most of them warm and fuzzy. However, after the Nazis were through with it, no one would ever look at it the same way again. Even Hindus and Buddhists understand that it now has a double meaning.

While neither the swastika nor the Totenkopf was unique to the Nazis, Walther Heck's lightning-bolt double runic logo was. The paired Sig runes of the SS became an emblem that, more even than the swastika itself, embodied the malice and brutality that would emanate from Germany to engulf Europe. Even today, the insignia has the ability to bring chills to the spine. To paraphrase Hitler, what a symbol it really was.

CHAPTER 6

Ballot Boxes
and Long Knives

—————

DURING 1933 AND 1934, two factors came into play in such a manner as to place Hitler into power, to secure that power, and to secure Heinrich Himmler's shadowy, sinister place as the second most powerful man in the reborn Reich.

It all began at the ballot box. Under its distinctive banner, the NSDAP rose to power far more quickly than anyone might have expected. From a fringe party with just a dozen of the Reichstag's 493 seats in May 1928, the party's number of seats had spiraled up to 107 in the September 1930 election. In the next election, held in July 1932, the Nazis won 230 seats, becoming, for the first time, the largest political party in Germany.

The Nazi party's rise was like a mythological tale of a serpent being born out of tumult. After the chaos of its early years, the Weimar Republic had stabilized in the mid-1920s. Currency reforms had brought an end to hyperinflation by putting the reichsmark on the gold standard. The global economic boom that resulted in the Roaring Twenties helped to stabilize the economy of Germany, although the severe reparations demanded of Germany by the hated Treaty of Versailles still held the country down like a schoolyard bully.

A certain amount of stability and continuity was provided by the image of the nation's president. Under the Weimar constitution, the role of the kaiser as head of both state and government had been superseded by an elected presi-

Adolf Hitler salutes the crowd in Nuremberg in November 1935, flanked by slouching, brown-shirted SA men on the left and helmeted SS men, standing upright on the right. *U.S. National Archives*

dent, who served as head of state and who appointed the *Reichskanzler* (chancellor), who headed the government. While the president was more of a figurehead, the chancellor ran the government. In 1925, the people had elected the strong and familiar Paul von Hindenburg as president. He had come out of retirement in 1914 to serve as chief of the general staff during World War I, and he came out of retirement again in 1925. Though the country went through a revolving door of chancellors, the familiar, fatherly figurehead remained the same through a critical period of stabilization.

Had the rest of the world not collapsed suddenly in 1929, the history of Germany probably would have gone differently. The NSDAP probably would not have gotten those 107 seats in September 1930. Nor would there have been the succession of events that followed.

After a decade of prosperity in the Western world came Black Thursday. On October 24, 1929, the New York Stock Exchange crashed, and falling economic dominoes rippled across the world financial markets. The twenties no longer roared, but sobbed.

In Germany, it was the Munich of 1919 all over again. The nation needed a strong hand, but would it be gloved in the red of the communists, or the black of the Nazis? The answer came when it was the Nazis who displaced the centrist Social Democrats in first place among the nation's political parties, and the Communists remained mired in third place.

In March 1932, the Weimar Republic was due to hold a presidential election, and Adolf Hitler announced his candidacy. At age eighty-four, and with his health failing, Hindenburg had hoped to retire for the last time, but those who feared the Nazis realized that he was the only man who could beat Hitler. Hitler came in second in both the first and second rounds of the election. In the run-off on April 10, Hindenburg garnered 53.1 percent to Hitler's 36.7, while the Communist candidate, Ernst Thallman, was a distant third. The Nazis were held at bay, but three months later, they held the largest blocks of seats in the Reichstag. It seemed that Hitler was indeed accomplishing with

A "mass roll call" of SA, SS, and other uniformed Nazis at the annual Reichsparteitag rally inside the massive Luitpoldhain amphitheater in Nuremberg.
U.S. National Archives

ballots what he knew would have been impossible without bullets.

When Chancellor Franz von Papen called another Reichstag election in November, the Nazis lost some ground, but still remained the largest party. Because the Social Democrats and the Nazis distrusted one another—and the Communists—the government remained paralyzed. Because no party had a strong enough majority, nothing got done. The government was paralyzed, and the people demanded a strong hand. Finally, Papen convinced Hindenburg to appoint Hitler as chancellor—just to break the impasse.

On January 30, 1933, Hitler became Reichskanzler. As such, he was asked by the president, Hindenburg, to form a new government. Five weeks later, on March 5, 1933, the Weimar Republic held its last election—the last free election to include all of Germany for the next fifty-seven years.

It has been said that the Communists might have done better had it not been for a fire, set by a Communist, that gutted the Reichstag itself on February 27. A Dutch communist named Marinus van der Lubbe was arrested, convicted, and executed for the arson. He was almost certainly involved, but theories of a conspiracy have circulated for years. Though the Communist Party as a whole was blamed for the fire, it lost just 19 of the 100 seats it had held, and the Social Democrats lost only one. However, the Nazis won 92 and retained their majority. The tide had definitely turned.

Also passed in March 1933 was the *Ermächtigungsgesetz* (enabling act). It amounted to a mandate giving the chancellor the right to exercise near dictatorial powers. The dithering years of the revolving door of chancellors had brought forth a desire to put more power into the office in order to get things done. Had the new chancellor been someone other than Adolf Hitler, things would have been much different, but history is full of turning points and in 1933, Germany was overflowing with them.

Fifteen years after the humbling dissolution of the Second Reich, a new Third Reich emerged. With Hitler legally entitled to form a new government, there was no doubt that government would be a fusion of party and nation. It was, said Hitler, a Reich that would last a thousand years.

Under the Nazis, there was also a move toward consolidating power in the central government in Berlin and limiting the political and administrative authority of the sixteen German lander, or states.

As this new government was forming, Nazis from every corner of the party jockeyed for position, each staking out turf and grabbing for portfolios in the new government. Though lost in the crowd in any cursory view of the Third Reich hierarchy as a "minister without portfolio," Dr. Alfred Rosenberg now effectively wielded the portfolio of the Reich's "racial philosopher." The Estonian-born engineer Rosenberg had been a Thule Society member, an early confidant of Dietrich Eckart, and a member of the Deutsche Arbeiterpartei, the Nazi Party precursor, even before Hitler himself. A devotee of racial theorists such as Houston Stewart Chamberlain, he had aligned himself with Helena Blavatsky, Guido von List, and Jörg Lanz von Liebenfels in believing in a qualitative racial hierarchy that was topped by Aryans. Indeed, he had been among the first to use the term *untermensch* ("under man," or subhuman) to describe both Slavs and Jews. Rosenberg shared Hitler's disdain for both Jews and Bolsheviks, and he had developed a theory in which the two were parties to an overarching, international conspiracy against Germany. In the 1920s and early 1930s, Rosenberg helped create organizations such as the Militant League for German Culture and the Institute for the Study of the Jewish Question. A loyal NSDAP man, Rosenberg had earlier served as an ideological caretaker while Hitler was in Landsberg, and he was elected to the Reichstag in 1930 on the NSDAP slate. In January 1934, Hitler made him a sort of racial philosopher-in-chief for the party and for the Reich.

Many of the early philosophers who had influenced Hitler and Himmler in their formative years, and who been key figures in such influential organizations as the Germanenorden and Thule Gesellschaft, were still around, though their influence had waned. Hitler had deliberately distanced himself from Jörg Lanz von Liebenfels since World War I. This was probably because he wanted his ideas and racial doctrines to appear as though they flowed from him, not from anything he might have picked up from the old Ariosophist or from having read *Ostara* when he was still a starving student back in prewar Vienna. In *Mein Kampf,* Hitler mentioned only in passing that he had read some "anti-Semitic pamphlets" while he was a student in Vienna.

Rudolf Freiherr von Sebottendorff, the early member of the DAP who was also a conspicuous figure in the Germanenorden and Thule Gesellschaft around the end of World War I, had dropped out of sight in the 1920s, returning to Turkey, where he had lived and worked before World War I. There are stories that he also traveled to Mexico during these years. He reappeared on the scene in Germany after Hitler took power, hoping to reassert himself within the ranks of the NSDAP and with the all-powerful Hitler. He certainly went about it the wrong way. Intending to inflate his own importance to the DAP back in the party's early days, he wrote *Bevor Hitler Kam: Urkundlich aus der Frühzeit der Nationalsozialistischen Bewegung (Before Hitler Came: Documents from the Early Days of the National Socialist Movement),* which was published in January 1933. As the title suggests, the book focused on the pre-Hitler origins of the party, which was a focus that Hitler did not want. Hitler had the book banned, and the old Thulean left the Reich, retreating back to Turkey, where he watched the Nazi era from the sidelines.

Another mysterious man in the shadows of Adolf Hitler's rise to power was Hermann Steinschneider. Like Hitler, he was born in Austria in 1889. The son of a Jewish actor, he took a page from the books of List and Lanz, renaming himself and claiming aristocratic lineage. As Erik Jan Hanussen, Danish nobleman, he made a name for himself in the middle-class parlors and theaters in Weimar-era Germany as an astrologer, clairvoyant, and hypnotist. It has been claimed that Hanussen met Hitler and taught him methods for mass hypnosis and crowd control. However, Hitler's own skills at such oratorical tasks were already quite abundant—or, as we recall from Karl Alexander von Müller, "almost like hocus-pocus."

Hanussen's controversial prediction of the Reichstag Fire is considered to be either an amazing feat of fortune-telling or evidence of inside information. Some people say that Hanussen had hypnotized Marinus van der Lubbe to get him to set the fire, but others claim that Hanussen was just a man who knew too much. As often happens with men who know too much, he did not last long. Like Sebottendorff, he had worn out his welcome. Shortly after the fire, he was found murdered and lying in a shallow grave near Berlin.

The Third Reich was made up of both philosophers and warriors. Heinrich Himmler imagined himself with a foot in both camps. The pompous Hermann Göring had no such illusions; the former World War I air ace imagined himself a warrior. Having dropped into the shadows after the failed putsch of 1923, Göring now reemerged in the forefront of the NSDAP. His portfolio would be that of the Interior Ministry of Prussia, the largest of the German states. Prussia accounted for three-quarters of Germany's area and 68 percent of its population—and Berlin was within Prussia. Bavaria, the second largest state, comprised a quarter of Germany's area, but just 15 percent of the population. His appointment as head of Prussia gave Göring a turf that was commensurate with his grandiose ego.

Within Göring's turf was the very powerful Prussian state police, and within the police was a Göring inlaw named Rudolf Diels. He

Rudolf Hess (1894-1987) was the Third Reich's deputy Führer when he made a mystery flight to Scotland in May 1941. Hess spent forty-six years in custody, never saying a word about his motives for this trip. He took his reason for it to his grave.

U.S. Army art collection

A solemn Heinrich Himmler (left) shakes the hand of a disappointed Hermann Göring (right), who handed him control of the Geheime Staatspolizei (Gestapo) in April 1934. The Gestapo had been Göring's idea, and he had hoped to command this secret national police force. However, Himmler outmaneuvered him, taking unquestioned control of all German police, to become the Third Reich's top cop.
U.S. National Archives

suggested, and Göring enthusiastically embraced, the creation of a powerful and authoritative police and intelligence apparatus that would extend its tentacles beyond Prussia and throughout all of Germany. The Göring-Diels blueprint called for a force called *Geheime Staatspolizei* (Secret State Police), headed by Diels and answerable directly to Göring himself. Known universally as the Gestapo, this entity would become an all-powerful super–police force that would have authority superior to that of the police forces of the sixteen individual lander. As the Nazis consolidated their power, these lander police forces would be consolidated into a nationwide regular police force known as the *Ordnungspolizei* (Order Police). They would be in the same chain of command as, but *beneath,* the Gestapo.

Heinrich Himmler, a cool, calculating character, was a study in contrast to the loud, bombastic Göring. As such, he approached the turf war more carefully. In the immediate aftermath of the Nazi victory, his turf was small, but would not be for long. Systematically, he worked to solidify his own turf and his place within the Third Reich. As Hitler moved the epicenter of the NSDAP from Munich to Berlin, Himmler appointed his own man in the capital. To neutralize Kurt Daluege, who still reigned autonomously at the SS offices in Berlin, held a seat in the Reichstag, and had been appointed by Hitler to be a minister without portfolio, Himmler sent Standartenführer SS (Colonel) Reinhard Heydrich, the man destined to become his strong right hand.

Had Hollywood central casting been responsible for casting the dark roster of the Third Reich, Himmler would have been cast as a clerk, and Heydrich would have been cast in the role of Reichsführer SS. Tall and Nordic in appearance, Heydrich had a chiseled face, a strong jaw and icy-cold, serpentine eyes. Four years younger than Himmler, he too had missed combat in World War I, although he eventually became involved with a Nationalist freikorps. In 1922, he enlisted as a cadet in Germany's minuscule postwar navy and attained the rank of lieutenant before his insatiable desire for women got him into trouble with the wrong people. In this case, the father of a jilted lover was the friend of Erich Raeder, the navy's chief of staff, and Heydrich was booted for conduct unbecoming an officer. Heydrich wound up marrying Lina von Osten, the "other woman" with whom he had been cheating on the rejected daughter of Raeder's pal.

In 1931, a friend of a friend got Heydrich a face-to-face interview with Himmler, who hired him immediately to head his new SS intelligence and counterintelligence apparatus, which became the *Sicherheitsdienst* (SD, or Security Service), in June 1932. In 1933, Heydrich became Himmler's man in Berlin and part of his master plan. This master plan was nothing short of having Himmler become Germany's chief of police. In April 1933, one might have made the case for either Göring or Röhm achieving this goal, but nobody ever overestimated the calculating cleverness of Heinrich Himmler.

While Göring and Diels were dreaming of expanding the Prussian state police into a nationwide police force, Himmler was operating on a parallel premise. As Göring controlled the Prussian police, Himmler now controlled the police in Bavaria. With ruthless efficiency, he was turning that state into a model for the kind of police state that he planned for all of Germany. In March 1933, he established a *Konzentrationslager,* a prison facility in which to "concentrate" communists and other political enemies of the NSDAP and the Third Reich. Located in Dachau, near Munich, this concentration camp would become a model for much worse things to come.

Himmler was also reworking the Führer's bodyguard detail, the Stosstruppe Adolf Hitler, into a small but effective paramilitary force, headed by Gruppenführer SS Josef "Sepp" Dietrich, who had been part of Hitler's succession of bodyguard units since 1928. With his Völkisch interest in old-fashioned Germanic terminology, Himmler fixated on an antiquated term for bodyguard, *Leibstandarte,* and with the Führer's acquiescence, named himself to be the "Leibstandarte Adolf Hitler."

The immense eagle and swastika, the emblems of the Nazi Party, became the state emblems of Germany when Hitler took power. Here, Hitler addresses the Reichstag, Germany's parliament, in 1938 as the body's members give the Nazi salute. *U.S. National Archives*

By the end of 1933, with the aid of Wilhelm Frick, the Reich interior minister, Himmler had muscled nine additional lander police departments under SS control. By February 1934, he controlled all but two, one of which was Prussia.

On April 10, 1934, a checkmated Göring handed over the keys to Gestapo headquarters at Number 8 Prinz-Albrechtstrasse in Berlin. (Diels was hustled out the back door and exiled to a minor political post in Cologne, where he would remain under Göring's protection, safe but neutered.) Himmler would maintain his own offices at this address, while Heydrich would settle the SD into offices nearby at Number 102 Wilhelmstrasse.

Himmler now controlled both the SS and the Gestapo, although it would not be until February 1936 that Hitler formally decreed that Himmler was the *Chef der Deutschen Polizei,* or the police chief of the Third Reich.

As Hermann Göring had aspired to have the Gestapo emerge as a national constabulary under his control, Ernst Röhm imagined that his SA would soon supplant the rickety Reichswehr as Germany's national army. Indeed, while the Reichswehr had a strength of 100,000 men, the SA had half a million in its brown uniform. The NSDAP had built an army for a battle for power that had never come, yet this unnecessary army still remained.

There was no love lost between the old generals of the Reichswehr and the SA. The former regarded the SA as nothing more than a street gang—a characterization that was essentially correct. In the spring of 1933, the Reichswehr begrudgingly struck a cooperative agreement with the SA for the latter to provide training and a conduit for recruiting, but Röhm considered it only a matter of time before he—not the Reichswehr generals—ruled Germany's armed forces.

Once there had been the day when Heinrich Himmler had looked up at Captain Ernst Röhm and seen a powerful warrior, a man to be admired. Over time, as Himmler's own star in the NSDAP and within the Reich spiraled upward, the infatuation flickered and faded, resettling on a new Führer—*the* Führer. Nevertheless, Himmler had continued to believe that the SS and the SA could coexist. As Himmler himself described it, "The SA is the infantry of the line, the SS the Guards. There has always been a guard; the Persians had one, the Greeks, Caesar and Napoleon, Frederick the Great, right up to the world war; the SS will be the imperial guard of the new Germany."

By the beginning of 1934, however, Röhm's pretensions of grandeur were making coexistence impossible. Göring understood it as well. Indeed, part of the back-room deal that he cut in order to hand control of the Gestapo to Himmler was the latter's agreement to coexist with Röhm no longer. A clandestine plot to oust Röhm emerged. It was not merely a scheme involving more political maneuvering; it was an assassination plot. The conspirators included Göring and his inner circle allied with Himmler and his.

Röhm's own outspoken arrogance made it easy to convince the führer that Röhm was planning a putsch against Hitler himself. Though this was not literally true, it was not a stretch for Hitler to believe such a thing. Viktor Lutze, an SA officer loyal to Hitler, had been whispering in the Führer's ear about the derogatory things that Röhm was saying about him personally.

With Reinhard Heydrich and his SD playing the key role in operational planning, the scheme called for the simultaneous elimination of most of the SA hierarchy. Target lists were compiled by Himmler, Göring, and Heydrich, and then cross-checked with meticulous detail. It was a plan that was ambitious as it was sinister, and even Hitler was initially apprehensive at the thought of crossing the large and powerful SA.

On June 30, 1934, the operation code named *Kolibri* (Hummingbird) swung into action. Röhm and much of the key SA leadership had previously been summoned to the hotel Hanselbauer at Bad Wiessee, a spa resort located on the Tegernsee, south of Munich. Hitler himself, accompanied by Goebbels, led a large contingent of SS to the hotel to arrest Röhm and the others. Other raids were conducted simultaneously throughout Germany. Secret orders were given, and SS death squads, especially the men of the Leibstandarte Adolf Hitler, plied their trade with brutality and efficiency. The deliberate and ruthless carnage was called the *Nacht der Langen Messer* (Night of the Long Knives).

For those not killed in the raids that night, summary executions followed. The death toll included around eighty prominent SA leaders, as well as many other perceived enemies of Hitler's hopes and dreams. Some estimates put the total number in the hundreds. Taken to Stadelheim Prison in Munich, Ernst Röhm was given an opportunity to commit suicide. He refused and was shot on Hitler's orders on July 2. The next day, Hitler's cabinet promulgated a decree giving retroactive legal sanction to the bloodshed, proclaiming that these measures had been necessary to suppress a treasonous assault on the sovereignty of the Reich. The proclamation was signed by Reichskanzler Hitler himself.

In the aftermath, Hitler installed Viktor Lutze to head the SA. Thereafter, it declined greatly in membership and even more steeply in prestige. The SA never again threatened Hitler, the Nazi Party, or the primacy of the SS as the paramount elite warrior caste within the Third Reich.

During 1933, thanks to the ballot box, Adolf Hitler had finally achieved the power he craved. In 1934, thanks to everything that came to a head on the Night of the Long Knives, Hitler's power was secure and unthreatened from within.

Thanks also the Night of the Long Knives, Heinrich Himmler, the man whom Heinrich Hossbach called Hitler's "evil spirit," now wielded power, mainly still unseen, that assured him his place as the second most powerful man in the Third Reich.

A dramatic display of uniformed German troops at the 1937 Reichsparteitag rally at the massive Luitpoldhain amphitheater in Nuremberg. *U.S. National Archives*

As the Night of the Long Knives faded to black, the Nazis entered an era in which their power was celebrated in a night of an entirely different sort. Thanks to the award-winning documentary filmed just three months later by Leni Riefenstahl, an enduring image of the pagan splendor of the Third Reich entered and remained part of the lasting visual legacy of the civilization Hitler created for Germany. Riefenstahl's movie, *Triumph des Willens (Triumph of the Will),* considered one of the most effective propaganda films, documents the second of the annual *Reichsparteitag,* or mass rallies, that were held at the massive Luitpoldhain amphitheater in Nuremberg between 1933 and 1938, and prior to those years on a smaller scale in other cities.

The sight of more than a half million uniformed Germans, marching by torchlight beneath massive swastika banners to the sounds of stirring martial music and Hitler's hocus-pocus speeches, was a dramatic signal to the world that the Third Reich had arrived—and that the world was best advised to watch out.

CHAPTER 7

Black Knights of the Master Race

F AR FROM UNSEEN, the Black Knights of Himmler's Schutzstaffel now became as he had imagined them: the stern face of the new Germany, marching beneath their banners at Nuremberg, the sinister, flickering light of the torches playing upon their hard faces and their polished black leather. With their roots in the murky past of Germanic lore, they were like Armanen princelings or the warriors of the Nibelungenlied, suddenly reborn to a new calling.

The Night of the Long Knives turned out to be an extraordinary SS recruiting tool, in that it removed the SA as a rival to the SS in the minds of potential volunteers. Among those who flocked to the SS were the upper crust and nobility of the old elite of Imperial German society. Among them was Josias Waldeck, the hereditary prince of Waldeck and Pyrmont, a nephew of Wilhelm of Württemberg, cousin of Queen Wilhelmina of the Netherlands and of Charles Edward, Duke of Saxe-Coburg and Gotha, who was related to the British royal family. As an enthusiastic SS man, Waldeck rose quickly to the rank of *Oberturmbannführer* and later to general.

Young blonde men with the obligatory duelling scars on their cheeks and "vons" in their Nordic family names flocked to the SS as their fathers had to the best regiments of the old guard. Indeed, the stark flags with their runic heraldry and the stern and stirring martial music that accompanied SS rituals were reminiscent of the bygone days of knightly pomp. So too, of course, were the striking

The cap and dagger of the SS officer, emblazoned with winged Hakenkreuz and the Totenkopf. The latter had the dual symbolism of striking fear into enemies and affirming that the SS man would rather die than submit to his enemies. Many did. *Photo by Kris Simoens, used by permission*

uniforms, solid black from cap to jackboot, with their runes and death's heads.

The uniforms were designed by Walther Heck, the graphic designer that had come up with the runic SS logo, and Dr. Karl Diebitsch, an SS Oberführer at the time. Diebitsch had earlier taken a top ribbon at the 1938 Nazi art show at the *Haus der Deutschen Kunst* (House of German Art) in Munich with a painting celebrating heroic Germanic motherhood. Diebitsch was also the designer of much of the regalia that the SS used, including the dagger and chained scabbard that each SS man wore as part of his dress uniform to underscore the warrior image that Himmler craved in his Black Knights.

The uniforms themselves, nearly a million of them, were manufactured from 1933 through 1945, mainly at the textile factory in Metzingen owned by a man named Hugo Boss, who had joined the NSDAP in 1931. Boss died in 1948, and the company evolved into a respected manufacturer of very high-end apparel later in the twentieth century. The company's past SS involvement was forgotten—even within the company itself—until a Nazi-era Swiss bank account in Hugo Boss's name turned up in 1997. According to an article in the *New York Times* of August 15, 1997, "Before Hugo Boss AG became known for classic men's suits and flashy ties, the clothing manufacturer made uniforms for the Nazis."

"We are trying to get a handle on the situation," Boss spokeswoman Monika Steilen told the paper. "This is a very new theme for us. We have nothing in our archives."

Boss suits were flashy even in the 1930s and 1940s. For the Völkisch romantics, and to the nationalist on the street that yearned for the lost glories of another age, the SS men in black were a thrilling sight. For those who didn't fall within the strict parameters of Ariosophic doctrine, they would prove to be a nightmare.

In fact, many who had yearned to be part of the SS world felt the sting of disappointment when they discovered that they themselves didn't fall within the strict parameters of Ariosophic doctrine. Once Himmler had been strict about membership requirements, but now he could afford to actually purge the SS of those who did not meet his increasingly exacting standards. Of course, these precepts were not so much a man's IQ or the number of pushups that he could do, but the Aryan purity of the blood in his veins and his Nordic appearance. Had DNA testing existed in the 1930s, Himmler would have used it.

Himmler was at last in a position to exercise all of his notions of race and blood. Just as the nineteenth-century ethnocentrists had decided that Aryans were the superior race and, therefore, the master race, Himmler, like Hitler, could now proclaim that the Aryan race had the divine right—and duty—to "master" the inferior races. The knights of the SS would be bred as the vehicle of that mastery.

As Hitler was forming his government, Ricardo Walther Oscar "Richard" Darré reappeared on the scene. The author of the narrowly influential *Peasantry as the Life-Source of the Nordic Race,* who had spent the Nazi power-grabbing years organizing farm folk on behalf of the party, was brought to Berlin as the new Reichsminister of Food and Agriculture. His Blut und Boden (blood and soil) philosophy had gotten Himmler's attention earlier, and Darré would now be instrumental in crafting racial policies for the SS. Splitting his time between his ministry and Himmler's office, he helped come up with the specific criteria for guaranteeing Aryan credentials.

In the absence of the airtight credentials of DNA, the SS now required that an applicant prove that his family tree contained neither Slavs nor Jews

back to 1800. If one wanted to be considered as an SS *officer*, this proof had to be pushed back a couple of generations to 1750. The full genealogical chart was kept in a document called a *Sippenbuch,* a kinship or clan book, not unlike the sort of stud book that owners keep for racehorses. At one point, under the Sippenbuch rules, a non-SS man who'd had a Jewish ancestor in 1711 was forbidden to marry the daughter of an SS officer. Any drop of tainted blood kept a man out or was grounds for expulsion if he had somehow slipped into the SS.

The SS leadership, decked out in their black uniforms and Totenkopf caps. Heinrich Himmler is in the center of the front row, with glasses and mustache. The tall man to his right is Kurt Daluege. At the far right of the front row is SS Gruppenführer Josef "Sepp" Dietrich, who headed the Leibstandarte Adolf Hitler, the Führer's bodyguard detail. *Author's collection*

Die SS Ausleseprinzip
(The SS Selection Principle)
by Heinrich Himmler, 1943

We [the SS Order] are the result of the law of the selection. We have been selected from among our people. The [Germanic] people are the culmination of fate and history developed from long ago, from primeval times, through many generations and centuries. Over these years, other peoples have evolved, and their genetic make-up sidetracked. The other bloodlines have led into ours, but our people have nevertheless succeeded, despite most terrible challenges, and most terrible strokes of fate, because of the strength of our bloodline. With this, the whole people with Nordic-Germanic blood is held together, so that one could still speak of a German people. From this people, with variously mixed hereditary factors, we consciously select those with the Nordic, Germanic blood, since we can assume this blood to be the carrier of the life-supporting characteristics of our people.

We partly used outside appearance [in the SS selection process], and have continued to examine this appearance always through new means, always through new samples, physically and mentally. We selected again and again, and discarded those who were not suitable, which did not fit us. In addition, for a long time we have sought strength, so for the health of our Order.

We are obligated, whenever we meet, to deliberate on our principles of blood, selection, and hardness. The law of nature is evenly this: That which is hard, which is strong, is good.

Gentlemen, from you, the German people expect tremendous hardness.

(Translated from material in the collection of the United States National Archives in College Park, Maryland)

While Himmler specifically did not give extra consideration to the aristocrats, those with "vons" in their Nordic names, most such men were from families that passed the pedigree test. Eventually, between 10 and 20 percent of SS officers with ranks equivalent to generals were from the nobility. Then, too, such families were able and willing to contribute significantly to SS fundraising events. Himmler, the Aryan idealist, was a realist when it came to turning blue bloods into Black Knights when there was money involved.

From a membership of around 3,000 in 1930 and 50,000 in 1932, the SS grew to over 240,000 by 1939, not counting the Gestapo and a complex web of other police agencies that were under SS control.

Among these other agencies were the regular police, the Ordnungspolizei (Order Police), the national police force that superseded the formerly independent police forces of the individual lander. Though they were part of Wilhelm Frick's Interior Ministry, the Ordnungspolizei, like the Gestapo, answered to Himmler's chain of command. Also in Himmler's chain of command were the *Kriminalpolizei,* or criminal investigation police, and the *Sicherheitspolizei,* or Security Police.

Together with the Gestapo, the Sicherheitsdienst (SD), the Kriminalpolizei, and the Sicherheitspolizei comprised the *Reichssicherheitshauptamt* (RSHA, or Reich Main Security Office). Commanded by Himmler and managed by Heydrich, the RSHA was the coordinated security apparatus designed to protect the Third Reich from all threats, foreign or domestic, real or imagined. (At this time, Heydrich also became the head of Interpol, the International Criminal Police Organization. Originally founded in 1928, this well-known entity still exists and is now the second largest intergovernmental organization in the world after the United Nations.)

As the Geheime Staatspolizei was known as the Gestapo for short, the Ordnungspolizei, Kriminalpolizei, and Sicherheitspolizei were known respectively as Orpo, Kripo, and Sipo. As such, they sound almost comical, like a gaggle of missing Marx brothers. However, there was nothing amusing about these organizations or the work they did in keeping Hitler's subjects from becoming enemies of the state.

Often characterized as an SS inside the SS, Heydrich's sinister SD fiefdom kept tabs on potential threats to the NSDAP and its leadership from whatever source—even from within the party itself. In this role, Heydrich and his faithful counterintel man, Walther Schellenberg, maintained a vast network of over 50,000 spies, counterspies, and snitches. These rats infested every corner and every level of the elaborate NSDAP and Reich government hierarchy. Schellenberg was an attorney who joined the Nazi Party and the SS in 1933.

Heydrich was one of the Third Reich's most cunning characters. His ruthless methods would earn him the name "Hangman of Europe." Even the SS feared Heydrich. His own protege, Schellenberg, described him as a man with

Young and Aryan, an SS man gazes away from the camera, as if toward future glory—or an ancient magnificence of which he fancies himself an inheritor. Note the Totenkopf insignia on his collar. *Author's collection*

"a cruel, brave and cold intelligence" for whom "truth and goodness had no intrinsic meaning." Though a firm believer in the Ariosophy doctrine of the Nazi Party, Heydrich payed but lip service to the cult of adoration that most of its elite felt toward the Führer. Heinz Höhne writes in *The Order of the Death's Head: The Story of Hitler's SS,* "Heydrich obviously had none of that blind faith in Hitler which was the elixir of life to Himmler, the stimulant enabling the small-timer to grow to supernatural size."

A colorful story of SD intrigue that is often retold is that of Salon Kitty. A high-class Berlin whorehouse that catered to the domestic and international political and diplomatic elite, it was taken over and operated by the SD. This house of pleasure was like any other, but with a microphone in every room. The secrets whispered by ministers and ambassadors while *in flagrante* at Salon Kitty all wound up in transcription on Heydrich's desk. The microphones worked 24/7—except of course when Heydrich or Schellenberg made a personal "inspection tour."

Heydrich's marriage to Lina von Osten, quite an attractive woman in her own right, never stopped the Obergruppenführer from stepping out and about. He was a bit like contemporary celebrities who, though married to beautiful women, cannot control their addictive hunger for call girls and cocktail waitresses. Lina, meanwhile, used Reinhard's position to usurp power for herself on the Berlin social scene.

The dossiers that Heydrich kept on everyone in Germany made him the third most feared man in the Third Reich—after his boss and his boss's boss, the Reichsführer and the Führer.

Heydrich's dalliances notwithstanding, within the SS, there was a code of conduct analogous to that of a religious order. There were vows to be made and holy days to be kept sacred. There were rituals to attend, oaths to repeat, and chants to be recited. It was as though the Völkisch solstice rituals of the

Guido von List Gesellschaft or Jörg Lanz von Liebenfels's New Templars were reborn for thousands of acolytes instead of mere dozens.

Like any growing organization, the SS had its own inhouse magazine. Known as *Das Schwarze Corps (The Black Corps),* the SS house organ was edited by Gunter D'Alquen, an eager young former staffer on the NSDAP rag, the *Völkischer Beobachter;* the SS weekly began publication in March 1935. During the first two years, circulation mushroomed from 40,000 to nearly 190,000, and SS membership grew. As it was required reading for an organization whose members did what was required, *Das Schwarze Corps* was eventually selling between one-half and three-quarters of a million copies every week. Editorially, *Das Schwarze Corps* obviously toed the party line, with articles glorifying the Völkisch and decrying all the sinister faults that the Nazis found in the Jews. The paper also closely served the SD. D'Alquen dutifully published scandalous gossip about supposedly upstanding Germans that was "leaked" to the paper by the SD. This gossip served to keep potential enemies of the state off balance and in line.

The SS "lightning bolt" flash from the collar of an SS officer's uniform. *Photo by Kris Simoens, used by permission*

Joining the SS was an act of religious conversion. Allegiances were pledged to Adolf Hitler, and the traditional Catholic or Protestant religions in which men had been raised were renounced. Christmas observances—a traditional favorite for Germans—were now superseded by solstice observances, just as they would be in the secular atmosphere later in the century.

Heinrich Himmler, the Catholic who had attended Mass regularly through his years at the University of Munich, had long since reinvented himself as a born-again pagan. He was now the chief priest of a religion far different from that of the young Heini who once stood in line beneath the twin towers of Munich's cathedral for his communion wafer. The new altar of the SS, like the altar at which Guido von List had experienced his epiphany at age fourteen, was erected to Wotan and the Nordic pantheon.

However, the anti-Christian policy was largely ignored by the SS rank and file. According to records from the Reichsführer's own office, now preserved in the United States National Archives, 54.2 percent of SS personnel continued to attend Protestant churches, while 23.7 continued to be practicing Catholics. This, of course, left up to 22 percent of SS men worshipping at the altar of Armanism.

The SS men were forbidden to have church weddings. Rather, they were encouraged to wed their brides in pagan wedding consecrations called SS Eheweihen, which had been created by Himmler himself. These wedding bonds were no less solemn that those exchanged in a church wedding. In fact, as marriage morphed into a pagan sacrament, even the desire to be married became a Nazi urge. As an unnamed SS wife wrote in 1939, in the pages of that year's sixteenth issue of *Das Schwarze Corps,* "This instinct, which in us women is stronger than any other capability, was awakened because the Führer touched as a whole man upon those strings of our womanhood, its sound dedicated to the sacred concepts of sacrifice and of selflessness, because [Adolf Hitler], in short, awakens in us that which is eternal and unalterable in the German concept of woman: the heroic love that is a vocation to save eternal life for the German people, beyond need and death."

In other words, an SS marriage was a tool in the perpetuation of both the Aryan race and the SS as a sacred order.

Naturally, in order to properly "save eternal life for the German people," the SS men were required to marry women whose pedigree was as Nordically homogenous as their own. Under the SS Marriage Code cooked up by Darré and Himmler, prospective wives, like their husbands, were required to have a Sippenbuch that traced their lineage back to the eighteenth century. Himmler even went so far as to reserve the right to approve or deny marriage licenses for SS personnel.

As Gudrun Schwarz points out in her 1997 book *Eine Frau an seiner Seite: Ehefrauen in der SS Sippengemeinschaft (A Wife at his Side: Wives in the SS Clan Community),* "Heinrich Himmler thought of and formed [the SS] as a Sippengemeinschaft [clan society] of men and women. In 1929, shortly after taking office as Reichsführer SS, Himmler said about the SS Sippengemeinschaft that it was intended to be a 'racial upper strata of a Germanic people,' a leading elite of a Europe ruled by the Nazis. According to a 'Marriage and Betrothal Command' issued in 1931, SS men were allowed to marry only women that had submitted themselves to a racial and political review."

According to the *Anleitung für die SS Ahnentafel (Guidelines for the SS Genealogical Table)* cooked up by Darré and his staff, "an SS leader and his future bride, alone for the entries into the SS Genealogical Table, had to provide at least 186 documents each [including birth or christening certificates for themselves and their ancestors] as evidence of the accuracy of the claims. . . . [I]n addition there were still the death certificates of the forebears, which, although not strictly proscribed, were nevertheless desired."

Once married, SS couples were encouraged to have multiple children because doing so would perpetuate the racial ideals of the Aryan race. In this propagation effort, the wives were subordinated to their husbands just as is the case even today in many fundamentalist religious sects that decree the wife's primary duty as motherhood.

"Father and mother are the purveyors of the family concept," wrote the anonymous female author in that 1939 issue of *Das Schwarze Corps*. "Thereby the man is assigned naturally the spiritual direction of the family. He founds it, he leads it, he fights for it, he defends it. In contrast, the woman gives the family the inner attitude, she gives it soul. In quiet, rarely noticed fulfillment of her duties she upholds what the man created and builds the quiet motive in the family relationship."

Himmler decreed that SS couples should each have four children, but this target was not met. Many SS personnel had no children. According to records in the United States National Archives, through 1939, SS officers had each produced an average of 1.41 children, while the SS as a whole had an average of just 1.1 per family.

In 1935, in order to encourage even more genetically ideal Aryans, Himmler created a program called *Lebensborn,* which means "fountain of life" in Völkisch Old German. Originally this program was intended to be a network of maternity homes for Aryan mothers having the children of Aryan fathers. These mothers included married SS personnel, as well as unwed Aryan mothers whose children had been fathered by certified Aryans.

After the war, it came to light that the Lebensborn had also contained a ghoulish selective-breeding program. Citing the work of French journalists Marc Hillel and Clarissa Henry, *Time* magazine reported on October 28, 1974, that "thousands of carefully selected German women were encouraged to have intercourse with SS men, who were presumed to be among the racial as well as the political elite. Once pregnant, the women were signed into one of twelve special maternity centers, where they received lavish medical and personal care. When one of his 'new breed' babies got sick, Himmler would fret and demand daily bulletins until the child was well." The *Time* article went on to say that "new light is now being cast on a darker and less well-known phase of Lebensborn: the wholesale kidnapping of hundreds of thousands of blonde, blue-eyed foreign children for the purpose of adding to Germany's breeding stock." Again, *Time* cited the research done by Hillel and Henry, which revealed that Himmler had issued orders to have "racially acceptable" children in countries later occupied by German armies—such as Czechoslovakia, France, Norway, Poland, and Yugoslavia—"brought to the Fatherland to be raised as Germans" in Lebensborn orphanages or by adoptive German parents.

"How can we be so cruel as to take a child from its mother?" Himmler asked rhetorically. "How much more cruel to leave a potential genius with our natural enemies."

Himmler was particularly interested in the bloodlines of Norway, which he considered to be the most Aryan of the countries that Germany would later occupy. There were at least as many Lebensborn homes in Norway as in the much larger German Reich, and, it has been reported, an equal number of children involved—around 8,000 each—in Norway and Germany. Because of the lack of documentation, the exact numbers of children involved in either the breeding or kidnapping programs will never be known.

As he was finally able to carry out his cravings for an order of racially ideal warriors with racially ideal progeny, Himmler was also now able to realize his Völkisch Blut und Boden, blood and soil, fantasy. However, fulfilling this fantasy would not involve Himmler getting any dirt under his own manicured finger-nails. In fact, he no longer had his farm. When Himmler had moved his offices from Munich to Berlin after the NSDAP takeover, he sold the chicken ranch at Waldtrudering. He then moved Margarete and five-year-old Gudrun to idyl-lic Lindenfycht bei Gmund, a resort town on the Tegernsee, not far from Bad Wiessee, where the central events of the Night of the Long Knives had occurred.

Also doing his part for the ideals of the Lebensborn, Himmler took in a young boy named Gerhard von Ahe, the son of a deceased SS man, to live with his family at Lindenfycht. Some sources suggest that he formally adopted the boy, but he probably did not. In fact, Himmler had little contact with Gerhard and with his own family. Margarete remained at the Tegernsee, consciously avoiding the social maelstrom of Berlin. She wrote to her husband often, cyni-cally prodding him to pay attention to his family, but he spent most of his time in Berlin while she wiled the way the hours on the lake. Occasionally though, Gudrun, whom he had nicknamed Puppi (meaning "Dolly," not "Puppy"), was flown to Berlin for a well-orchestrated photo op. The Reichsführer SS, the photo cutlines insisted, was a family man. Naturally, the pictures of Puppi and her papa occasionally appeared in the newspapers, including *Das Schwarze Corps*.

While Walther Darré was setting himself up as the godfather of Third Reich agrarian policy, Himmler had other ideas in mind for his old Artamanen brother. He tapped Darré to head up the *Rasse und Siedlungshauptamt* (Race and Settle-ment Office), or RuSHA. The dual mandate of the RuSHA could literally be described as blood and soil. The race part of the mandate was to safeguard the "Aryan purity" of the German population. The settlement part was a goal not unlike that of the Völkisch utopianism of the old Artamanen Gesellschaft: to put more city dwellers onto the land.

As the Lebensborn came under the race side of the house, the settlement part settled on *Lebensraum* (living space), a theme that had been explored at length by Hitler in *Mein Kampf*. In his book, the Führer had wailed on and on about how Germany needed more living space for its growing population, more land for its Völkisch farmers. This idea would remain theoretical until 1941, when German armies began to conquer vast tracts of territory within the Soviet Union.

CHAPTER 8

Father Confessor to the New Order

———

MANY ORGANIZATIONS, from service clubs to fire departments, to armies and navies, have their chaplains. In military service, they are the priests, rabbis, ministers or other ordained clergy who provide pastoral and spiritual support to the troops. In secret and not-so-secret societies, they have been the traditional keepers of the faith, the interpreters of metaphysical mysteries. Often they have the ear of the leader of an organization, functioning as his close-at-hand spiritual advisor, his father confessor.

Within the SS, this role was held by a man named Karl Maria Wiligut. He was the conduit by which the pagan arcana of Guido von List, Jörg Lanz von Liebenfels, and their spiritual cronies was filtered into Heinrich Himmler's views of the real world and spirit world.

Wiligut's role in Himmler's life is often compared to the role played by the controversial spiritualist Grigori Rasputin in the life and outlook of Russian tsar Nicholas II and his wife, the tsaritsa Alexandra. Often called the Mad Monk, Rasputin, like Lanz, actually spent only a short time in a monastery. Most of his life he spent as a self-styled visionary healer. In fact, he was a skilled hypnotist with a sexual appetite that would have made Reinhard Heydrich blush. Rasputin would have disappeared without a trace into the sands of time had he not found his way into the Russian family, summoned to "heal" the young hemophiliac son of the tsar and tsaritsa. His apparent success led to his being treated by the royal family—especially her highness—as an infallible prophet.

Himmler's "Rasputin," Wiligut, was born in Vienna in 1866, three years before the real Rasputin and seven years before Lanz. When he was a child, his father recited Völkisch proverbs called Halgarita, which formed a sort of neo-pagan primer for the impressionable boy.

He became a military cadet when he was fourteen, and three years later, he was mustered into the imperial army of Austria-Hungary. He began his military career in Herzegovina, then part of the empire. His first posting with the 99th Infantry Regiment took him to Mostar, the city that was to be a center of conflict in the Balkan wars more than a century later. In 1889, he joined the Schlaraffia fraternity, a German-speaking organization erroneously compared to Freemasonry, which had been formed in Prague three decades earlier by a group of German artists. (Having been repressed in the German-speaking world by the Nazis and Soviet communism for much of the twentieth century, the Schlaraffia still exists as a service club, with members from Europe to Australia to North America.)

Over the years, Wiligut developed an interest in Völkisch paganism. Like Madame Helena Blavatsky and Erik Jan Hanussen, he started to think of himself as having a mystic "gift." In Wiligut's case, the gift was imparted to him through a connection to an ancient civilization.

Like Guido von List, Wiligut became interested in ancient Germanic runes around the turn of the century, imagining them as being expressive of the platitudes of the Halgarita. He went on to publish his first book on rune lore, *Seyfrieds Runen,* in 1903, a full five years before List's own book, *Das Geheimnis der Runen* was published. For this work, he used the *nom de plume* Lobesam, the first of many assumed names by which Wiligut would be known during his life.

In 1908, he formalized his beliefs about his connection to an ancient priesthood in a book called *Neun Gebote Gots (Nine Requirements of God).* Whereas List had his Armanen, his primeval priestly cult of Germans, Wiligut called his priests Irminen. Both terms were derived from *Irminones,* the name of the Germanic tribes who were untamed by Roman civilization and discussed by

Gaius Cornelius Tacitus in his first-century work *De Origine et Situ Germanorum* (*The Origin and Situation of the Germans*). In other words, Wiligut's Irminen were derived from the same source, and for all practical purposes were identical to, Guido von List's Armanen.

While List enjoyed the devotion of a secret society that swarmed to his teachings, Wiligut went it alone. While List led dramatic, firelit solstice pilgrimages to holy sites, Wiligut merely communed with Irminist spirits in the privacy of his own small world. Spiritualists such as Madame Blavatsky had been speaking with "departed spirits" in middle-class drawing rooms for some time, but Wiligut's connection to ancient Irminism had more in common with the late twentieth-century New Age practice of channeling. In channeling, the medium receives ancient wisdom from a specific departed or otherworldly spirit guide.

List's Armanen derived their powers from Wotan, while Wiligut's ancients were organized around a heroic deity named Irmin, a name that, coincidentally, was the ancient Saxon term for "strong." Some scholars of ancient Germanic literature have suggested that Irmin may actually have been merely an avatar or pseudonym for Wotan, as this name does not come up in German writing until relatively recent times. Irmin's name in Old Norse is Jörmunr, which is an alternate name for Wotan. Nevertheless, Wiligut continued to believe in Irmin's unique identity as he believed that the ancient Irminists communicated with him. The spirits told Wiligut that the German people had originated about 2,300 centuries before, in a time when giants, dwarves, and mythical beasts moved about beneath a sky filled with three suns. The same or similar theme would be revisited by a number of later twentieth-century science-fiction authors, including Poul Anderson. For Wiligut, though, it was the real deal.

The Irminen went on to whisper to Wiligut that their religion dated to 12,500 BC, and they insisted it had evolved distinct from Wotanism. They told him that the Irminist god was named Krist, and that the Christians had stolen the term from them. (In fact, the word "Christ" was taken from the Greek word "Kristos," meaning the "chosen one.") In addition to feeling violated by Christianity, the Irminen had their long-running feud with the Wotanists, which—according

to Wiligut's belief—came to its head when the Wotanists destroyed the Irminen holy city near what is now Goslar in Lower Saxony.

Another sacred site that especially interested Wiligut was that of the Irminsul, or "Irminen ascending pillar." Belief in the Irminsul had been current in Völkisch neo-pagan circles for some time, and mythologists have often linked this belief with that of the great tree known in Old Norse as the Yggdrasil—named again for Wotan, as "Ygg" is

Karl Maria Wiligut, walking stick in hand, was the center of attention as he led Heinrich Himmler and a bevy of SS officers on a tour of the Externsteine, circa 1935. Note the large daggers that were such a conspicuous part of the SS raiment. *Author's collection*

Karl Maria Wiligut was not alone among Völkisch German neo-pagans in believing that the strange rock formations of the Externsteine were filled with mystical importance. Located near Detmold, in an area otherwise devoid of rocky outcroppings, the pillars rise as high as 120 feet. A pagan religious site for centuries, the site was thought by Wiligut to have been the "Irminsul," or "Irminen ascending pillar," of the primordial Aryan race known as the Irminen. *Author's collection*

another of the names by which he is known. The legend of the Yggdrasil, or "world tree," is by no means unique to northern Europe. Indeed, the world tree, the sacred leafy pillar that holds up the world, is common to cultures all across the breadth of ancient Indo-European civilization. Ancient shamanic scriptures from Hungary to Siberia include the world tree. In Hindu mythology, it is the Ashvastha, or sacred fig tree, while it was incorporated into Buddhism as the Bodhi tree, under which Siddhartha Gautama achieved enlightenment and became the Buddha. Not only do the Nordic Eddas mention the tree, but a Tree of Knowledge also figures prominently in the Bible's book of Genesis.

In *De Origine et Situ Germanorum,* Tacitus describes an actual stone edifice, rather than a metaphorical tree. Though he notes that it was located in a part of what is now Germany that had not been explored by Romans, he named the edifice the Pillars of Hercules. Anything so monumental, he reasoned, had to have some connection to Hercules, the Roman hero of heroes.

Whomever it was who told Tacitus about this stone edifice was not making up its existance. Such a thing exists in the countryside near the city of Detmold in the *Fürstentum* Lippe (principality of Lippe), now part of the German state of Nordrhein-Westfalen (North Rhine-Westphalia). Known as the Externsteine, it is a peculiar rock formation comprised of five naturally occurring, early Cretaceous, sandstone pillars similar to those found at the Pinnacles National Monument in central California. Located in an area otherwise devoid of rocky outcroppings, the Externsteine pillars rise as high as 120 feet.

Apparently the place had been a pagan religious site for centuries before a twelfth-century Christian artist carved a bas relief into one of the pillars. This carving shows a man, identified as Nicodemus, whose name comes up in the New Testament in connection with the Resurrection of Jesus. The carving shows him removing Christ from the cross while trampling the Irminsul. In the nineteenth century and early twentieth century, the Externsteine experienced renewed interest among the Völkisch neo-paganists, including Wiligut.

Meanwhile, back in the real world, Karl Maria Wiligut lived the more or less normal life of an Austrian army officer. He did not marry until the age of forty, wedding Malwine (Malvina) Leuts von Teuringen in 1906. As far as we know, this woman from the Austrian city of Bozen (now Bolzano in northern Italy) was his first wife. They had three children: a pair of twins—a boy and a girl—and a second daughter.

When World War I began, Wiligut served first with the 30th Infantry Regiment against the Russian forces in the Carpathian Mountains of Eastern Europe. Between June 1915 and June 1916, he was assigned to Southern Tyrol, on the mountainous southern front facing Italy. Thereafter, the fifty-year-old lieutenant colonel was posted to a reserve training command near Salzburg, and he ended the war running convalescent camps around Lemburg (now L'vov in Ukraine). Having been promoted to full colonel, he was retired from the army of the collapsed Austrian empire in 1919.

Karl Maria Wiligut believed that the old castle at Goslar in Lower Saxony had been built at or near an Irminen holy city that was destroyed many millennia ago in a great struggle between the Irminen and the Wotanists. In 1940, after he retired, Wiligut was taken by Elsa Baltrusch, a member of the Reichsführer SS personal staff, to live in Goslar. *Author's collection*

The Wiligut family, minus their son, who had died as a young child, retired to a small town near Salzburg. Here, Karl would lose himself in his imaginary pagan world, communing with his Irminist ancestors. He imagined his own ancestors had been Irminen ice kings, who were the fruit of the intermarriage of Vanir and Aesir (or Aesynja), gods and goddesses associated with wisdom, fertility, and fortune-telling. According to the mythology, they settled a long running feud through a fusion of bloodlines.

Malvina took a dim view of her husband's hobby. This was not surprising; many wives would become perturbed with a husband who has decided that he is a king descended from gods. She was also frustrated with his often-uncontrolled anger over the death of his son. Most people would react badly to the death of a child, but Wiligut's fury came because, without a male heir, he would be unable to pass on his kingliness and godliness to another generation.

The whispering voices of the Irminen had told Wiligut to despise the Christians, and he did not need the Ariosophists to tell him to mistrust the Jews. Of course, a distrust of both of these established religions was prevalent throughout the Völkisch New Age of the early twentieth century. Like many like-minded individuals within the indistinct parameters of this movement, he began to imagine a conspiracy against Irminists such as himself. As the Christians and Wotanists had once persecuted the Irminen, the Christians and Jews were now conspiring for this same purpose.

In his spare time, which in retirement he had in abundance, he even started a newspaper. As Jörg Lanz von Liebenfels had his *Ostara,* Karl Maria Wiligut had his *Der Eiserne Besen (The Iron Broom).* The theme was similar: the superior Aryan race was being threatened by its inferiors. The god-king Wiligut felt it his duty to communicate this dire threat to his fellow Aryans in print.

The retired colonel became increasingly abusive at home, estranging himself from the mistreated Malvina as he withdrew into his obsessions. Verbal abuse turned more serious, and death threats followed. Finally, she could take it no longer. Karl had to be locked up.

Having been diagnosed as a schizophrenic, he was legally declared incompetent by the courts, snatched from a Salzburg cafe in November 1924, and hustled off to the rubber room. Wiligut would remain in a mental institution 1927. His dossier called him delusional, a diagnosis that had to have really insulted this man, a god-king who communed with ancient Irminen spirits.

When he was finally released, Wiligut drifted into the welcoming arms of friends in Austria and Germany with whom he had corresponded—friends who were members of Lanz's Order of the New Templars. Among them were Ernst Rüdiger, Käthe Schäfer-Gerdau, Friedrich Schiller, and Friedrich Teltsher. By now, the venerable Wiligut was regarded as a sort of patriarch, an elder states-man of Irminism. When he said that the spirits spoke to him, his friends hung on every word, convinced the voices in his head spoke the truth. At last he was being taken seriously. In the eyes of his new devotees, he had been locked up not because he was an abusive husband, but because he was a martyr being per-secuted for his neo-pagan religious beliefs. Schäfer-Gerdau welcomed him into her Bavarian home as a sort of a permanent houseguest.

As Wiligut was communing with Lanz's New Templars, he had also been communicating with Jörg Lanz von Liebenfels himself. It was in 1927, the same year that Wiligut got out, that Lanz resumed limited publication of *Ostara*, mainly reissuing earlier editions.

At this time, with Hitler on the rise within a movement that embraced the catechism of Ariosophy, it would seem logical that the great comeback of Lanz would be pending. But it never happened. Though Lanz heard from Wiligut, he never heard from Hitler. Like an aging silent movie star put out of business by the talkies, Lanz spent the coming decades waiting for a call that never came. Hitler had moved on. On the notion of Aryan superiority, Lanz and Hitler could agree, but in the orgiastic obsessions and the complicated zoology of primordial life forms, Hitler had no interest. Hitler's vision lay in the future, not in the past, and his eye was on a much more tangible, much more political prize.

In 1932, as the neo-pagan NSDAP, with its swastikas and torchlight rallies, was climbing toward political power in Germany, the neo-pagan Wiligut made his way to Munich. The former brooding, solitary loner became a joiner. At last, he had found a movement to which to attach his star—or his rune, as the case may be. It was to be a mutual attraction.

In January 1933, the same month that Adolf Hitler was named Reichskanzler, a sixty-seven-year-old former Austrian colonel was ushered into the office of Heinrich Himmler. The man told Himmler that he communicated with the spirits of Germanic heroes of a bygone era of Nordic greatness, and Himmler hung on every word. Willigut spoke of runes and kings, of gods and ancient ancestors, mysterious and arcane—and the reborn Heinrich I was smitten.

The old colonel and the Reichsführer SS had each found a kindred spirit. Himmler saw Wiligut as a conduit into the ancestral memory of Germanic mythology, a window into a past with which he longed to forge a connection. In Himmler, Wiligut at last had found someone of great power who took him seriously.

When Wiligut finally formally joined the SS in September 1933, he did so under the pseudonym Karl Maria Weisthor, a surname that can be translated, eerily, as "Thor Knows." Shortly after, Himmler assigned him to head up the Department of Ancient and Prehistory within Walther Darré's Rasse und Siedlungshauptamt (Race and Settlement Office). The old Austrian officer's climb up the SS ladder was quick. When he joined the SS, Himmler had given him the rank of *Standartenführer*, a rank equivalent to his old imperial rank of colonel. In October 1934, Himmler's mystic was upgraded to SS Oberführer, the equivalent of general.

CHAPTER 9

The Dark Temples of the Schutzstaffel

WATCH ANY HOLLYWOOD FILM of a sinister brotherhood with roots in an ancient, mysterious time and place, and there will be a cold, dark castle situated on a hilltop. Deep within that castle, there will be circular room, with high stone walls, blazing torches, and dark-clad members of a secret society speaking in an archaic and arcane language.

Such a scene did not originate with Hollywood. Nor did it originate with J. R. R. Tolkien, who certainly used such medieval trappings to great effect, nor with Geoffrey de Monmouth, the man who first started writing about the Knights of the Round Table back in the twelfth century. Nor did it originate in the samurai legends of Japan.

In Nordic mythology, such places were Fólkvangr and Valhalla, the great halls of slain warriors. The better-known Valhalla appears prominently in the Nibelunglied and has been celebrated in song by composers and musicians from Richard Wagner to Led Zeppelin. Valhalla was ruled over by Wotan himself, while Fólkvangr was the hall of Freyja (or Freya), whom the Eddas call the most beautiful of the Nordic goddesses. The patron goddess of war, magic, and prophecy, she was a popular and recurring figure in Nordic literature from the cold shores of Iceland to the dark and forbidding forests of northern Germany. She is often seen as a Mother Earth figure of the type that is still worshiped by various neo-pagan groups.

The image of a great hall of slain warriors is an age-old archetype, the sort of thing that Carl Jung would call part of our collective unconscious. Other psychologists would say that it is a fantasy born out of fear and insecurity, or from the need of adolescent moviegoers to scare themselves.

The dark-castle archetype certainly figured in the fantasy world of Heinrich Himmler as he grew up looking up at the towering, thirteenth-century Burg Trusnitz. It fired the imagination of Guido von List as he and his followers romped amid the torchlit ruins of ancient Carnuntum. It certainly drove Jörg Lanz von Liebenfels to acquire Burg Werfenstein, which he used as a mystic party house and as the place to first fly the swastika on a banner celebrating Ariosophy. While none of these men would ever know Led Zeppelin, they all had heard Richard Wagner's operas, and they all thrilled to the thought of a Valhalla ruled by Wotan himself.

The SS would establish a number of specialized officer training facilities throughout Germany. In 1932, for example, Himmler organized the first of several SS *Junkerschulen* (leadership schools) at Bad Tölz, the alpine resort in Bavaria. However, the Reichsführer SS had something even more specialized and more special in mind.

As Lanz had made Bad Werfenstein his Aryan clubhouse, Himmler desired such a place for his own black-clad order of dark knights. Himmler wanted his cold, dark, brooding edifice. He wanted a castle. On a cold winter day in November 1933, when the shadows were long and the days short, he found such a place.

As the story goes, Karl Maria Wiligut accompanied Himmler on his first visit to the place that would become their SS Valhalla. The castle toward which the men drove, like a pair of typical house-hunters, albeit in a chauffer-driven Mercedes-Benz, was located in the Westphalian district of Paderborn. It was called Schloss Wewelsburg, meaning "the castle of Wewel," as in the robber baron Wewel von Büren. Also known as Wifilisburg, the same site had been the location of another castle in the time of Heinrich I in the ninth century. This would have appealed to the twentieth-century Heinrich, who probably imagined that he had visited this hilltop in his other lifetime.

Wewelsburg was also thought to be close to the possible site of the celebrated Battle of the Teutoburgerwald (Teutoburg Forest), fought in AD 9. The actual site of this great battle had continued to elude archaeologists, but the importance of the Battle of the Teutoburgerwald was unquestioned. In this contest, the great Germanic warlord Hermann ambushed, defeated, and destroyed three Roman legions under the command of Publius Quinctilius Varus, a favorite of Emperor Caesar Augustus. In his *Carnuntum,* Guido von List had developed the thesis of conflict between the Germanic peoples and the Roman intruders, and in no other battle had the ancient Germans achieved such a resounding victory over the armies of Rome. In the popular image of the battle that was generally held in Germany through the nineteenth and early twentieth centuries, it marked the end of Roman expansion into Germany.

As the Mercedes climbed the hill to the castle, Wiligut was no doubt discussing the pivotal battle with the Reichsführer SS. While both men are aware of the Battle of the Teutoburgerwald, Wiligut also surely mentioned the legend of the *Schlacht am Birkenbaum* (Battle at the Birch Tree). In this mythological saga, Paderborn is predicted to be the site of a future battle in which the armies of the East will be defeated by the armies of the West in a great apocalyptic struggle. Keen on symbolism, Wiligut saw Schloss Wewelsburg as a bastion in this monumental battle between East and West.

The Externsteine, the strange rock formations that the Irminists and neopagans—like Wiligut—believed to be the Irminsul, the tree of the world, were also in the Teutoburgerwald. Wiligut and Himmler probably discussed the Externsteine on their drive out to Wewelsburg, and perhaps even stopped by.

Wiligut had taken Himmler to the Externsteine before. Friedrich Franz Bauer, the Munich photographer who was a favorite of the Reichsführer, took a number of frames of Himmler and his entourage at the alleged Irminsul. There are photographs of Wiligut and Himmler studying the bas relief of Nicodemus, and of Himmler climbing among the rocks in his SS black leather, looking very serious. Himmler had been so intrigued by the rocks that a year earlier, he had established the *Externsteine Stiftung* (Externsteine Foundation) as a pseudoscientific entity to study the history and prehistory of the place.

Looking so benign on its hilltop in the Paderborn hills, Schloss Wewelsburg was Himmler's Black Camelot. The north tower (at left) was the focal point of the castle complex and the sacred center of secret SS rites and ceremonies. *Photo by Kris Simoens, used by permission*

Had he and Wiligut stopped by on that cold November day, they might have chatted briefly with Wilhelm Teudt, the seventy-four-year-old, self-taught archeologist and neo-pagan who was in charge of the official excavations at the Externsteine. Like Wiligut, he had the "gift" of channeling the spirits of his ancient Germanic ancestors. As he put it, he felt their "vibrations."

Arriving at Wewelsburg at last, Himmler knew that the castle from the time of Heinrich I was gone. The one that he beheld in 1934 had been completed by *Fürstbischof* (prince-bishop) Dietrich von Fürstenberg in 1609. This structure had functioned as a country home for the Fürstbischofen of Paderborn, who had owned the property since the beginning of the fourteenth century.

The footprint of the castle and its walls was triangular, rather than rectangular, an unusual configuration necessitated by its location on a narrowing hilltop. The north tower sat atop the steepest part of the hill like the prow of a ship, a fact that certainly appealed to Himmler's sense of the dramatic. He is reported to have been thrilled by Schloss Wewelsburg's triangular shape.

No castle is complete without its myths and legends, and stories of the thousands of witches who were racked and executed at Wewelsburg abounded in local folklore. Records existed of at least two witch trials, and a dungeon existed

Karl Maria Wiligut (center) lectures to a group of SS officers outside the walls of Schloss Wewelsburg. Reichsführer Heinrich Himmler (foreground) and another officer examine a stone in the foreground as Wiligut explains the significance.
U.S. National Archives

in the basement, all of which had to have excited Himmler's imagination. He could probably almost *smell* the bonfires.

Taken over by the state of Prussia early in the nineteenth century, Schloss Wewelsburg was owned by the government of Paderborn. It was in a deteriorating state when Himmler found it, the north tower in ruins since a fire in 1815. Only part of the structure was habitable, and that part was being used as a Catholic rectory. The place was in only slightly better condition than the ruins of Burg Werfenstein had been when Jörg Lanz von Liebenfels had taken them over three decades earlier. As at Burg Werfenstein, it would not be long before the new owner ran up a swastika flag.

Himmler was able to cut a good deal with the Paderborn government. Who would try to cut a *bad* deal with the Reichsführer SS? He signed a one-hundred-year lease for one reichsmark per annum, and the Catholic rectory became a pagan shrine. Though his rent was a pittance, Himmler went on to spend 11 million reichsmarks on remodeling and reconstruction in the first year alone. While much of the southern part of Schloss Wewelsburg was rehabilitated and placed into use fairly quickly, reconstruction of the north tower, under the direction of architect Hermann Bartels, was ongoing throughout the 1930s.

The guardhouse at the entrance to Schloss Wewelsburg. Note the partially obliterated SS Sig rune insignia carved into the panel above the gate. *Photo by Kris Simoens, used by permission*

Work began in January 1934, and the labor was supplied at first by the Freiwilliger *Arbeitsdienst,* or FAD (Volunteer Labor Service). Later, construction crews and skilled craftsmen were supplied by the *Reichsarbeitsdienst,* or RAD (Reich Labor Service). The RAD was the German equivalent of the American Civilian Conservation Corps (CCC), which included historic restoration work among its many projects in the United States during the 1930s.

Himmler needed to finance the project without skimming funds directly from the SS budget. While the SS could, in fact, do anything it wished, it was a government agency to which donations could not be made legally. Himmler wanted to keep everything straight with regard to his schoolhouse, so he created a "nonprofit" fundraising foundation in 1936. He named it the *Gesellschaft Zur Fürderung und Pflege Deutscher Kulturdenkmäler* (Society for the Advancement and Maintenance of German Cultural Artifacts). How could donors say *nein* to a foundation that was going to maintain their Germanic patrimony?

The first stage of the renovations was complete on September 22, 1934, and Schloss Wewelsburg was officially turned over to Himmler and the SS.

Officially, the place was to be called SS *Schule Haus Wewelsburg.* It was an understated name, Völkisch to the point of being folksy, which could be translated as "SS Schoolhouse."

The phrase actually meant "the SS School at Wewelsburg House," but if there had been a plan for Wewelsburg to be an SS Junkerschule like the one at Bad Tölz, this plan was quickly superseded by Himmler's scheme to turn it into what has been characterized as a Black Camelot.

The focal point of castle was a 14,500-square-foot dining hall, configured as a meeting place for the Black Knights of the SS Round Table. Each of the chosen knights would have his own high-back, pig-leather chair, with his name engraved on a silver plate. Here, at this table, SS officers would sit and meditate in a trancelike state. The overall theme of the interior decorators naturally revolved around pagan symbolism—the swastika, the SS "lightning bolts," and the runes of the Armanen Futharkh.

In the great hall there would be dining and rituals, performed in the torchlit splendor. Pagan rituals replaced traditional religious holiday celebrations. For example, the winter solstice replaced Christmas and was celebrated with feasts of fish, goose, and wild boar—chosen to represent the primordial elements of water, air, and ground. The fourth element, fire, was present in the roaring conflagration that warmed the room and cooked the meat.

SS Eheweihen, or wedding ceremonies, were also held at Wewelsburg, as were pagan baptisms. Over the coming years, many of these would be conducted by Wiligut. Whenever he was in residence at Wewelsburg, he functioned as sort of a high priest of the SS neo-pagan religion.

One can imagine the castle as the setting for seances that would have done Madame Blavatsky proud. There is no record that Heinrich Himmler ever communicated directly with the spirit of his former self in castle, but this is certainly grist for the many fanciful stories that have swirled about the place over the years. The rumor mill has been further stoked by the fact that Himmler drew

In the heart of Wewelsburg was a 14,500-square-foot dining hall in which the Black Knights of the SS each sat in his own high-back, pig leather chair, with his name engraved on a silver plate. *Photo by Kris Simoens, used by permission*

a curtain of secrecy over Schloss Wewelsburg, forbidding the interior of the castle and the rituals to be photographed. Only a handful of photographs exist, probably taken by the architects to show specific details to the Reichsführer SS during construction.

Among the stories about Schloss Wewelsburg, suggested by the Round Table parallel, were those that intimate that it was the site of rituals involving either a pagan Holy Grail or *the* Holy Grail of Arthurian legend. (Those who consider the works of Richard Wagner to function as an operatic soundtrack to Germanic mysticism need no reminder that Wagner's opera *Parzival*—based on the thirteenth-century work of the same name by Wolfram von Eschenbach—is the story of the Round Table's knight Percival and his quest

Officially known as SS Schule Haus Wewelsburg, the sacred castle of the SS Order was also intended to serve as a pagan seminary for the study of Germanic mysticism. *Photo by Kris Simoens, used by permission*

for the original Holy Grail.) Indeed, one of the many oak-paneled reading rooms constructed within the castle for the study of Germanic esoterica was named *Gral*, the German word for "grail."

The presence of these reading rooms demonstrates that the purpose of Schloss Wewelsburg was as a center of Germanic studies. In addition to Gral, there was a room named Arier, meaning "Aryan," and one named Deutsche Sprache, named for the German language. Others were named for great medieval Germanic warriors, including König (King) Heinrich der Löwe, Christian the Younger, Widukind, and of course, Himmler's own former self, König Heinrich I der Vogler. As if there were any doubt that Himmler and his cronies had a Round

Table parallel in mind for Schloss Wewelsburg, there was a room named König Artus, for King Arthur himself. Curiously, there was also a room named for Christopher Columbus.

In the wings of the reconstructed Wewelsburg, apartments were prepared for the use of SS leaders, including Himmler, who visited at least two or three times each year. Far beneath the main castle, in the ancient crypt, with its stone walls five feet thick, was the circular grotto with a large fire pit in the center and a swastika centered in the ceiling. Known as the *Obergruppenführersaal* (General's Hall), it was surrounded by twelve pillars, twelve niches, and a sun wheel with twelve spokes. The number twelve was oft-used in Nordic mythology. (Twelve rivers are mentioned in ancient Nordic scriptures, for example.) This room was set aside for the worship of glorious SS martyrs, making the crypt a sort of Black Valhalla. Ashes of such SS personnel were taken here, and it has been suggested that a vault for Himmler himself may have been built here.

In her 1977 book *The Nazis and the Occult,* Dusty Sklar mentions that she learned of secret U.S. government interviews with SS men who observed human sacrifices at Wewelsburg. According to C. Scott Littleton, an anthropology professor at Occidental College in California, SS men were beheaded, and their blood was drunk from the severed heads as part of a ritual related to the "Secret Masters of the Caucasus." In addition to his academic work, Littleton is well known in esoteric circles for his study of paranormal phenomena, the Knights of the Round Table, whom he believes were real, and the Holy Grail.

Himmler had a personal safe installed at a secret location in the basement of Schloss Wewelsburg's west tower. The whereabouts were said to be known only to the Reichsführer SS himself and to the commandant at Wewelsburg.

To be the first *burghauptmann,* or commandant, of Wewelsburg, Himmler picked SS Obersturmbannführer Manfred von Knobelsdorff, a friend of Wiligut's who happened to be Walther Darré's brother-in-law. While Wewelsburg never became a school with a practical leadership curriculum, Knobelsdorff oversaw its transformation into a pagan seminary for the likes of Armanen and Ariosophic mysticism. It would be an institute for *Germanische Zweckforschung*

(Germanic Applied Research) and a center for Völkisch archeology projects in Germany and adjacent countries. In addition to the reading rooms, or study halls, there were a photo lab, archives, and a library with a growing collection of musty old tomes and rare documents related to Germanic lore and the arcane sciences. A planetarium was planned, but never built.

Among the SS Schule Haus Wewelsburg's "faculty" were medieval historian and Völkisch folklorist Karl (a.k.a. Karlernst) Lasch, as well as Völkisch archaeologists Wilhelm Jordan and Hans Peter des Coudres, who conducted research projects in the area, using Wewelsburg as a base.

As had Guido von List at Carnuntum and Jörg Lanz von Liebenfels at Bad Werfenstein, commandant Knobelsdorff and his successor, Siegfried Taubert, presided over solstice events at Wewelsburg, and Himmler and Wiligut attended from time to time.

The art that decorated the SS Schule Haus Wewelsburg consisted of a profusion of paintings and objects celebrating Völkisch, as well as heroic Nazi and SS, ideals. These included works by portraitist Wolfgang Willrich, as well as porcelain statuettes by Dr. Karl Diebitsch, a Waffen SS Obersturmbannführer who, as an industrial designer, had been responsible for the dagger and chained scabbard that was standard gear for every SS man.

By 1936, Diebitsch had gone into business with the industrialist Franz Nagy, manufacturing porcelain ware at a factory near Munich. Their firm, Porzellan Manufaktur Allach, produced more than two hundred different patterns of statuettes depicting various Nazi and SS themes. These included SS men in heroic poses and were designed by Diebitsch and others, including Theodor Karner. Himmler was a staunch patron of their work, and he granted Nagy and Diebitsch permission to use the SS lightning bolt runes as a maker's mark on the bases of their ware. The design differed from the SS insignia in that the two Sig runes were interlocking, rather than side-by-side.

Wolfgang Willrich's credentials as a Nazi artist were also quite impeccable, as he had played a leading role in organizing the 1937 *Entartete Kunst* (Degenerate Art) exhibition in Munich. This infamous art show had been arranged at Hitler's behest and was designed to mock modern or avant-garde art, or art that was deemed insulting to Völkisch ideals such as motherhood, heroism, or rural life. As an artist himself, Willrich had been commissioned by Walther Darré to create portraits illustrating and celebrating Völkisch German peasantry and those blonde, blue-eyed physical features that Darré and Himmler considered representative of the Aryan archetype. Willrich's first book of portraits, appropriately entitled *Bauerntum als Heger Deutschen Blutes (Peasantry as the Keeper of German Blood)* was published in 1935 by Blut und Boden Verlag (Blood and Soul Publishing) and was easy to find on coffee tables around Wewelsburg. Another Willrich collection, *Des Edlen Ewiges Reich (The Noble, Eternal Reich),* was published four years later.

Even as the artwork was being moved in and the SS elite sat in the dining hall to savor their goose and boar, construction work continued around the castle. The southern and western of the three wings were rebuilt between 1934 and 1938 by Reichsarbeitsdienst crews, and the third wing was renovated between 1936 and 1938. The biggest focus was on the complete restoration of the north tower, the focal point of SS ritual at Schloss Wewelsburg.

Meanwhile, in 1935, an ironworks was even built on site for the manufacture of wrought iron fittings that were used throughout the castle. Dishes and flatware were designed and manufactured specifically for the Schloss Wewelsburg dining hall, to be used nowhere else.

Karl Maria Wiligut was no stranger to the halls at Wewelsburg

In 1937, a year after his millennium celebration for Heinrich I, Heinrich Himmler was back in black, this time to reinter the remains of Heinrich I in a special crypt at the Quedlinburger Dom. Himmler (center in helmet) staged another dramatic procession, accompanied by such Nazi luminaries as Martin Bormann and Dr. Robert Ley, as well as dozens of SS officers. As stirring martial music was played, they marched through the castle and cathedral complex, their route flanked by an honor guard of hundreds of SS men in full black regalia. *U.S. National Archives*

Reading Rooms at SS Schule Haus Wewelsburg, and the Significance of Their Namesakes to the Imagination of Heinrich Himmler and the Mythology of the SS

1. *Arier:* The name literally translates as "Aryan."

2. *König Artus:* Named for King Arthur, the mythical British king of the legendary Round Table. He and his table are said to be prototypes for Heinrich Himmler's conception of Wewelsburg as a mystical meeting place of his own black knights.

3. *Christoph Kolumbus:* Named for Christopher Columbus (1451–1506), the Italian navigator working for Spanish monarchs who confirmed the existence of a continental landmass west of Europe and east of Asia.

4. *Deutsche Sprache:* The name literally means "German Language," an important element in Germanic identity.

5. *Deutscher Orden:* The name literally means "German Order," but it has been suggested that it is a reference to the Teutonic Order (the Teutonic Knights, or *Orden der Brüder vom Deutschen Haus St. Mariens* [the Order of the Brotherhood of the German House, St. Mary's Hospital]) in Jerusalem. Founded in the twelfth century during the Crusades, the order was often seen by the mystic German nationalists of the twentieth century as the original Germanic secret society of warriors.

6. *Fridericus:* The term is generally assumed to refer to Frederick the Great, or Friedrich II of Prussia (1712–1786), probably Germany's most prominent and most highly regarded monarch.

7. *Gral:* The name literally translates as "Grail," meaning the Holy Grail. This confirms the interest in the grail on the part of Heinrich Himmler and the SS.

8. *König Heinrich:* The name literally translates as "King Henry," and the specific Henry is Heinrich I der Vogler (Henry I the Fowler) (876–936), who Heinrich Himmler believed himself to be in a previous life. The duke of Saxony, Heinrich I is considered the founding father of the Ottonian Dynasty of German kings and emperors and first king of the medieval German state.

during these years, as he was a ubiquitous fixture throughout the SS universe. He continued to serve as the mystic advisor to the Reichsführer SS, and he was even called upon to design the official SS *Ehrenring* (SS honor ring) for the Black Knights. Known as the *Totenkopfring* because of the death's head that was placed at the center, it was initially conceived by Himmler as a means of recognizing the founding members of his order of dark warriors, but it was eventually awarded to most senior SS leaders.

Like many ceremonial items that Himmler introduced into the SS, the

9. *Heinrich der Löwe:* The name literally translates as "Henry the Lion" and is a reference to the Heinrich (1129-1195) who ruled as both Heinrich III, Duke of Saxony, and Heinrich XII, Duke of Bavaria.

10. *Jahrlauf:* The term literally means "Annual Run," and is translated to mean the "Course of the Seasons."

11. *Reichsführer SS*: Heinrich Himmler's title as the supreme leader of the Schutzstaffel.

12. *Reichsführerzimmer:* The term literally means the "Room of the Reichsführer," or the supreme leader of the Schutzstaffel. It is the name of Heinrich Himmler's room.

13. Runen: The term literally means "Runes," a subject of obvious interest within SS mysticism. Runes were also a key element in the decorating scheme at Wewelsburg.

14. *Tolle Christian:* The term, which literally means "Mad Christian," refers to Christian the Younger (1599-1626), the duke of Braunschweig-Lüneburg and the bishop of Halberstadt. A German military leader during the Thirty Years' War (1616-1648), he had a reputation of being a dangerous maniac. It is recalled too that the Braunschweig-Lüneburg uniform used a *totenkopf*, or death's head, insignia—just like that used on SS uniforms.

15. *Westfalen:* The German name is that of the German state of Westphalia, where Wewelsburg itself was located.

16. *Widukind*: The name is probably a reference to the Saxon warrior leader Widukind (a.k.a. Wittekind, or "White Child"), who lived in the later eighth and early ninth centuries in the area around Wewelsburg and Paderborn. A principal antagonist of Charlemagne, he came to represent Saxon independence. Through the years, he became an archetype of the Germanic warrior hero. There is a story that he had one blue eye and one black eye—a physical characteristic that has esoteric mystical significance to some. His coat of arms was a black horse, which he exchanged for a white one after his conversion to Christianity. His white horse appeared on the flag of Westphalia and still appears on the flags of the modern German states of North Rhine-Westphalia and Lower Saxony.

Totenkopfring was firmly grounded in ancient Germanic mysticism, right down to its Armanen runes. They were straight from the "vision" of Guido von List, although Wiligut had been dabbling in creating a runic system of his own. On the ring, the death's head was flanked by Sig runes. The SS "lightning bolts" appeared at the back, opposite the death's head, flanked by a rune that was a combination of the Tyr and Os runes from List's Armanen Futharkh. The iconography was rounded out with a swastika on one side, and the rune Hagal, symbolizing conviction and *esprit de corps*, on the other.

Approximately 14,500 of the rings were manufactured by the Gahr jewelry firm in Munich between 1938 and October 1944, when production was halted because of the economic difficulties of World War II. Each ring was engraved with the name of the individual to whom it was presented and the date it was issued. Himmler later decreed that the Totenkopfrings of deceased SS men should be returned to Wewelsburg, where they were to be enshrined as a symbol of their owners' eternal membership in the order of the SS.

Heinrich Himmler's long-term plan for Schloss Wewelsburg involved its becoming the center of a vast complex that was to be called the *Zentrum der Neuen Welt* (Center of the New World) by the 1960s. The Zentrum was never built, although blueprints and architectural models still exist to show the monumental scope of this scheme. The north tower was to be the hub of a great semicircular complex half a mile in diameter, surrounded by sixty-foot-high stone walls, and punctuated by eighteen towers. It was to have been a Nazi Stonehenge.

Within the complex would be large, stark buildings, including the *Saal des Hohen Gerichtes der SS* (Hall of the High Court of the SS), accommodations for various levels of SS hierarchy, and even cultivated land to appeal to the Völkisch predilections of these people. Also inside the semicircular complex, interior walls would extend from the two walls of the triangular castle that met at the north tower. As viewed from the air, these radiating walls would form a giant arrowhead or spear point, with the north tower as its point.

In turn, this semicircle was to have been surrounded by a highway circle nearly a mile in diameter. A broad boulevard lined with four rows of trees would have in turn connected this highway with the autobahn leading to the city of Kassel. This boulevard was aligned in such a way as to visually form the shaft that attached to the spear point. This spear, of course, pointed north, toward the mythological origins of the Germanic race in the imaginary land of Thule.

According to the tale that has circulated in pop-mythological circles for decades, the Wewelsburg complex spear motif represented the so-called Spear of Destiny. Also known as the Holy Lance, this weapon was said to have been used by a Roman legionnaire (named Longinus in some legends) to pierce the side

A smiling Reichsführer Himmler looks on happily in the midst of a solstice party for children held at Schloss Wewelsburg. It was almost like Christmas, but only almost. The SS made a point of not celebrating holidays with Christian significance. *Author's collection*

of Jesus Christ during the Crucifixion. According to various stories, the lance was preserved and later recovered as a holy relic. There, the story forks. In one version, the spear was brought back to France during the Crusades by King Louis IX (later St. Louis) and preserved for over 500 years until it disappeared during the French Revolution. In an alternate story, the lance was in Germany at the time of Otto III, but taken to Vienna during the French Revolution. Adolf Hitler is said to have seen this lance in Vienna, and he was said to have believed the story that if he possessed it, he would rule the world. He later got his hands on it, but never ruled the world. Himmler's SS architects were so taken with their Führer's fantasy that they designed the Spear of Destiny motif into their never-realized site plan for Wewelsburg.

Though Wewelsburg was dear to Heinrich Himmler's heart, he also had a special fondness for another cold stone edifice at Quedlinburg in what is now the German state of Saxony-Anhalt. Schloss Wewelsburg was being remade as the creation of the reborn Heinrich, but Quedlinburg was the creation of the widow of his former self. Even before the death of Heinrich I der Vogler, his wife, Queen Mathilde, later canonized as St. Mathilde, was notable for her pious devotion to prayer. She often left Heinrich's side in the middle of the night to go to the chapel to pray. She was also one to put her money (and her husband's) where her mouth was, endowing various religious institutions. Among these was a school and *frauenstift* (religious community for women) near Heinrich's castle on Quedlinburg's castle hill.

When Heinrich I died in 936, he was interred at Quedlinburg, where his widow and his son, Otto I, established the Abbey of Quedlinburg. Construction of a Romanesque basilica on the remains of earlier churches began at the site sometime before 997, three decades after Mathilde's death, and was completed in 1021. This church, known as Quedlinburger Dom (Quedlinburg Cathedral), although it was never officially a cathedral (the seat of a bishop), incorporated a crypt for Heinrich I and his queen.

Naturally, Heinrich Himmler was quite attracted to this site. As colorfully described in the *New York Times* of March 31, 1996, "So extraordinary is the city's historical and artistic patrimony—in the 10th and 11th centuries it was often the residence of the Saxon German emperors, thus a magnet for works of art—that during the Nazi years, Heinrich Himmler, leader of Hitler's SS, turned Quedlinburg into a shrine to the country's Germanic past. SS troops took over the cathedral and installed a Romanesque-style apse window emblazoned with the German eagle and the Nazi swastika."

The *New York Times* did not mention that Heinrich Himmler's redesign of Quedlinburg Dom also included a prominently placed "König Heinrich Window," a stained glass window created by the Reichsführer's favorite artist, Karl Diebitsch. Nor does it mention that Himmler brought a young anthropologist named Bruno Beger to examine the alleged remains of King Heinrich I. Recruited into the SS in 1935, Beger was an attractive candidate both for his impeccable Aryan pedigree and for his anthropology credentials. High among the latter was his being a disciple of Hans Friedrich Karl Günther. It was while he was a young anthropology student at the university in Jena that Beger had fallen under the spell of Professor Günther, the Völkisch anthropologist and racial theorist who had written *The Racial Elements of European History,* among other works. Hitler himself attended Günther's lectures and had even endowed a chair for him at the university. By the late 1930s, Günther's name was so entwined with the concept of Aryan racial superiority that he had been nicknamed *Rassengünther,* or "Race" Günther.

Using rulers and calipers, the standard tool kit of early twentieth-century physical anthologists in Western countries from Britain to the United States, Beger measured the alleged skull of Heinrich I and decreed it genuine. It is not known if he compared the measurements to Himmler's skull.

On July 2, 1936, exactly one millennium had passed since the death on Heinrich I, so his reincarnation naturally planned a special commemoration. As reported in the SS weekly newspaper *Die Schwarze Corps,* Himmler staged a dramatic procession to the Quedlinburg Dom and its crypt.

Himmler was there, of course, accompanied by such Nazi luminaries as Martin Borman and Dr. Robert Ley, as well as dozens of SS officers. As stirring martial music was played, they marched through the castle and cathedral complex, their route flanked by an honor guard of hundreds of SS men in full black regalia. Himmler wore his Reichsführer SS uniform, complete with helmet.

The Nazis, especially the SS, thrived on putting on a good show, but the crypt beneath Quedlinburg Dom did not become Heinrich I's final resting place until 1,001 years after his death. The mortal remains of the man whom Himmler thought of as himself would be interred in the crypt during another solemn spectacle in July 1937.

Quedlinburg Cathedral, in what is now the German state of Saxony-Anhalt, was founded by St. Mathilde, the queen of Heinrich Himmler's former self, Heinrich I der Vogler. It therefore became a sacred site for the SS. The building still exists, although the peaked roofs of the towers are currently much shorter than shown here in Himmler's day.
Author's collection

According to SS economist Enno Georg, the crypt became "a sacred spot to which Germans make pilgrimage to do honor to King Heinrich." Georg is remembered as the author of *Die Wirtschaftlichen Unternehmungen der SS (The Economic Enterprises of the SS),* published in 1963, which is considered the definitive work on the history of SS business activities. According to the *New York Times,* "Beginning in 1936, the SS celebrated King Heinrich Day here on the second of each July to commemorate the death of Heinrich I, or Henry the Fowler, the 10th-century Saxon duke who united several German-speaking states, a forerunner of the German nation." For Himmler, the camp and kitsch of Wewelsburg and Quedlinburg represented the ceremonial trappings of a pagan religion that he and Hitler assumed would last at least until the 2,000th anniversary of Heinrich I's original interment.

When the teenaged Guido von List had visited the literal underworld of Vienna and had beheld what he just *knew* was an altar of Wotan, it was a religious experience. The chills ran up his spine, and he was changed forever. The thrill was like a drug that powered the rest of his life. It's not hard to imagine that when Heinrich Himmler visited Quedlinburg, he could *feel* the presence of his former self. When he gazed upon the Armanen runes, or the runes that were carefully selected by graphic designers such as Walther Heck, he could *hear* the ancients from the court of Wotan as though they were whispering in his ear.

When the Reichsführer SS drove through the Teutoburgerwald on his way to his castle, his *magic* castle at Wewelsburg, the ancient history of Germanic roots that went back for millennia—to Hermann's glorious victory and beyond—was swirling all around him, cloaking him like the warm air from the Mercedes's heater. In the Obergruppenführersaal, he felt the presence of the past and saw the future.

The chills that ran up Heinrich Himmler's spine at Quedlinburg and Wewelsburg were the drug that powered him, and the quest for that thrill drove him on. He was obsessed by an ancient Germanic past that became ever more real each time he found and touched a concrete artifact of that past.

CHAPTER 10

Das Ahnenerbe

—

I N 1935, AS ADOLF HITLER was consolidating his power in Berlin and dreaming of future expansions of the Third Reich, Himmler was consolidating the Aryan sense of identity. He was a believer, and he surrounded himself with believers. The next step was to institutionalize the credo of Aryan superiority, turning it from a passionate belief into an unquestioned dogma. At the turn of the century, the Lithuanian archeologist Gustaf Kossinna had shaped an understanding of the Aryan race by announcing that it had originated in Northern Europe, and he had backed up his assertion with tangible artifacts. Himmler needed tangible facts and an institute to validate a firm academic footing.

In July 1935 Himmler and his Irminist colleague, Walther Darré, founded the Ahnenerbe, an umbrella agency for a broad range of scientific and pseudo-scientific organizations directed to study ancient Germanic cultural history and its holy pagan roots, with the goal of proving the mythology of Aryan superiority that Himmler and Darré just *knew* was true. A U.S. Army overview of Ahnenerbe documents, now in the U.S. National Archives, says, "The stated aim of the Ahnenerbe was the systematic exploration of the Northern Indo-Germanic race and its achievements. This was to be accomplished by the unified coordination of all separate disciplines of letters and sciences bearing upon the 'living space,' spirit, achievements and heritage of the Indo-Germanic people."

Originally designated the *Studiengesellschaft für Geistesurgeschichte Deutsches Ahnenerbe* (Study Society for Primordial Intellectual History, and German Ancestral Heritage), it was renamed two years later as the *Forschüngs und Lehrgemeinschaft das Ahnenerbe* (Research and Teaching Community for

"Die Schmiede Grossdeutschland" ("The Forge of Greater Germany"). As Völkisch workers forge steel weapons, a Germanic warrior draped in swastikas dons her helmet and prepares to take her sword. Fire, runic heraldry, steel, and heroic warriors were all elements of the ancient Nordic culture that the Ahnenerbe sought to rediscover, reinterpret, and reassert into the psyche of the Third Reich. *U.S. Army art collection*

Ancestral Heritage). For short, this organization was simply known as *Das Ahnenerbe,* or "the Ahnenerbe." Though Himmler was officially in charge of the Ahnenerbe from its beginning, it was not formally integrated into the SS until 1939.

Its center, located at 35 Widmayerstrasse in Munich, became a sort of Smithsonian Institution of strange artifacts and dubious science. It came to incorporate spiritualism and many of the favorite parlor pseudosciences that had been coffee-house diversions for the early twentieth-century Germanic New Age. One of the many practitioners of the spurious arts who drifted through the Ahnenerbe in those days was the astrologer Wilhelm Wulff, who had earlier claimed to have discovered an astrological "DaVinci code," while studying DaVinci's drawings in Italy. According to Wulff's own account, he worked on an Ahnenerbe project aimed at harnessing "supernatural forces."

Although the Ahnenerbe as an umbrella organization covered all manner of shady and esoteric undertakings, from musicology studies aimed at "confirming" the inferiority of Hebrew musical traditions to grisly human medical experiments, the agency was primarily tasked with archeological research.

The nominal head of the Ahnenerbe, and a founding father along with Himmler and Darré, was a fifty-year-old, Netherlands-born German named Hermann Wirth. He was a nonacademic scholar of Völkisch culture, religion, and runes who had recently published several books supporting the the godly origins of the Aryan race. Among these were *Der Aufgang der Menschheit (The Stairway of Mankind)* and *Die Heilige Urschrift der Menschheit (The Holy Origins of Mankind)*. Obviously, this line of thought was in keeping with the deified-ancestor school of thought proclaimed by List, Lanz, and Wiligut. What most attracted Himmler to Wirth was the fact that the latter had just translated the ancient *Ura Linda*, or *Oera Linda Book,* into German. This book, like the fruits of Gustaf Kossinna's neolithic excavations, was a tangible artifact that offered a concrete bridge from the German present to the Nordic past.

As the story goes, there was an old manuscript that had been in possession of a Dutch family in the Netherlands province of Friesland for centuries. In 1867, Cornelis Over de Linden, a member of the family, donated it to the provincial library. It appeared to be written in the ancient Frisian language that had been spoken in the coastal regions from what is now northern Netherlands, northwest Germany, and southwest Denmark. Dated to the year 1256, the manuscript described itself as a compilation of earlier works that had been written in northern Europe between the twenty-second century BC and the early ninth century AD. The *Ura Linda* was a chronicle of ancient Völkisch priestesses going back to the goddess Freya herself. The book not only describes a Nordic origin of the Aryan race, but also indicates that the Aryan race was the master race for Middle Eastern civilizations. For Aryan-centrics such as Hermann Wirth or Heinrich Himmler, the content of the book seemed almost too good to be true.

Many believed that it *was* too good to be true. When the book was first translated into Dutch in 1872, two years before the death of Cornelis Over de Linden, there was a good deal of controversy. It was had been denounced as a hoax because it contained various nineteenth-century idioms that were not in use in 1256. Further, it seemed that the Frisian language in which it was written bore too much resemblance to the nineteenth-century Frisian dialect. Nevertheless, it had its coterie of believers, and Wirth was one. So, too, was Heinrich Himmler.

To be the *Reichsgeschäftsführer,* or business manager, of the Ahnenerbe, Himmler appointed Wolfram Sievers, who, like Himmler and Darré, had been a member of the Völkisch, back-to-nature Artamanen Gesellschaft. In 1933,

when Himmler first set up the Externsteine Stiftung (Externsteine Foundation) to study the ancient Irminsul rock formations in the Teutoburgerwald, he
assigned Sievers to the project. The mandate of the Externsteine Stiftung was a
sort of prototype for that of the Ahnenerbe. In other words, subjects that were
related to ancient Nordic literature, or theories based on Nordic and Völkisch
themes, or theories that Himmler merely wanted to believe were true, were to
be researched archaeologically and documented scientifically.

Karl Maria Wiligut, meanwhile, functioned as a free agent as part of
Himmler's personal staff and had the Reichsführer's blessing to follow any mystical lead that struck his fancy—or that of the voices in his head. While the old
pseudoarcheologist Wilhelm Teudt was feeling the Völkisch vibes of the ancients
at the Externsteine, Wiligut was chasing other primeval phantoms. Hermann
Wirth, who fancied himself to be a "serious" amateur archeologist, never took
well to the old, hard drinking mystic. He regarded Wiligut as little more than a
crank. Of course, it never mattered what Wirth thought, so long as Wiligut had
the blessing of Heinrich Himmler.

In 1934, even as he was getting the Reichsführer excited about Wewelsburg,
Wiligut directed the attention of both Himmler and Darré to the "work" being
done by the Völkisch prehistorian and Nibelungen scholar Günther Kirchhoff.
Like Wiligut, Kirchhoff believed in the Irminen, their importance in Nordic lore,
and the presence of their holy sites within Germany. Like Teudt, Kirchhoff had
been feeling "vibrations." According to correspondence now preserved in the
German Bundesarchiv in Koblenz, Teudt had mapped intercontinental "energy
lines." He had even gone so far as to map an important energy-line intersection
point that coincided with an important Irminen holy center. This site was in the
Schwarzwald (Black Forest), conveniently not far from where Kirchhoff lived.

In 1936, reportedly with the Ahnenerbe footing the bill, Wiligut accompanied Kirchhoff on a dig in the Schwarzwald's Murg Valley. They uncovered
a number of old stone ruins, which were, of course, interpreted as being of
Irminen origin. They calculated that the crumbling old wreck of Schloss Eberstein (now called Alt Eberstein) was a former power center for the Irminen.
Conventional archaeologists date the ruin to around the eleventh century, when

it was built by the minor nobility of Eberstein. Wiligut and Kirchhoff considered it to be thousands of years older, and unlike conventional archaeologists, they could count on the authority of what the vibrations were telling them.

Wiligut also spent a great deal of time studying the maypoles and solstice festivals of the Völkisch people of the Schwarzwald and elsewhere in rural Germany. His idea, shared by Himmler and Darré, was that these people of German blood, so close to the German soil, still possessed some of the original unblemished spirit that had been present in their ancient Nordic ancestors.

Over several years, the Ahnenerbe continued its work in the Black Forest. In 1937 and 1938, the agency sent academically trained archeologist Gustav Riek of the University of Tübingen to the Heuneburg, a prehistoric complex near the towns of Herbertingen and Ulm. Dating back to at least twelfth century, Heuneburg had a succession of occupants, including an important early Celtic settlement established around the seventh century BC. Rediscovered in the nineteenth century, it continues to be the site of various digs, including a major excavation between 1950 and 1979, and another initiated in 2004. Riek poked around the burial mounds for a couple of seasons, but apparently found no Irminen.

In 1937, the Ahnenerbe digging did, however, make an archaeologically important discovery. Dr. Assien Bohmers, a Dutch citizen on the Ahnenerbe payroll, discovered a Cro-Magnon site in the Jura Mountains of Bavaria that was among the oldest yet discovered in Europe.

Meanwhile, Wirth sent Ahnenerbe teams abroad to remote corners of Nordic Scandinavia in 1936. The 22,000-verse *Kalevala* is a work with a very long history within

Wolfram Sievers (1905–1948), strikes a mystical pose with his handlebar mustache and Völkisch jacket. In 1935, Heinrich Himmler named him Reichsgeschäftsführer, or business manager, of the SS think tank known as the Ahnenerbe. The agency encompassed a broad range of scientific and pseudoscientific organizations directed at the study of ancient Germanic cultural history and its holy pagan roots. Though the Ahenenerbe had academic figureheads, it was Sievers who actually ran the agency. *U.S. National Archives*

Very much in his element, Karl Maria Wiligut leads a tour to the Externsteine, the ancient Irminsul rock formations in the Teutoburgerwald. He is in the center, barely visible in the midst of the pack of SS dignitaries to whom he is lecturing. On the rock face above is the twelfth-century Christian bas relief of Christ being taken from the cross, as the Irminsul is trampled beneath. It was actually Wolfram Sievers, rather than Wiligut, who headed up the Ahnenerbe's Externsteine Stiftung (Externsteine Foundation), which conducted ongoing studies of the ancient site. Heinrich Himmler is on the right, next to the unidentified woman. Sievers may be in the group as well.

U.S. National Archives

Finnish literature. Indeed, fresh in the minds of Wirth and Sievers was its having been credited with inspiring Finland's declaration of independence from Russia in 1917. (Among other distinctions, the old rune scholar J. R. R. Tolkien identified it as a source for his book *Silmarillion*.) Himmler had read about the *Kalevala* and the Völkisch, northern peoples who still subscribed to the ancient pagan mythology that it celebrates. Excited by the prospect of a folklore that may have been virtually unchanged since the most ancient past of the early Aryans, he insisted that the pagan dirges of the people in the Karelian woodland region of Finland be recorded so that he could hear them.

In 1935, the German electronics firm Allgemeine Elektrizitäts Gesellschaft (the still extant AEG company), an innovator in magnetic-tape technology, had just rolled out the Magnetophon, one of the first reel-to-reel tape recorders. The Ahnenerbe teams Himmler sent to Scandinavia obtained one of these cumbersome beasts for their trip. It was an example of leading-edge, twentieth-century technology in the service of pagan spiritualists who yearned to grasp the ethos of a culture older than time.

On their Nordic trip, the Ahnenerbe men did make contact with the legendary seer—often called a witch—Miron-Aku. There was talk that she, like Karl Maria Wiligut, could communicate with the spirits of past civilizations. The Ahnenerbe are known to have photographed her for the first, and possibly the last, time. Aside from this chance meeting, little was ever documented of the enigmatic oracle.

Himmler's interest in runes was the catalyst for the other Ahnenerbe archeology boondoggle of 1936. Hermann Wirth had shown Himmler some slides of ancient petroglyphs that he had taken on an earlier trip to the Bohuslän area of southwestern Sweden, just below the Norwegian border. In August, Himmler sent Sievers and Wirth to check out these petroglyphs and investigate other sites, including the German island of Rügen, in the Baltic Sea.

By the time that he returned from the Bohuslän junket, Wirth's tenure at the helm of the Ahnenerbe was running out. Himmler was bothered by his budget overruns, accusations of his having faked certain artifacts from Bohuslän, and especially by his being more of a hobbyist than a scholar. Like a schoolboy who snubs a former friend after entering a higher cliche, Himmler bounced the nonacademic Wirth from the Ahnenerbe in 1937. Wirth's being fired by Heinrich Himmler was like Lanz von Liebenfels being ignored by Adolf Hitler. Once upon a time, both Wirth and Lanz had been the man of the hour, but the momentum of the Third Reich had moved past and left them in its wake.

Replacing Wirth in Himmler's favor was the Dr. Walther Wüst of Ludwig Maximilians Universität (Ludwig Maximilian University) in Munich, which today is still the second largest university in Germany. According to U.S. Army Occupation Headquarters documents (National Archives Record Group 260), Wüst was "the dean of the philosophical faculty and later rector" of the university. He became president and curator of the Ahnenerbe, though "for all practical purposes, Sievers was the acting head of the organization."

The ideal Ahnenerbe figurehead, Wüst was a heavily credentialed academic insider whose claim to fame was that

The Externsteine was a favorite destination for SS ritualistic field trips. Heinrich Himmler (center) liked having his SS men get in touch with their pagan ancestors. He often visited Wilhelm Teudt, the archeologist in residence here, who had the gift of channeling the spirits of ancient Germans. As Teudt put it, he could feel their vibrations. *Author's collection*

A Partial List of Scientific Research Organizations and Institutions Set up in Germany Under the Umbrella of the Ahnenerbe

Alte Geschichte (Ancient History)

Angewandte Geologie (Applied Geology)

Astronomie (Astronomy)

Ausgrabungen (Excavations)

Biologie (Biology)

Botanik (Botany)

Darstellende und Angewandte Naturkunde (Descriptive and Applied Natural History)

Deutsche Volksforschung und Volkskunde (German Ethnic Research and Folklore)

Entomologie (Entomology)

Externsteine Stiftung (Externsteine Foundation)

Forschungsstatte für Innersasien und Expeditionen (Research Institute for Intra-Asia and Expeditions)

Geologische Zeitmessung (Geochronology)

Geophysik (Geophysics)

Germanisch-deutsch Volkskunde (Germanic-German Folklore)

Germanische Kulturwissenschaft und Landschaftskunde (Germanic Cultural Studies and Landscape Science)

Germanische Sprachwissenschaft und Landschaftskunde (Germanic Linguistics and Landscape Science)

Germanisches Bauwesen (Germanic Architecture)

Gesamte Naturwissenschaft (Natural Science)

Griechische Philologie (Greek Philology)

Hausmarken und Sippenzeichen (House Brands and Family Marks)

Sven Hedin Institut für Innerasien Forshung (Sven Hedin Institute for Intra-Asian Research)

Indogermanisch-arische Sprach- und Kulturwissenschaft (Indogermanic-Aryan Language and Cultural Studies)

Indogermanisch-Deutsche Musik (Indogermanic-German Music)

Indogermanische Glaubengeshichte (Indogermanic Faith History)

he was a respected orientalist. He had studied and lectured on Middle Eastern and Indian cultures, but he also was a believer in the notion of the Aryan race being the master race for Indo-European ethnicity and civilization. It also didn't hurt that, before being named to head the Ahnenerbe, he had been a low-level consultant to the SS. Not long after being named president of the Ahnenerbe, Wüst was promoted to SS *Hauptsturmführer.*

Wüst revamped the image of the Ahnenerbe, giving it the academic legs that Himmler desired and providing it with the appearance of an important institute

Indogermanische Rechtsgeschichte (Indogermanic Historical Jurisprudence)

Indogermanisch-Finnische Kulturbeziehungen (Indogermanic-Finnish cultural relations)

Indogermanisch-Germanische Sprach- und Kulturwissenschaft (Indogermanic-Germanic Language and Cultural Studies)

Karst und Höhlenkunde (Speleology)

Keltische Volksforschung (Celtic Ethnic Research)

Kernphysik (Nuclear Physics)

Klassische Altertumswissenschaft (Classical Antiquity)

Klassische Archäologie (Classic Archaeology)

Lateinische Philologie (Latin Philology)

Mittellatein (Medieval Latin)

Mittlere und Neuere Geschichte (Middle and Modern History)

Naturwissenschaftliche Vorgeschichte (Scientific Prehistory)

Nordwestafrikanische Kulturwissenschaft (Northwest African Cultural Studies)

Orientalistische Indologie (Oriental Indology)

Ortung und Landschaftssinnbilder (Location and Landscape of Symbols)

Ostasien-Institut (East Asian Institute)

Osteologie (Science of Bone Structure)

Pferdezucht (Horse Breeding)

Pflanzengenetik (Plant Genetics)

Philosophie (Philosophy)

Runen, Schrift und Sinnbildkunde (Runes, Alphabets, and Symbols)

Tiergeographie und Tiergeschichte (Animal Geography and Animal History)

Ueberprüfung der Sogenannten Geheimwissenschaften (Survey of Alleged Secret Sciences)

Urgeschichte (Prehistory)

Volkserzählung, Märchen und Sagenkunde (Folktales, Fairytales and Myths)

Volksmedizin (Folk Medicine)

Vorderer Orient (Near East)

Wehrwissenschaftliche Zweckforschung (Institute for Military Scientific Research)

Wurtenforschung (Dwelling Mound Research)

doing important work. A foundation was created, and fundraisers brought in corporate contributions to perpetuate this important work. The board members of BMW, Daimler-Benz, and Deutsche Bank all chipped in. Nobody, it seemed, wanted to say nein to the Reichsführer SS. Though small by comparison to Himmler's other dominions—the SS and the Gestapo, for instance—the Ahnenerbe was his dream come true, his happy place. As Himmler had always known, the past and future are inexorably linked through the present. As he had always believed, he who interprets the past shapes the future.

CHAPTER 11

Archaeologists
in Black

AS PART OF HEINRICH HIMMLER'S interest in firmly establishing a foundation for Nazi mythology, the Ahnenerbe sponsored numerous archeological expeditions aimed at "discovering" the ancient roots of the Aryan race. In the planning of such expeditions, the inspiration was Heinrich Schliemann, the German archeologist who had discovered the city of Troy.

Schliemann had discovered something that literally was not supposed to exist. In the eighth century BC, Homer had written in his epic poem, the *Iliad,* about the Trojan War, a monumental event in Greek history. Subsequent ancient historians had discussed it as fact, but by the nineteenth century, more rational and scientifically "enlightened" historians had written the Trojan War off as mere legend. Conventional wisdom held that it was all a big myth. To shorten a long and complicated story to its essentials, in the 1870s, Schliemann, a self-taught, amateur archeologist, excavated a site in Turkey called Hisarlik—and he found Troy.

Heinrich Himmler and his Ahnenerbe archaeologists went after the ancient roots of the Aryan race as the master race, just as Schliemann had gone after Troy. They "knew" they were right, so it was just a matter getting their hands on some tangible artifacts to support their beliefs.

If Schliemann inspired the fathers of the Ahnenerbe, the Ahnenerbe itself would serve as an inspiration to future generations of fiction writers and filmmakers. Nothing stirs the imagination more than truth that is literally stranger than fiction. Many people consider the Nazi archaeologists who served as foils for Indiana Jones in the popular Stephen Speilberg films to have been an interesting, if unrealistic, plot device. In fact, the idea of Nazi archaeologists, specifically *Ahnenerbe* archaeologists, racing around the world in quest of the Holy Grail was not far fetched, but *true.*

Though the roster of the Ahnenerbe is filled with the names of myriad archaeologists and pseudoarchaeologists, the man whom pop culture had anointed as a possible prototype for the Indiana Jones fiction is a man from Michelstadt named Otto Rahn. He grew up a fan of Wagnerian opera and thrilled to the Nibelunglied. He devoured Wolfram von Eschenbach, fantasizing about Parzival and his obsession with the Holy Grail.

According to John Preston, writing in the May 22, 2008, issue of the London daily, *The Telegraph,* Rahn was "small and weasel-faced, with a hesitant, toothy smile and hair like a neatly contoured oil slick."

While at the University of Giessen, Rahn developed an interest in the Cathars, the breakaway Christian sect with roots in the Black Sea rim and which was centered in the Languedoc region of western France between the eleventh and thirteenth centuries. The Cathars believed in the dualism of two powerful gods, a physical one who embodied violence and evil, and a spiritual god who personified goodness and peace. The Cathars rejected the divinity of Jesus Christ because in order to have embodied goodness, he could not have been made flesh. The Catholic Church labeled the Cathars as heretics and launched a Crusade to crush them. This culminated in a massacre of Cathars in 1244 at their last stronghold, the mountaintop castle at Montségur.

Rahn theorized that the Cathars had found and hidden the Holy Grail, as it was linked to the physical Christ. Rather than leaving his ideas as campus coffee-house chatter, Rahn decided to go look for the Holy Grail in a place where he was sure he could find it: at Montségur.

He arrived in 1931. He searched the castle, and he quested high and low, on mountains and in caves, all across the Pyrenees. Though he did not find the Holy Grail, he did accumulate the material for a book, *Kreuzzug*

Heinrich Himmler, his SS dagger prominent at his side, greets a young German skier around the time of the 1936 Winter Olympics, which were held in Bavaria. Fit, young mountaineers and outsdoorsmen were characteristic of Himmler's ideal Nordic type—and of the cadre of archaeologists he sent on expeditions to Tibet and other far-flung places in search of the cold, icy origins of the Aryan race. *Author's collection*

gegen den Gral (*Crusade Against the Grail*), which was first published in 1933.

As Preston writes, "One day in 1933 he received a mysterious telegram offering him 1,000 reichsmarks a month to write the sequel to *Crusade Against the Grail*. The telegram was unsigned, but he was instructed to go to an address in Berlin—Prinz Albrechtstrasse. When he arrived, he was understandably surprised to be greeted by the grinning figure of Heinrich Himmler. . . . Not only had Himmler read *Crusade Against the Grail*; he'd virtually committed the thing to memory. For the first time in his life Rahn met someone even more obsessed with finding the Grail than he was."

Within a few weeks by Preston's reckoning, or a couple years according to other sources, Rahn was in the black uniform of an SS Sturmbannführer. He continued his search for the Holy Grail under the Reichsführer's patronage, traveling to various sites throughout Europe. Again, he came up empty-handed so far as the Grail is concerned, but he did accumulate the material for a second book. In *Luzifers Hofgesind (Lucifer's Court)*, originally published in 1937, Rahn wrote "My ancient forbears were heathens, and my ancestors were heretics. For their exoneration I collect the pieces that Rome left over." It was a sentiment straight out of the canons of Guido von List or Karl Maria Wiligut.

Gradually, Rahn lost favor in the Reichsführer's court, partly for his apparent indifference to Nazism, partly for being too openly gay, but mainly for promising too much in his search for the Holy Grail. "He came back empty-handed," wrote Nigel Graddon, Rahn's biographer. "That was his biggest offence."

Himmler was interested in tangible artifacts.

In March 1939, Rahn went hiking near Soll in the Austrian Tyrol and never came back. When his frozen corpse was found, the formal ruling was suicide. The man was dead, but the conspiracy theories lived on. There were stories of an SS hit squad and of his having made contact with British intelligence. There

The German island of Rügen in the Baltic Sea was the objective of a 1936 archeological expedition involving both Wolfram Sievers and Hermann Wirth. Heinrich Himmler sent them to scour these cliffs, as well as a site in the area of Bohuslän in southwestern Sweden, looking for petroglyphs that might have been related to ancient runic lore. *Author's collection*

were even rumors that the body was a ringer, and Rahn was still alive. Preston writes, "Hollywood has conferred a strange kind of immortality on Otto Rahn. But it's not only Hollywood; on the Internet, his memory continues to be bathed in a richly speculative glow, fanned by ever more outlandish theories about his fate."

Still waiting for a very well deserved Hollywood moment is the legacy of the tireless husband and wife team of Dr. Franz Altheim and Erika Trautmann. The son of a Frankfurt sculptor who committed suicide on Christmas Day in 1914, Altheim joined the Imperial German Army during World War I and was stationed in Turkey. During this time, he took an interest in history and archeology, which he pursued academically after the war, eventually serving as a professor at the University of Halle. Erika Trautmann was a photographer who had once spurned the romantic advances of Hermann Göring.

Having vacationed in northern Italy, Altheim was intrigued by the vast number of prehistoric petroglyphs that exist in the Valcamonica region of Lombardy. The valley stretches for nearly sixty miles from Tonale Pass to Corna Trentapassi near Lake Iseo, and contains one of the largest concentrations of petroglyphs in the world. Designated in 1979 as the first UNESCO World Heritage site in Italy, Valcamonica was then thought to encompass 140,000 carved pictographs, although current estimates exceed double that number.

In 1937, by showing parallels between the rock art and the runes that Himmler and friends loved so much, Altheim was able to convince the Ahnenerbe to send him and his then-girlfriend to Italy. They also made a convincing argument that many of these glyphs were carved by ancient Nordic alpine dwellers.

In the quest for academic credibility, the Ahnenerbe apparently got its money's worth. Altheim and Trautmann actually made some scientifically important discoveries, and they got published. *Die Welt als Geschichte (The World as History)* published their *Forshungsbericht zur Romischen Geschichte: Von den Anfanggen bis zum Tode des Pyrrhos (Research Report to Roman History: From the Beginning to the Death of the Pyrrhos)* in 1936, and *Nordische und Italische Felsbildkunst (Nordic and Italian Rock Picture Art)* in 1937. *Neue Felsbilder aus der Valcamonica: Die Sonne im Kult und Mythos (New Petroglyphs from Valcamonica: The Sun in Cult and Myth)* was published in 1938 by Worter und Sachen. Not only were Altheim and Trautmann published in contemporary journals, but their work is also still being quoted in the academic media today.

In 1938, the couple submitted an even more ambitious proposal to the Ahnenerbe. While Guido von List had held true to conventional historic thinking when he waxed romantically about the struggle between ancient Rome and the Germanic people, Altheim and Trautmann picked up a theory that the Romans were successful precisely because they *were* a Nordic people. The thesis was that there had been a struggle in the Middle East between Nordic, Indo-European people and Semitic populations. Altheim wanted to go to the Middle East and prove it.

Altheim was preaching to a choir predisposed to believe that Aryans were pioneers in the Middle East. Ahnenerbe boss Walther Wüst imagined the Aryan race to have been the originator of all Indo-European civilization, and men such as Alfred Rosenberg believed that Aryan paganism was the mother religion of the Middle East's oldest religions. Then, too, there was Houston Stewart Chamberlain's idea that Jesus Christ was a member of the Nordic community in the Middle East that was at war with the Jews. Trautmann's old friend Hermann Göring was so excited by the project that he reportedly put up 4,000 reichsmarks to fund it. Not to be outdone, the Ahnenerbe matched his offer.

The well-financed expedition passed though Romania, a future ally of Germany in World War II, where the archaeologists looked briefly at sites connected with the ancient Indo-European people called Dacians, who lived in the region before the Romans—the namesake of Romania—arrived in the first century. From here, the couple traveled across Turkey to Iraq, with which Germany was then angling for a political alliance to counter British influence elsewhere in the Middle East. Against the backdrop of the political intrigue, Altheim and Trautmann were treated by Iraqi archaeologists to tours of various archeological sites in the country in scenes that could easily have been outtakes from an Indiana Jones film. They visited Babylon and drove out to Hatra (now al-Hadr), an ancient city founded in the third century BC under the Seleucid Empire, a fragment of the former empire of Alexander the Great.

Altheim found no evidence that the Romans were a Nordic tribe, and it is probable that he knew going into his adventure that he wouldn't. However, the time that he did spend investigating Türkic runes provided him with grist for several later monographs. As later scholars, such as O. G. Tichzen, have pointed out, the origin of the Türkic runic alphabet remains uncertain, and there indeed is a resemblances between Türkic runes and the Gothic runes of the Germanic futharks. Another rune scholar, N. M. Yadrintsev, saw in such runes "an Indo-European alphabet [reminiscent of] Phoenician, Gothic, Greek, etc. letters." Altheim's runic findings were finally published in the Hallische Monographien series as *Hunnische Runen (The Runes of the Huns),* but not until 1948.

For Göring and the Ahnenerbe, which were no longer around by 1948, the results of the expedition may have been as disappointing as Otto Rahn's search for the Holy Grail, although in retrospect Altheim and Trautmann's expedition probably served as a useful cover for covert German efforts to shore up relations with pro-Axis factions in both Romania and Iraq. Romania was allied with Germany during World War II, while Iraq was briefly affiliated with Germany in 1941 during a half-hearted anti-British uprising across the Arab world. Thereafter, Iraqi leader Rashid Ali headed an Iraqi government in exile based in Berlin. Unlike Otto Rahn, who ended up in a snowbank, Franz Altheim had a long and successful postwar academic career.

As Himmler's desire to prove an Nordic link to the ancient civilizations of the Middle East continued unabated, so too did plans to investigate other archeological sites in the area. One such objective was the so-called Bisutun, or Behistun, Inscription, located on a mountain of the same name in the western Iranian province of Kermanshah. Carved between 522 BC and 486 BC, the inscription discusses the life and ancestry of the Achaemenid Persian emperor Darius I, also known as Darius the Great. In the text of the narrative, Darius is thought to have described himself as being an Aryan. Proving that a historic figure of the stature of Darius the Great was one of his own certainly would have thrilled Himmler.

In 1938, Walther Wüst began pulling the logistics together for an expedition to Iran, but it had not gotten off the ground by the fall of 1939, when most Ahnenerbe junkets were put on hold because of World War II.

As Altheim and Trautmann were heading toward the Middle East in 1938, another, even more challenging project to investigate the Aryan connection with Asia was percolating within the halls of the Ahnenerbe. Once again, it was a story that could have been pulled from an Indiana Jones script. Indeed, the protagonist of this enterprise could easily have been stand-in for Harrison Ford in his prime. The young outdoorsman named Ernst Schäfer was leading-man handsome and an experienced hunter and mountaineer. Among his other adventures, Schäfer had been part of expeditions into the remote mountains of Tibet and Western China with Brooke Dolan II of Philadelphia's Academy of Natural Sciences in 1931 and 1934–1935. Schäfer's 1933 book, *Berge, Buddhas und Bären (Mountains, Buddhas and Bears),* was a popular and exciting tale of man-against-nature of that genre always popular with armchair adventurers.

A natural Völkisch mountain man, Schäfer was the kind of perfect Aryan specimen bespectacled clerks such as Heinrich Himmler drool over. Schäfer had been recruited into the SS in 1933. It was here that he would meet another diligent young example of the Völkisch ideal, Bruno Beger. The man who had measured the skull of Heinrich I at Quedlinburg Cathedral, Beger was now employed by Walther Darré's Rasse und Siedlungshauptamt (Race and Settlement Office). He was also an attractive candidate for the Tibet expedition because of his impeccable Aryan pedigree, his anthropology credentials, and his connection with Völkisch anthropologist Hans Friedrich Karl "Race" Günther.

Like most in the Aryan superiority camp, Günther was convinced that the Aryan race originated in northern Europe, not in Asia as believed by the linguists studying the Indo-European family of languages. He agreed with Wüst and Rosenberg that the Nordic Aryans had later migrated across Asia, through Persia and into India. He believed that the Aryans gave the Hindus the Vedic scriptures. What Beger found particularly compelling was Günther's idea that threads of this original Aryan influence might still exist in remote regions of Asia, such as in Tibet. Like Thule, that favorite mythical hunting ground of the Völkisch fringe, Tibet was certainly a remote and icy world. There were stories of light-skinned, blue- and green-eyed people living in these isolated areas of the Himalayas and the Hindu Kush. Indeed, there are many such people in this part of the world. (One is reminded of the famous photo of the green-eyed "Afghan Girl," twelve-year-old Sharbat Gula, who was photographed by Steve McCurry in 1984 and who appeared on the cover of the June 1985 issue of *National Geographic.*)

Another story, somewhat at odds with Günther's theory, that interested the Ahnenerbe was the old theory, possibly originating with Arab geographers of the Middle Ages, of *Jabal al-Alsinah*, the Mountain of Tongues. This place, real or allegorical, was supposedly the origin of Indo-European languages and possibly of the Aryan race. The stories placed it in the Caucasus, but the Himalayas were higher and icier, so perhaps the Mountain of Tongues was in Tibet?

Going around at the time was also yet another theory that suggested that the common origin of plant and animal species in both Asia and Europe existed somewhere up there on the roof of the world. If the master, or common source, species of plants and animals were there, what about the master race of *people?* The Ahnenerbe couldn't afford *not* to take a look.

It was over the subject of Aryans in Tibet that Schäfer and Beger crossed paths. Schäfer, the inveterate outdoorsman, had been there and wanted to go back. Beger, the Aryan anthropologist, wanted to study the Aryans of this mysterious place for himself. At the time, Tibet was indeed one of the most remote nations on earth. A traveler could neither fly there nor travel there by train. There were no highways that crossed the Himalayas to reach this far-off land. Claimed by China and coveted by Britain, it was a defacto Buddhist theocracy beyond the practical political control of outsiders. Indeed, foreigners were rarely granted permission to enter the country.

Ever since he returned in 1935 from his mainly American expedition, Schäfer had been casting about for a funding source to mount an all-German trip that would travel all the way to Lhasa, Tibet's forbidden capital and Buddhist spiritual center. Himmler heard about his efforts and summoned the twenty-six-year-old explorer to Prinz Albrechtstrasse in the summer of 1936 to let him outline his proposal. Though Himmler was keen on the idea, the price tag that Schäfer quoted was more than the Ahnenerbe budget could afford.

Nevertheless, the idea proved so appealing that Schäfer was able to raise the cash from outside fundraising. Corporate contributors, such as the IG Farben chemical conglomerate, stepped up and kicked in sizable sums. The German industry advertising council—a de facto subsidiary of Goebbels's Reich propaganda ministry—recognized the public-relations value of the project and footed most of the tab. The image of brave young Nordic explorers raising the swastika flag on a Himalayan mountaintop would be a wonderful coup for Germany's international prestige.

How the research aspect could greatly advance the goal of the Ahnenerbe is less clear. The expedition was probably not going to find a race of blonde, blue-eyed Tibetans. Schäfer knew better. He had been there. The tenuous goal was to prove that Aryans were the mother race of the

A 1942 newspaper clipping from the "Who-Where-Which" column on the entertainment page discusses the Ernst Schäfer film *Geheimnis Tibet (Secret Tibet)*. The film, gleaned from "exceptional, on-the-spot material, is finished [was shown] by the director/conductor of the expedition, Dr. Ernst Schäfer, last evening in Hamburg, approximately two months before it was to be released by the Tobis [film company]." The movie was cut from more than 60,000 feet of 16mm motion-picture film that had been shot in Tibet by filmographer Ernst Krause. *Author's collection*

Tibetans, thus demonstrating a Nordic racial hegemony over the whole swath of the Indo-European world.

If Schäfer was cast in the role of the strong, handsome leader, Beger was cast as the essential scientist. Beger's mission as the anthropologist was to assess the "Aryaness" of the people whom he encountered. How would he know, in the absence of DNA testing, and in the anticipated absence of blonde, blue-eyed subjects? He would use the time-tested methods of twentieth-century Western anthropologists everywhere—he would measure their heads and bodies. Every quack racial anthropologist and Social Darwinist from Arthur de Gobineau to "Race" Günther had been quite specific with the physical characteristics that defined each race within their hierachy of races. By using rulers and calipers, the standard tools of early twentieth century physical anthropologists, these features could be measured. In addition to his measuring, Beger would make plaster casts of people's faces.

The team, which also included Edmund Geer, geologist Karl Wienert, and filmmaker Ernst Krause, was also asked to assess more exotic aspects of Tibetan culture. During his last meeting with Himmler at Prinz Albrechtstrasse before they departed in April 1938. Karl Maria Wiligut took Beger aside. He whispered that he had heard stories of Tibetan women keeping magic stones in their vaginas. Wiligut asked Beger to check to see if this was true.

After a bizarre interval of intrigue and rejection, the team managed to obtain permission from the British to cross through India to get to Tibet. (The Brits finally decided that it was wise to keep the Nazis where they could see them.) The team set out across India in June 1938 without receiving permission from the Tibetans to enter their country, but correctly predicted that this detail could be worked out at the border.

Along the way, Schäfer, a passionate hunter, was determined to collect specimens of animal life to ship back to the dissecting tables of Berlin. With Schäfer busy killing wildlife, some of which were rare and seldom seen, the expedition wound its way across the roof of the world with their long pack train of gear and small army of local bearers. The Germans were quite impressed with the Sikkimese, Nepalese, and Tibetans they met—and many of whom Beger measured. The people were strong and innovative, as is often the case of people who live in extreme climates, and their agrarian lifestyle was best described as Völkisch. They lived the back-to-nature ideal of the German romantics. The hardy people were like the Alpine folk of the Bavarian or Tyrolian Alps, but even more so.

In the hundreds upon hundreds of meters of film shot by Krause—most of it held now by the United States Library of Congress—Beger is seen measuring faces, arms, and other parts of Tibetan anatomy, generally with the full cooperation of his good-natured subjects. Though he almost smothered one man while plaster casting, most of his inquiries were unmarred by serious incident. It is unclear whether he undertook the specific research requested by Wiligut, although the explorers apparently did have numerous off-camera contacts with the women of the mountains.

In January 1939, after seven months of trekking across some of the most difficult terrain in the Indo-European world, the five Germans finally reached the holy city of Lhasa. Here, the Nazis probably felt right at home given that banners with the Buddhist swastika were everywhere to be seen. The German responded by proudly displaying their own swastika livery in an effort to bond with their hosts. The Tibetans regarded them with caution or amusement, not as men from a superior race, although they did load the Germans down with gifts of food and Buddhist artifacts.

The expedition accumulated benign geographic, climate, and weather data and gathered many crates of animal specimens. Krause took 40,000 photos, including many in Agfacolor, and 60,000 feet of 16-mm motion-picture film. The latter was edited into the film *Geheimnis Tibet (Secret Tibet)*, which was released in Germany in 1942. Among his numerous photographs were attempts to capture the mysterious, frosty aura of Tibetan priests and lamas.

Beger had made measurements of 376 people, and in his measuring, the SS race expert was gradually becoming convinced that this hardy, Völkisch race actually *were* "Europoid" descendants of Nordic Aryans. He published an unconvincing paper to this effect, but not until 1943. As author and adventurer Christopher Hale wrote in his 2004 book *Himmler's Crusade: The True Story of the 1938 Nazi Expedition into Tibet,* "Beger's own attempts to make sense of his Tibetan data were inconclusive and fragmentary. They did not tell the story of Nordic expansion that he wanted to bring back to his professors and the expedition's patron [Himmler]. Much of what he reported simply showed what any visitor to the market in Gangtok would have seen—that the people of India and Tibet were highly diverse."

Having been granted permission to visit Lhasa for two weeks, the Germans ingratiated themselves to their cordial hosts and remained for two months, finally departing on March 20. When they finally reached Calcutta at the end of July, the more relaxed relations with the British that had prevailed a year earlier had evaporated in the heat of war paranoia. Indeed, Heinrich Himmler was so fearful that his archaeologists in black would be interned by the British that he used SS funds to send an airplane to pick them up and shuttle them back to Berlin, where they finally arrived on August 4, 1939, less than a month before the start of World War II.

Another German showpiece expedition into the Himalayas met either more or less fortunate fate than Schäfer's, depending on how one looks at it. In May 1939, the German Himalayan Foundation sent noted Austrian mountaineer and champion skier Heinrich Harrer to make an attempt to be the first to climb Nanga Parbat (Naked Mountain), the 26,660-foot, ninth-highest mountain in the world. Considered one of the most difficult climbs over 8,000 meters on earth, it had never been climbed, although many had died trying. Though this expedition had nothing to do with the Ahnenerbe or its goals of pseudoscientific wishful thinking, Harrer himself was a member of the SS.

Having been unsuccessful in his climb, Harrer was nabbed by the British in October 1939 when he came off the mountain, which was located within British India. Because World War II had begun, he was interned in India for the duration. Though he was recaptured after several thwarted escape attempts, Harrer finally got away for good in May 1944. He slipped across the border into Tibet, where he remained until 1951. His 1952 book, *Seven Years in Tibet,* featured an introduction by the Dalai Lama and became an international bestseller. Brad Pitt portrayed Harrer in the second of two movies based on the book. As for

Nanga Parbat, it was first successfully climbed by in 1953 by another Austrian, Hermann Buhl.

Another individual who went in search of Aryans in Asia, but without the aid of the Ahnenerbe, was the French writer Maximine Julia Portaz. She became a convert to Nazism in or around 1929, and a convert to Hinduism three years later when she traveled to India. She created a theory, an interesting corollary to Jörg Lanz von Liebenfels's notion of superhumans versus subhumans, that described men as being in, above, or against time. According to Portaz, men in time act from selfish motives and are destructive forces in the world; men above time are enlightened mystics, too detached from the real world to cause change; and men against time combine the mystical knowledge of men above time with the strength of men in time to become heroes able to restore a golden age. Of course she considered Adolf Hitler to fall into the latter category and once declared that he was the reincarnation of the Hindu god Vishnu. (She would be dubbed "Hitler's Priestess" by historian Nicholas Goodrick-Clark.) She remained in India through World War II, changing her name to Savitri Devi, meaning "sun goddess," and working as a pro-Nazi advocate of Indian independence from Britain.

CHAPTER 12

A World of Ice

H EINRICH HIMMLER had carefully monitored Ernst Schäfer's Tibetan expedition through wireless messages that the team was sending. Indeed, he was so excited that he promoted Schäfer to Obersturmbannführer while he was still on the faraway, icebound roof of the world. At the same time, the Reichsführer was also obsessing about the icy origins of the Aryan race on the icebound roof of primeval Europe. Both Hitler and Himmler had become believers in an ideology that would be written off as bizarre nonsense were it not for its sizable number of adherents. *Welteislehre* (World Ice Theory) was an idea that would have been destined for a legacy as a footnote to a footnote in the annals of pseudoscience had the Reichsführer not become fixated upon it.

Welteislehre was the brainchild of an engineer whose earlier credentials planted his feet firmly in the terra firma of the real world. Born in Austria in 1860, Hanns (sometimes called Hans) Hörbiger had invented a compressor valve that greatly increased the efficiency of blast-furnace engines. His valve revolutionized the steel industry and was also adapted for the chemical industry. Eventually, his Austrian company had branch offices in Britain and Germany, and he became a rich man exporting his invention throughout the world. By the time Hörbiger handed off management of his successful engineering company to his son Alfred in 1925, he had already been tinkering with his astronomical theories—and leading a scientific double life—for three decades.

As was the case with Guido von List and his Armanen runes, Hörbiger came about his theory through a self-described vision. An amateur astronomer, he was staring at the moon one night when he decided that it and the planets were actually made of ice. He went on to receive a "vision" that made him believe that the basic building block of the universe is water-ice. The Milky Way, for example, was seen a vast archipelago of icebergs. (Jupiter's moon Europa, the sixth largest moon in the solar system, does have a more or less solid ice surface, but this fact was unknown in Hörbiger's lifetime.)

Working with backyard astronomer Philipp Fauth, Hörbiger concocted his theory about how the icy universe had been formed, and published it in his 1912 book *Glazial-Kosmogonie (Glacial Cosmogony)*. In Hörbiger's view of things, the universe had indeed been formed by a big bang—in this case, an explosion that sent chunks of ice hurtling in all directions. Most of the stars and planets are, he said, ice fragments from that big bang. This idea of the origin of the universe came nearly two decades before 1929, when Edwin Hubble began making the observations that led to the big bang theory of the creation of the universe.

Just as Karl Maria Wiligut believed that there had once been several suns, Hörbiger believed that the earth once had several moons. One by one, they fell out of the sky, hitting the earth. The original humans, the master race, had descended to earth thusly, cloaked in "cosmic ice." The ancient city of Atlantis had been a casualty of a subsequent impact, and Noah's biblical flood had been the result of another.

Hörbiger's ideas initially attracted only scorn from the academic establishment. After World War I, however, as the Austro-German New Age opened up a floodgate of counterculture interest in alternative dogmas, Hörbiger's name started cropping up a lot in coffee-house conversation. Glacial Cosmogony, now renamed Welteislehre, suddenly had a following. Even that old Völkisch racist Houston Stewart Chamberlain began singing Hörbiger's praises. Glazial-Kosmogonie was particularly resonant with the Völkisch neo-pagans who believed that the Nordic origins of the Aryan race's supermen had been in a world of ice. Naturally, Glazial-Kosmogonie coincided nicely with the idea of the primordial Thule.

As often happens with such fads, a flurry of magazines and newspapers cropped up for devotees of one aspect of Glazial-Kosmogonie or another. There were even films and radio programs about it. In turn, these media probably

Hanns Hörbiger (1860–1931) was the Austrian engineer who originated Glazial-Kosmogonie (Glacial Cosmogony), or Welteislehre (World Ice Theory). He believed that the first humans, the master race, came to earth cloaked in "cosmic ice." His idea was right in line with many notions swirling around the German mystical counterculture, which linked icy worlds with ancient Aryan supermen. *Author's collection*

inspired some early science fiction, as ice men and ice planets became pop-culture icons. (One is reminded of the later New Age hysteria that swept the counterculture in 1973 and 1974 as the icy Comet Kohoutek swept past the earth. As in the 1920s, magazines and radio programs devoted much space and time to Kohoutek's mysterious portents. All but forgotten today are the proto–New Age gurus whose followers were led to believe Kohoutek heralded an imminent doomsday, which never happened. Then too, there was the Heaven's Gate cult, whose members committed mass suicide in 1997 so that they could catch a ride on the ball of ice known as Comet Hale-Bopp.)

As Guido von List had seen his followers form the Guido von List Gesellschaft in 1908, Hanns Hörbiger watched organizations being formed around his theory. There were the *Kosmotechnische Gesellschaft* and the Hörbiger Institute, both founded in postwar Vienna, the latter being headed by Alfred Hörbiger.

Hörbiger died in 1931, leaving his legacy and his Glazial-Kosmogonie to his fans and their world ice clubs. In turn, Hörbiger's followers saw an opportunity in the rise of national socialism. The NSDAP and like-minded parties were keen on new scientific ideals that were independent from a scientific mainstream, which was perceived to be dominated by Jews.

Though the Nazis appreciated Glazial-Kosmogonie for all the right, icy, Völkisch reasons, they abhorred the independence of the Kosmotechnische Gesellschaft and the Hörbiger Institute. As soon as Germany annexed Austria in 1938, the Kosmotechnische Gesellschaft was closed down, and the Hörbiger Institute—including Hörbiger's library and his own extensive astronomical archives—was swallowed into Heinrich Himmler's Ahnenerbe.

At the same time that Ernst Schäfer and Bruno Beger were tramping through the ice and snow of Tibet in 1938 and 1939, another German expedition was making its way toward the ultimate land of ice and snow—Antarctica.

The idea behind the *Deutsche Antarktische* expedition originated with Hermann Göring rather than with Heinrich Himmler and the Ahnenerbe. The idea, at least on the face of it, was another "scientific" expedition to promote German prestige. In the early years of the twentieth century, nationally sponsored polar expeditions were popular headline-grabbers. France and Norway had each sent teams to Antarctica, while the British sponsored eight teams between 1901 and 1937, during which men such as Robert Falcon Scott and Ernest Shackleton became household names. The United States had sent Admiral Richard Byrd on an extended expedition from 1928 to 1930, during which he had flown over the South Pole and become a national folk hero.

Germany had sent two expeditions to the Antarctic, but the last had returned in 1912. Göring felt that it was high time to go again. The stated objective of the new expedition was to survey a location for a whaling station. Germany was short of necessary oils for the production of cosmetics, soaps, and even margarine. Somehow, the Nazi economists had decided that harvesting whale oil in the Antarctic made more sense than buying it from the Norwegians, who controlled the market.

Equipped with swastika flags to raise over polar ice, the team, under the command of Kriegsmarine captain Alfred Ritscher, departed from Hamburg in December 1938 aboard the research ship *Schwabenland*. The ship's name was no coincidence as it was the intention of the Third Reich to claim sovereignty over a 230,000-square-mile slice of the ice continent and name it *Neuschwabenland* (New Swabia). ("Old" Swabia, or Schwabenland, is that part of Germany that roughly corresponds to the modern state of Baden-Württemberg.) This assertion raised diplomatic eyebrows, especially in Norway, because Ritscher and his crew staked out part of Norway's previously claimed Queen Maud Land region.

In the United States, the event was reported on page eleven of the *New York Times* on April 13, 1939, where the narrative read, "Judging from the claims advanced in the press, Great Germany has just staked out her first colony outside Europe and is proposing to take possession."

By the summer of 1939, the world was increasingly edgy about German territorial claims, and U.S. President Franklin Roosevelt went so far as to order Admiral Byrd to take an American expedition south. The headline in the *New York Times* on July 8, 1939, read, "Germany's Moves in Antarctica Spur Action to Validate Our Territorial Claims There . . . Admiral [Byrd] Says Area Is Rich in Natural Resources." The article went on to say, "President Roosevelt moved today to prevent possible extension of Germany's claims to Antarctic areas into the Western Hemisphere by directing Rear Admiral Richard E. Byrd to leave early in October on another South Polar Expedition."

A week later, on July 14, the *New York Times* reported: "Rear Admiral Richard E. Byrd, disclosing plans for his coming expedition in the Antarctic, said today that six army tanks and a unique 45,000-pound snow cruiser would be used for transport over the South Pole's icy wastelands." But because of World War II, Byrd's expedition never happened.

During the war, German naval activity in the South Atlantic and the Antarctic continued. Both U-boats and surface warships did battle with the British navy there, and Germans were also active in Australian waters. As Walter Sullivan wrote in an article on Antarctica in the *New York Times* on March 9, 1955, "Disguised German raiders attacked allied shipping there in World War II."

Rumors of a secret German base in Antarctica persisted after the war, and today there are a vast array of "Nazis in the Antarctic" stories alive on the world wide web. These stories range from interaction between the Germans and otherworldly beings to Hitler's having taken up residence in Neuschwabenland after the war.

Meanwhile, Himmler had approved an Ahnenerbe project aimed at seeking a lost Nordic civilization in the icy peaks of the Andes. In this case, the man with the theory was an author and amateur archeologist named Edmund Kiss. A devotee of Hanns Hörbiger and his Glazial-Kosmogonie, Kiss was also among those in the Völkisch New Age movement who believed that Thule had been a real place, a northern Atlantis. He discussed this theory at length in his book

Die Letzte Königin von Atlantis (The Last Queen of Atlantis), explaining in detail how the people of Thule had traveled throughout the world.

In 1928, after winning a great deal of money in a writing contest, Kiss made a trip to the Bolivian Andes. While there, he visited the ancient ruins of Tiahuanacu (also called Tiwanaku), a place that had been a major city long before the rise of the Inca civilization. The architecture of the ruins reminded him so much of ancient European architecture that he decided it was built by Aryans from Thule. While most mainstream archaeologists date the heyday of Tiahuanacu to around AD 500, Kiss was convinced that the Nordic Thuleans had built the place at least sixteen thousand years earlier. (Coincidentally, Kiss visited Bolivia at the same time that Heinrich Himmler's old friend, Ernst Röhm, was living in the country. Late of the NSDAP's SA paramilitary freikorps, Röhm was in the midst of a five-year stint as an adviser to the Bolivian army.)

When Kiss returned to Germany, he spent the next decade telling his tale of Thuleans traveling to icy Bolivia to anyone who would listen. After the Nazis came to power and the Ahnenerbe was formed, Kiss finally found someone who would do more than listen. He told his story to Walther Wüst, and in 1939 pitched him on the idea of a year-long, full-scale expedition, involving a large team of field archaeologists and aerial surveys of the area. Wüst, and presumably Heinrich Himmler as well, were delighted by the idea and planning got underway. Unfortunately for Kiss, though, World War II began just as the expedition was packing its gear to embark. Had the project not been postponed indefinitely, Kiss's aerial survey might have observed the mysterious Nazca Lines— manmade geoglyphs visible only from the air—that stretch across fifty miles of nearby Peru. The largest of these stylized animal and geometric shapes are over six hundred feet across. There's no way of knowing what Kiss would have thought of them , but they would later be described by Swiss amateur archeologist Erich von Däniken as landing sites for spacecraft from another planet. Von Däniken's controversial bestseller *Chariots of the Gods?: Unsolved Mysteries of the Past* was published in 1968, eight years after Kiss died. The icy, Thulean counterculture of the 1920s and 1930s had almost intersected with the spacy counterculture of the 1960s.

CHAPTER 13

Black Knights in an Army of Field Gray Pawns

———

WHILE AMATEUR AND PROFESSIONAL Ahnenerbe archaeologists were scampering around the world in real-life precursors to the Indiana Jones saga, far more serious events were unfolding in Europe.

Adolf Hitler was preparing the Third Reich for war. It had been the tidal wave of humiliation over the egregious Treaty of Versailles that had swept him to power, and he was not about to disappoint his fans. National pride and rearmament were his platform, and he was out to make good on it.

When German president Paul von Hindenburg died on August 2, 1934, Reichskanzler Hitler assumed the office of president in addition to his current office of chancellor, becoming both the head of state as well as the head of government. As such, he became to the German Reich what he had been with the Nazi Party—der Führer.

By assuming the office of president, Hitler became—under the provisions of the 1919 Weimar constitution—the legal commander in chief of the German armed forces. As stated in Article 47, *"der Reichspräsident hat den Oberbefehl über die gesamte Wehrmacht des Reiches"* ("the national president holds supreme command of all armed forces of the nation"). Every soldier, sailor, and airman now swore his allegiance directly to Hitler. In March 1935, Hitler reinstated conscription, in violation of the Treaty of Versailles, and began rearming Germany, remaking the feeble Reichswehr into the robust *Wehrmacht*. The civilian ministry overseeing the armed forces was superseded by the *Oberkommando der Wehrmacht* (Armed Forces High Command), which coordinated the three branches of the armed forces: the *Oberkommando des Heeres* (Army High Command), *Oberkommando der Marine* (Navy High Command), and *Oberkommando der Luftwaffe* (Air Force High Command).

Where within this chain of command was a place for the Black Knights of Heinrich Himmler's SS?

The answer was nowhere. The SS, specifically the SS subcomponent known as the Waffen SS (Armed SS), was destined to be an independent army of its own, not in the chain of Oberkommando der Wehrmacht command, but answerable directly to Himmler and, of course, ultimately answerable to the Führer. The Waffen SS has often been described as the fourth branch of the German armed forces. As befitting its image of itself, this Waffen SS was conceived as, and became, the elite of the German armed forces. It was a fight-to-the-death, take-no-prisoners outfit that was often disliked, distrusted, and feared by the regular Wehrmacht. The Waffen SS had its origins in the SS contingent that was named for Hitler himself.

Reflecting on the brutal efficiency of Sepp Dietrich's Leibstandarte Adolf Hitler on the Night of the Long Knives in June 1934, Himmler began to grow this organization from its initial status as a bodyguard for the Führer into a private army loyal to the Führer. Unlike the SA, it was not a freikorps of ill-bred thugs and goons, but a freikorps that embodied all the heavily ordered, disciplined, *and pagan* ideals of the SS. Himmler dreamed fondly of the Teutonic Knights of old and imagined his sacred pagan knighthood not merely as a secret society, but also as a warrior caste. It was to be a knighthood Heinrich I der Vogler would have been proud of.

In September 1934, the Führer himself authorized Himmler to create his SS army. It was originally known as the SS *Verfügungstruppe* (Ordered Troops), as distinct from the regular or general SS, known as the *Allgemeine SS,* which included Reinhard Heydrich's SD. Meanwhile, the SS concentration-camp guards were later organized into a third subcomponent of the SS, appropriately given the grisly designation *Totenkopfverbände* (Death's Head Federation). The

Adolf Hitler's favorite photographer, Heinrich Hoffman, took this picture of German troops marching into Imst, Austria, in March 1938. Germany annexed German-speaking Austria, incorporating its people into the greater German Reich. *U.S. National Archives*

SS Verfügungstruppe then evolved into the Waffen SS, which came into existence in 1940 as the Kommandoamt (command office) der Waffen SS, an umbrella for a growing number of armed SS units. The core unit within this new army was the Leibstandarte Adolf Hitler.

To command the SS Verfügungstruppe, Himmler picked SS Brigadeführer Paul Hausser, a former general in the old imperial army and later in the Reichswehr. As he took his new job in October 1936, Hausser had orders from the Reichsführer SS to turn the SS Verfügungstruppe into an autonomous army second to none—including the Wehrmacht.

Practical military training for this pagan warrior caste took place at the SS Junkerschule (leadership schools) in Bad Tölz, as well as at other Junkerschulen in Braunschweig and Klagenfurt. (After World War II, the Bad Tölz site was the headquarters of the United States Third Army when it was commanded by General George Patton, and it remained a U.S. Army facility until 1991.) The emphasis at the Junkerschulen was on the practical, ranging from the traditional marching and presenting arms to physical-fitness and weapons training. Submachine guns took precedent over infantry rifles. The SS were to be Germany's shock troops, as Hitler got the nation marching inexorably toward its next war.

This march began in 1936, when the Wehrmacht occupied the German Rhineland, which had been demilitarized by the Treaty of Versailles. The world cried foul, but the lack of active opposition by Britain and France encouraged Hitler.

In 1938, Hitler annexed Austria in a move that was called *Anschluss,* or "Connection." This annexation fulfilled the Völkisch dreams of Germanic ethnocentrists in both countries who wished to see all German-speaking, or *Völksdeutsche,* people in a single Reich. (The term "Völksdeutsche," which entered the lexicon early in the twentieth century, described ethnic Germans who were citizens of other, especially adjacent, countries. This contrasted with the *Reichsdeutsch,* who were ethic German citizens of Germany.) Before World War I, Austria had been the center of a multiethnic empire. After World War I, Austria was a sliver of the former empire, but populated mainly by people whom the Germanic ethnocentrists would call Völksdeutsche.

This contact strip included snapshots taken of an SS man enjoying himself with some local women during the 1941 push by German forces into the Balkans and Greece. *U.S. National Archives*

There were also large numbers of such "Germans" in Czechoslovakia and Poland. Having absorbed the Völksdeutsche of Austria, Adolf Hitler next demanded that Czechoslovakia's German-speaking Sudetenland region also be folded into his Third Reich.

In September 1938, at the now infamous summit conference, Britain's prime minister, Neville Chamberlain, and France's president, Edouard Daladier, flew to Munich, the mother city of the NSDAP, to meet with Adolf Hitler. The Führer told them that the Sudetenland should properly be part of Germany, and he promised that this was the end of his territorial ambition. Czechoslovakia naturally complained, but Chamberlain and Daladier ignored the Czechs and acceded to the Führer's demands. When Chamberlain flew home, he happily announced that he had helped to negotiate "peace for our time."

When the uniformed German troops marched into Austria and the Sudetenland, smiling to the cheers of German-speaking, pro-Hitler crowds, most but not all, were wearing the field gray *(feldgrau)* uniforms of the Wehrmacht. At the head of the column, as the troops entered Vienna, were the Black Knights of the Leibstandarte Adolf Hitler. The SS Verfügungstruppe also contributed a symbolic contingent in the Sudetenland. In addition to these units, small SS/SD special operations task forces called *Einsatzgruppen* or *Sonderkommandos* were assigned to specific tasks such as securing government buildings.

In March 1939, Hitler decided that he wanted the rest of Czechoslovakia. The price tag for "peace for our time" had gone up. Chamberlain and Daladier were willing to go to almost any lengths to appease Adolf Hitler and avoid war. Czechoslovakia had no choice. The poor country was chopped into bits. Slovakia was sliced off as a quasiautonomous satellite of Germany, while the remainder of Czechoslovakia became the Reich Protectorate of Bohemia and Moravia.

Two months later, Hitler inked a deal with Italy's Fascist "duce," Benito Mussolini. Known as the Pact of Steel, the agreement called for cooperation in time of war—a war that seemed all that much closer because of the pact.

On August 24, Hitler sent his foreign minister to Moscow. There, Joachim von Ribbentrop signed a nonaggression pact with the Soviet Union's own brutal strongman, Josef Stalin. Much to the surprise of the global media, which demonized and caricaturized both leaders, the right-wing demon Hitler had tumbled into bed with the left-wing demon Stalin.

A week later, Hitler, the man who held the best hand at the table of European politics that year decided that negotiating had taken him as far at it could. It was time for war.

German bombs began falling on Poland the morning of September 1, 1939, as German troops raced across the border. In London, Neville Chamberlain proposed more negotiations. Chamberlain consulted with Daladier, and together they came to realize that the time for negotiating was indeed over. On September 3, Britain and France declared that a state of war between them and the Third Reich had existed for two days.

World War II had begun, and the SS had fired the opening volley.

Seen here shaking hands, Adolf Hitler and Hermann Göring were all smiles in 1940 and early 1941 as their armies remained undefeated and apparently invincible in every land campaign that they had fought so far. *U.S. National Archives*

In case one might labor under an illusion that Himmler's disciplined and elite warrior caste was somehow as noble or as righteous as it imagined itself, one has only to look at the despicable circumstances of this opening volley. Himmler had even agreed that it should be named after *himself*.

Operation Himmler had been cooked up by himself and Reinhard Heydrich, even as the former was making the arrangements to fly his boys home from Tibet. The idea was to use mainly SD troops to generate the illusion that Poland was attacking Germany. It was much the same as on the Night of the Long Knives in 1934 when the SS faked a putsch against Hitler by Röhm and the SA as an excuse to smash Röhm and the SA. Dressed in Polish uniforms, Heydrich's men attacked German border areas, shooting wildly and leaving behind bodies—of inmates from Himmler's Dachau concentration camp—also dressed in Polish uniforms. This way, Hitler was able to point to an "attack" on Germany.

At the time Germany invaded Poland, the Wehrmacht, especially its Luftwaffe, was the most well-trained, best-equipped and overall superior military force in the world. Among them, or rather, alongside the Wehrmacht, were three regiments of a growing SS Verfügungstruppe. It was a small force, but it was no longer merely symbolic, to the consternation of the Oberkommando Wehrmacht, who would like to have seen the black-shirted army disbanded and sent back to being a party police force. (It should be pointed out that the SS combat troops wore military-style camouflage uniforms in combat. Black, symbolizing their image as "black knights," was reserved for their dress uniforms.)

The coordinated German air and ground offensive, known as the *Blitzkrieg* (lightning war), was the most rapid and efficient mode of military attack the world had ever seen. The use of fast-moving tanks, mobile forces, dive bombers, and paratroop units, all working together as one tight, well-disciplined force, stunned the world, especially the Polish defenders. Germany was able to subjugate Poland in just three weeks.

Meanwhile, SS *Einsatzgruppen* (special operations groups) commanded by Reinhard Heydrich undertook the sinister task of eliminating those members of Polish society and the intelligentsia who might be problematic to the occupation. Functioning essentially as hit men, they systematically murdered

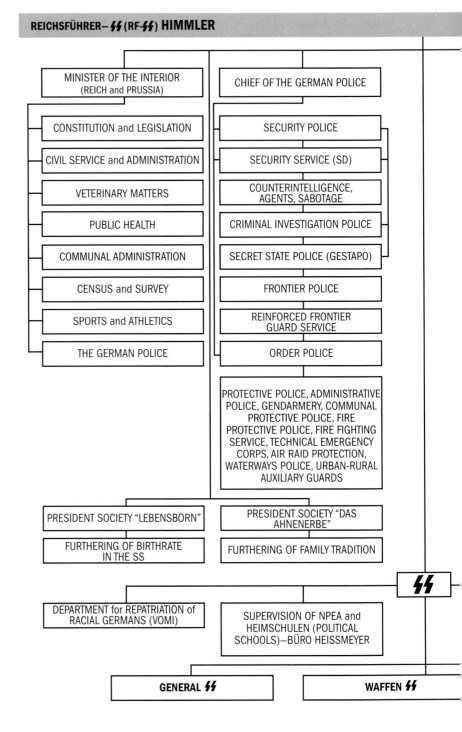

REICHSFÜHRER—SS (RF-SS) HIMMLER

MINISTER OF THE INTERIOR (REICH and PRUSSIA)	CHIEF OF THE GERMAN POLICE
CONSTITUTION and LEGISLATION	SECURITY POLICE
CIVIL SERVICE and ADMINISTRATION	SECURITY SERVICE (SD)
VETERINARY MATTERS	COUNTERINTELLIGENCE, AGENTS, SABOTAGE
PUBLIC HEALTH	CRIMINAL INVESTIGATION POLICE
COMMUNAL ADMINISTRATION	SECRET STATE POLICE (GESTAPO)
CENSUS and SURVEY	FRONTIER POLICE
SPORTS and ATHLETICS	REINFORCED FRONTIER GUARD SERVICE
THE GERMAN POLICE	ORDER POLICE

PROTECTIVE POLICE, ADMINISTRATIVE POLICE, GENDARMERY, COMMUNAL PROTECTIVE POLICE, FIRE PROTECTIVE POLICE, FIRE FIGHTING SERVICE, TECHNICAL EMERGENCY CORPS, AIR RAID PROTECTION, WATERWAYS POLICE, URBAN-RURAL AUXILIARY GUARDS

PRESIDENT SOCIETY "LEBENSBORN"	PRESIDENT SOCIETY "DAS AHNENERBE"
FURTHERING OF BIRTHRATE IN THE SS	FURTHERING OF FAMILY TRADITION

| DEPARTMENT for REPATRIATION of RACIAL GERMANS (VOMI) | SUPERVISION OF NPEA and HEIMSCHULEN (POLITICAL SCHOOLS)—BÜRO HEISSMEYER |

| GENERAL SS | WAFFEN SS |

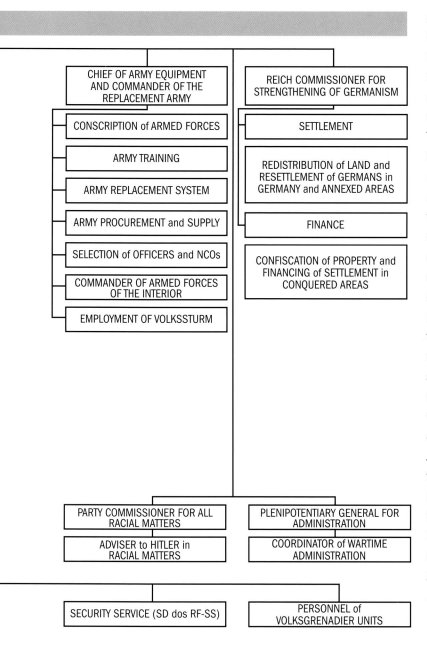

As shown in this chart, Heinrich Himmler, as Reichsführer SS, held eight separate offices besides those resulting directly from his position as commander of the SS proper. They included Reich and Prussian minister of the interior (*Reichs und Preussischer Minister des Innern*), under which Himmler controlled a department for constitutional and legislative matters; the administration of the German civil service, veterinary matters, and public health; the federalized communal administration, census, and survey; and the administration of sports and athletics. As German chief of police, (*Chef der Deutschen Polizei*) since June 1936, he federalized former state and local police organizations into the SS. These included the Sipo, Orpo, and Kripo, as well as the Gestapo. *U.S. War Department Technical Manual 30-451, March 15, 1945*

CHIEF OF ARMY EQUIPMENT AND COMMANDER OF THE REPLACEMENT ARMY

CONSCRIPTION of ARMED FORCES

ARMY TRAINING

ARMY REPLACEMENT SYSTEM

ARMY PROCUREMENT and SUPPLY

SELECTION of OFFICERS and NCOs

COMMANDER OF ARMED FORCES OF THE INTERIOR

EMPLOYMENT OF VOLKSSTURM

REICH COMMISSIONER FOR STRENGTHENING OF GERMANISM

SETTLEMENT

REDISTRIBUTION of LAND and RESETTLEMENT of GERMANS in GERMANY and ANNEXED AREAS

FINANCE

CONFISCATION of PROPERTY and FINANCING of SETTLEMENT in CONQUERED AREAS

PARTY COMMISSIONER FOR ALL RACIAL MATTERS

ADVISER to HITLER in RACIAL MATTERS

PLENIPOTENTIARY GENERAL FOR ADMINISTRATION

COORDINATOR of WARTIME ADMINISTRATION

SECURITY SERVICE (SD dos RF-SS)

PERSONNEL of VOLKSGRENADIER UNITS

DEATH'S-HEAD FORMATIONS

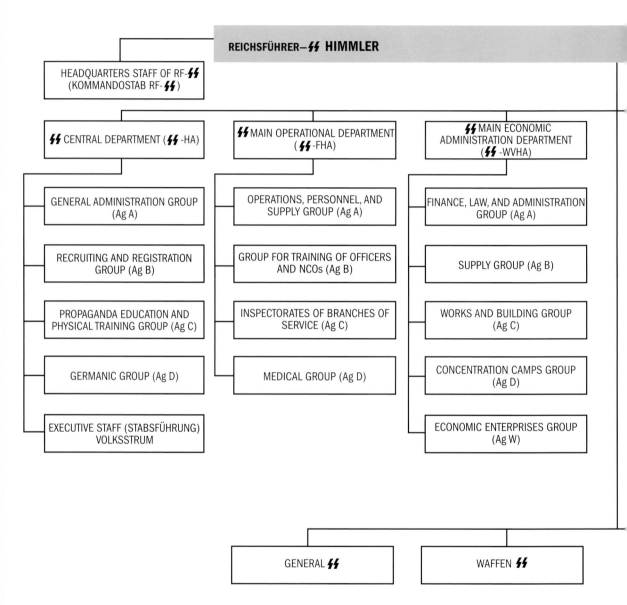

REICHSFÜHRER— **HIMMLER**

HEADQUARTERS STAFF OF RF-
(KOMMANDOSTAB RF-)

CENTRAL DEPARTMENT (-HA)

MAIN OPERATIONAL DEPARTMENT
(-FHA)

MAIN ECONOMIC
ADMINISTRATION DEPARTMENT
(-WVHA)

GENERAL ADMINISTRATION GROUP
(Ag A)

OPERATIONS, PERSONNEL, AND
SUPPLY GROUP (Ag A)

FINANCE, LAW, AND ADMINISTRATION
GROUP (Ag A)

RECRUITING AND REGISTRATION
GROUP (Ag B)

GROUP FOR TRAINING OF OFFICERS
AND NCOs (Ag B)

SUPPLY GROUP (Ag B)

PROPAGANDA EDUCATION AND
PHYSICAL TRAINING GROUP (Ag C)

INSPECTORATES OF BRANCHES OF
SERVICE (Ag C)

WORKS AND BUILDING GROUP
(Ag C)

GERMANIC GROUP (Ag D)

MEDICAL GROUP (Ag D)

CONCENTRATION CAMPS GROUP
(Ag D)

EXECUTIVE STAFF (STABSFÜHRUNG)
VOLKSSTRUM

ECONOMIC ENTERPRISES GROUP
(Ag W)

GENERAL

WAFFEN

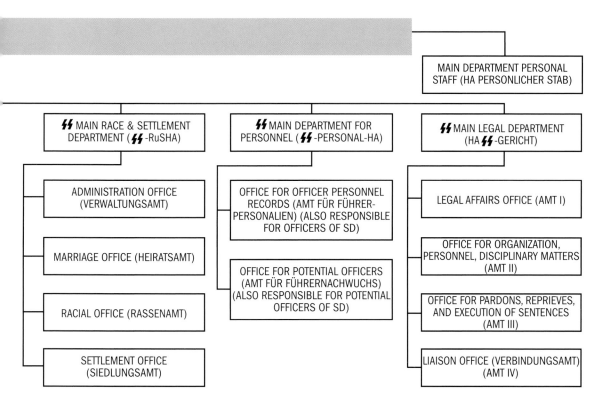

◢◢ MAIN RACE & SETTLEMENT DEPARTMENT (◢◢-RuSHA)	◢◢ MAIN DEPARTMENT FOR PERSONNEL (◢◢-PERSONAL-HA)	◢◢ MAIN LEGAL DEPARTMENT (HA ◢◢-GERICHT)
ADMINISTRATION OFFICE (VERWALTUNGSAMT)	OFFICE FOR OFFICER PERSONNEL RECORDS (AMT FÜR FÜHRER-PERSONALIEN) (ALSO RESPONSIBLE FOR OFFICERS OF SD)	LEGAL AFFAIRS OFFICE (AMT I)
MARRIAGE OFFICE (HEIRATSAMT)	OFFICE FOR POTENTIAL OFFICERS (AMT FÜR FÜHRERNACHWUCHS) (ALSO RESPONSIBLE FOR POTENTIAL OFFICERS OF SD)	OFFICE FOR ORGANIZATION, PERSONNEL, DISCIPLINARY MATTERS (AMT II)
RACIAL OFFICE (RASSENAMT)		OFFICE FOR PARDONS, REPRIEVES, AND EXECUTION OF SENTENCES (AMT III)
SETTLEMENT OFFICE (SIEDLUNGSAMT)		LIAISON OFFICE (VERBINDUNGSAMT) (AMT IV)

MAIN DEPARTMENT PERSONAL STAFF (HA PERSONLICHER STAB)

DEATH'S-HEAD FORMATIONS

This table shows the organization of the SS high command (Reichsführung SS), consisting of the Reichsführer SS, his staff, and the chiefs of the main departments administering the internal affairs of the three functional subdivisions of the SS, the General SS, Waffen SS, and the Death's Head Formations (*Totenkopfverbände*) . *U.S. War Department Technical Manual 30-451, March 15, 1945* business leaders, professors, politicians, and even doctors. A special target was the Catholic Church. In one diocese, a third of the priests were executed, and another third were arrested.

Adolf Hitler had not forgotten Drang Nach Osten. He had not forgotten that the creation of Poland itself was one of the insults cast against Germany by the Treaty of Versailles, which he reviled so much.

Having defeated Poland, he and his new ally, Stalin, put Poland out of existence. Western Poland disappeared into the Third Reich, while eastern Poland was permanently absorbed into parts of the Soviet Ukraine and what was then the Byelorussian (White Russian) Soviet Socialist Republic (now Belarus). Meanwhile, their secret deal also allowed Stalin to absorb Estonia, Latvia, and Lithuania in one fast swoop.

According to documents later captured by the Allies, 10 percent of Polish farmland in the western part of the country was handed over to Völksdeutsche settlers, and 20 percent of Polish businesses were confiscated and handed to German or Völksdeutsche owners.

Of course, the Soviets were not above ruthless slaughter in the part of Poland that they swallowed. In an incident known as the Katyn Massacre, 21,768 soldiers, priests, business owners, politicians, and professionals were murdered. Under orders given by Stalin himself and rubber-stamped by the Soviety Politburo, they were rounded up by the Soviet secret police, taken to Russia, and executed, mainly in the Katyn Forest.

In the aftermath of Poland's collapse, Britain and France dispatched a few bombers over Germany, but for the most part, took no offensive action. A lull in the action of World War II descended over Europe. Throughout the winter of 1939–1940, Allied and German troops sat and stared at one another across the heavily fortified Franco-German border. So little was happening, that newspaper writers dubbed the situation "the *Sitzkrieg,*" or the "phoney war."

For the SS Verfügungstruppe, it was far from phoney. During the "sitzing" time, the SS army was growing. Three SS regiments, named Der Führer, Deutschland, and Germania were combined into an SS Verfügungs *division.* Some of the Totenkopfverbände death camp guards were organized into a second division. The Leibstandarte Adolf Hitler remained as an independent regiment until it was expanded to brigade, then achieved division status in 1941.

All through the winter and into the spring, Europe waited and wondered what would happen next in this conflict called World War II. On April 9, 1940, the other shoe—or the other jackboot to be more accurate—in Europe's nervous standoff finally dropped. Germany went on the offensive. Sitzkrieg became Blitzkrieg once again.

The German armed forces quickly occupied Denmark, and by the end of the month, Norway had also been swallowed. On May 10, with the Leibstandarte Adolf Hitler in the spearhead into the Netherlands, the Germans began a great offensive to the west that duplicated their advance on Belgium and France in 1914 at the beginning of World War I. The most battle-ready of the units in the still relatively small British army were dispatched to France as the British Expeditionary Force (BEF) to help the French stem the German tide.

By the end of May, Luxembourg, Belgium, and the Netherlands had surrendered, and German forces were pouring into France. The French army and the BEF were outmaneuvered and quickly routed by the German Blitzkrieg. The latter found themselves surrounded at the French port of Dunkirk, with their backs to the English Channel. Between May 26 to June 4, a hastily assembled fleet of more than 800 boats, including fishing boats, pleasure craft, and lifeboats, made numerous crossings of the English Channel, rescuing nearly 200,000 British troops and more than 100,000 French soldiers from capture by the Germans.

The rest of the French army was not so lucky. By June 14, Germany had seized control of Paris, having accomplished in five weeks what it had been unable to do in four years of protracted fighting in World War I. France surrendered a week later, leaving Britain to face the onslaught of Germany's Blitzkrieg alone. Only about thirty miles of English Channel separated Germany's crack troops from a British army that had abandoned all of its equipment in France when it barely managed to escape from Dunkirk.

✳✳✳

ON JUNE 22, the attention of the global media was on the fall of France. Hitler had smugly arranged for the French to formally surrender at Compiègne Forest near Paris, in the same spot and in the same railway car where the Germans had surrendered in 1918. Hitler had achieved an astounding victory, and he would gleefully rub French noses in the filth of defeat.

Mussolini was so awed and impressed by Hitler's conquests that he sent the Italian army to invade southern France—but he did wait until after the Germans had beaten the French army.

Across the globe, Imperial Japan was so awed and impressed by Hitler's conquests that they asked to join Germany's Pact of Steel alliance with Italy. On September 27, 1940, the Tripartite Pact was signed, creating the three-nation Axis alliance.

Admiral Miklós "Nicolas" Horthy, the former Austro-Hungarian naval commander, who was now the regent of landlocked Hungary, was so impressed with Hitler's triumphs that he asked whether his kingdom could please join the Axis as well. He inked a deal to join the others on November 20.

In Romania, there was also interest in joining the Axis. General Ion Antonescu of the pro-Nazi Iron Guard, with whom the Ahnenerbe's Dr. Franz Altheim and Erika Trautmann had dined when they visited Bucharest in August 1938, became prime minister on September 6. He squeezed out King Carol II, installed his son as a puppet monarch, and joined the Axis three days after Horthy and the Hungarians.

Through the Axis alliance with Italy's Mussolini, Adolf Hitler now controlled virtually all of continental Europe from the border of the Soviet Union to the Atlantic Ocean. By virtue of the surrender of France and its African colonies, the Axis controlled all of North Africa from the Atlantic Ocean to the Egyptian border. Hitler would try, and later give up on, a defeat of Britain, but for the people of continental Europe, the dark shade of Nazi occupation and domination had been drawn.

As Germany consolidated its frighteningly quick conquests, the role of the SS in the occupation expanded. The heavy iron hand of the SS that had become familiar within the Third Reich was now felt throughout Europe. The conniving, furtive eyes and ears of the SD now snooped on foreign enemies of the occupier.

Europe had a new police chief, and his name was Heinrich Himmler.

The SS and SD were tasked with keeping tabs on potential resistors to German occupation and dealing with them as only such agencies can. Usually, the subjects of Nazi suspicion simply disappeared. Under Reinhard Heydrich, the SS adopted a *Nacht und Nebel* (night and fog) policy, meaning that the Black Knights would do their brutally efficient work discreetly under cover of darkness, striking the cold chill of fear (while providing the grist for countless exploitation films in the decades since World War II).

In 1941, Heydrich himself had a chance to personally wield his own iron fist in Bohemia and Moravia. Though they were permitted to have a puppet government, the Czechs were still uppity over their ignoble loss of sovereignty. They failed to appreciate their puppet government, and public opinion still supported the Czech government-in-exile in London. Hitler needed someone to throw a little fear of the pagan gods into these Slavic ingrates. Named as *Reichsprotektor* of Bohemia and Moravia, Heydrich instituted a bloody reign of terror on a scale not yet seen in Nazi-occupied Europe. The SS swept through the country, arresting, trying, convicting, and executing opponents with blistering speed and ruthlessness.

As quickly as he had done this, however, Bohemia and Moravia's "protector" increased the flow of foodstuffs and consumer goods, transforming himself and the Third Reich into an almost benevolent dictatorship. Having tasted Heydrich's wrath, Bohemia and Moravia now tasted his generosity. Fear turned to confusion, and confusion turned to acceptance. The Reichsprotektor had his subjects eating out of his hand—both literally and figuratively.

The brutality Heydrich demonstrated in his protectorate had been demonstrated by the Third Reich to some degree or another throughout Western Europe in 1940 and 1941. The Germans were here to stay, and their dark side was not a side that you wanted to see. For most people, it was time to keep your head down or taste the lash. For some people, however, no amount of keeping your head down would save you from the lash.

CHAPTER 14

Drang Nach Osten

I N HIS ASTOUNDING INUNDATION of Western Europe, Adolf Hitler had not forgotten Drang Nach Osten, the yearning of the Germanic Völkisch fringe for their destiny in the east. Lebensraum, the "living space" about which Hitler had waxed so romantically in *Mein Kampf,* was one of his favorite themes; now living space to the East seemed ripe for the taking, like low-hanging fruit. With his armies undefeated in every land battle thus far, Hitler made the decision to trash his nonaggression pact with Josef Stalin and invade the Soviet Union.

Strategically, the German invasion of the Soviet Union was the most enormous single-front military undertaking yet contemplated in world history. Consequently, it has been one of the most widely discussed. With twenty-twenty hindsight, military historians will call it Hitler's biggest battlefield miscalculation, although in the second half of 1941, that fact was far from evident. It was impudent and audacious, and there a million reasons why it failed—and half a million "ifs" justifying how it might have worked. But this discussion is beyond the scope of this work. The bottom line is that Hitler did it—because he really had no choice. He could no more elude the impulse to invade the Soviet Union than an unrepentant alcoholic can keep his hands off a drink. He *had* to do it. Drang Nach Osten was his destiny. Lebensraum was to be his sacred gift to his people.

As he had written in *Mein Kampf,* "We begin where we left off 600 years ago. We put an end to the perpetual Germanic march towards the South and west of Europe and turn our eyes toward the lands of the East. We finally put a stop to

Heinrich Hoffman took this photo of Reichsführer SS Heinrich Himmler inspecting Slavic Red Army prisoners, somewhere on the Eastern Front, sometime in 1941. Himmler couldn't wait to round up every Slav west of the Urals and turn the steppes over to Völkisch settlers. "It's the greatest piece of colonization the world will ever have seen," he told Felix Kersten. "Linked with a most noble and essential task, the protection of the Western world from an irruption from Asia."

U.S. National Archives

the colonial and trade policy of prewar times and pass over to the territorial policy of the future."

Hitler's theories, especially in *Mein Kampf,* are said to have been influenced by the geographer Karl Ernst Haushofer, whose assistant had been Rudolf Hess, Hitler's friend and now the deputy Führer. A pre–World War I officer in the kaiser's army, Haushofer had served as an advisor to the Japanese army for a year and a half in the early twentieth century and had been a student of the Greek-Armenian mystic George Gurdjieff. Haushofer's theory saying that a thorough understanding of geography was one key to future German greatness is credited by some as an inspiration for Hitler's Lebensraum concepts. Some say that Haushofer had even visited Hitler in Landsberg prison while the latter was writing his book. Others say that Haushofer's experiences with the samurai in Japan influenced Heinrich Himmler as he designed his own warrior society, the SS.

It has also been said that Haushofer may have played a role in forging the alliance between Germany and Japan. While working in Japan as a military advisor, he had met the emperor, albeit the previous emperor, and he had developed and maintained many contacts within the Japanese military establishment.

By 1941, the seventy-two-year-old Haushofer was ensconced as a senior lecturer in the geography department at the Universität München, but he was still influential in the inner sanctums of Hitler and Himmler. As Frederic Sondern wrote in the June 1941 issue of *Current History and Forum* magazine:

> Dr. Haushofer and his men dominate Hitler's thinking. That domination began 17 years ago when the World War general flattered the ex-corporal by paying him visits in prison. Haushofer saw possibilities in the hysterical agitator who had launched an unsuccessful beer-hall revolution. The prison visits became frequent; the distinguished soldier-scientist fascinated Hitler, then finally made him a disciple. The ascendancy has grown as Dr. Haushofer again and again has proved the accuracy of his knowledge and the wisdom of his advice. . . . It was Haushofer who taught the hysterical, planless agitator in a Munich jail to think in terms of continents and empires. Haushofer virtually dictated the famous Chapter XVI of *Mein Kampf* which outlined the foreign policy Hitler has since followed to the letter.

Sondern clearly believed the stories that Haushofer had actually visited Hitler at Landsberg.

Thinking back through those "600 years," of which he wrote in *Mein Kampf*, Hitler picked an appellation for the invasion of the Soviet Union that had venerable, even mystical, connotations. He named the operation "Barbarossa," after Friedrich I, the twelfth-century Holy Roman emperor and a successor to Heinrich I der Vogler as king of Germany. The name "Barbarossa," meaning "Red Beard," was a nickname given to Friedrich I by the northern Italians against whom he campaigned. Indeed, Friedrich I, Barbarossa himself, had led a great European campaign against the East in 1189—specifically the Third Crusade. Flanked by Philip II of France and Britain's famous, French-speaking King Richard Lionheart, Friedrich I Barbarossa rode toward the Holy City of Jerusalem at the head of an army that legend estimates at 100,000 troops. In picking this nickname as their operational code name, the Völkisch Nazi leaders demonstrated their attentive cognizance of their German medieval military heritage. (One wonders, however, how many of the men of 1941 thought about Barbarossa's last moments as they passed around the operation's paperwork. On June 10, 1190, near what is now Antakya, Turkey, the red-bearded Holy Roman emperor stumbled while going to bathe in the shallow Saleph [now Göksu] River and drowned.)

On June 22, 1941, Operation Barbarossa began. More than three million German troops achieved quick and decisive victories, pushing deep into the Soviet Union across a 1,800-mile front. The German operational objective was a swift conquest of the Soviet Union west of the Ural Mountains.

"When Barbarossa commences, the world will hold its breath," Hitler confidently predicted. "We have only to kick in the door and the whole rotten structure will come crashing down."

For a while it looked as though he was right. Within a week, the German spearhead was a third of the way to Moscow. Tens of thousands of Soviet troops had been captured within a matter of days, and around 4,000 Soviet aircraft were destroyed.

Waffen SS units went to battle attached to Wehrmacht army groups. The SS Totenkopf Division and SS Polizei Division were attached to *Heeresgruppe Nord* (Army Group North) for the offensive against Leningrad by way of the Baltic states of Latvia, Lithuania, and Estonia. The SS Das Reich Division joined in the *Heeresgruppe Mitte* (Army Group Center) attack toward Moscow, while the SS Wiking Division and the Leibstandarte Adolf Hitler joined with *Heeresgruppe Sud* (Army Group South) in the invasion of the Ukraine. The SS Nord Division participated in joint Operation Polarfuchs (Polar Fox) with the Finnish army in the far north.

By the first week of September 1941, the Germans had pushed more than 400 miles into the Soviet Union across the entire front. The area of the Soviet Union now occupied by Hitler's legions was more than double the size of Germany. Accompanied by nominal contingents of Hungarian and Romanian troops, and by the *Corpo di Spedizione Italiano in Russia* (Italian Expeditionary

Corps in Russia), the Germans conquered and occupied more territory faster than any army in history.

It was the manifest destiny of Völkisch German peasants to be masters of the land, and in the Soviet Union—in Russia, Byelorussia, and Ukraine— there was almost limitless land. Except for a sizable Völksdeutsche minority in Ukraine, most of this land was occupied by Slavs. However, as Adolf Hitler saw it, the Slavs were "subhuman," so they were a mere inconvenience. Now that the German armies were in control, it was time to turn these wide-open spaces into Lebensraum.

As Hitler had written, Germany's policy toward the Slavs and their "Jewish-Bolshevik masters" would be to "either sterilize these racially foreign elements to ensure that its own people's blood is not continually adulterated or remove them altogether and make over to its own people the land thereby released."

Hitler now turned to his racial philosopher, Dr. Alfred Rosenberg, the man who had compiled the Third Reich's official hierarchy of races and who had popularized the term "untermenschen" to describe the "subhumans." Rosenberg was named to head the new *Reichsministerium für die Besetzten Ostgebiete* (Reich Ministry for the Occupied Eastern Territories). The policy for the Eastern Territories would be for the steppes to be emptied of Slavs and Jews. The executioner of this policy would be Reichsführer Heinrich Himmler.

The Reichsführer SS had been working for more than a year on a meticulously detailed plan for dealing with the problem of what to do with these people. However, he had been thinking about this moment for most of his life. He had long dreamed of this vast clean slate, larger than Germany itself, that could be remade into a mystical Völkisch utopia, ruled over by the Aryan übermenschen of his SS.

"What a sublime idea!" Himmler told his Estonian-born masseur, Felix Kersten, as reported in Kersten's biography. "It's the greatest piece of colonization the world will ever have seen, linked with a most noble and essential task, the protection of the Western world from an irruption from Asia."

Another look into Himmler's personal perspective on what we would now call the ethnic cleansing of the East comes from SS Obergruppenführer Erich

Julius Eberhard von dem Bach, who cut a deal with Allied authorities after the war to give extensive evidence against his SS superiors. Known as Erich Julius Eberhard von dem Bach-Zelewski until he dropped his embarrassing Polish surname, Bach had been appointed by Himmler in 1937 as the *Höher SS und Polizeiführer* (HSSPF, or higher SS and police leader) for the eastern German state of Silesia. Having been involved in mass resettlements and confiscation of private property in Poland, he was reassigned by Himmler to serve as an HSSPF during Operation Barbarossa. In January 1941, at the SS Shangri-la at Wewelsburg, Himmler told Bach that the SS master plan for the East called for "eliminating" 30 million Slavs and deporting 14 million members of other races in order to make Lebensraum for German and Völksdeutsche settlers.

Dr. Alfred Rosenberg (1893–1946), Hitler's racial philosopher, codified the Third Reich's official hierarchy of races and popularized the term "untermenschen" to describe the Slavs and Jews in Russia. When Germany occupied huge areas of the Soviet Union, Rosenberg headed the new *Reichsministerium für die Besetzten Ostgebiete* (Reich Ministry for the Occupied Eastern Territories). *U.S. National Archives*

Himmler went on to effuse that a 100,000-square-mile swath of western Russia, roughly between Bryansk and Leningrad, would be devoid of Slavs by 1971. He added that 80 percent of Poles and two-thirds of the Ukrainians would be deported to Siberia, and that by 1961, there would be 2.4 million newly arrived German and Völksdeutsche people living in this area.

As Himmler told Kersten, the scheme was radical, but not without precedent. "Our measures are not really so original," the Reichsführer admitted to the masseur. He added:

> All great nations have used some degree of force or waged war in acquiring their status as a great power, in much the same way as ourselves; the French, the Spanish, the Italians, the Poles, to a great extent, too, the English and the Americans. Centuries ago Charlemagne set us the example of resettling an entire people by his action with

the Saxons and the Franks, the English with the Irish, the Spaniards with the Moors; and the American method of dealing with their Indians was to evacuate whole races. . . . But we are certainly original in one important point. Our measures are the expression of an idea, not the search for any personal advantage or ambition. We desire only the realization on a Germanic basis of a social ideal and the unity of the West. We will clarify the situation at whatever cost. It may take as many as three generations before the West gives its approval to this new Order, for which the Waffen SS was created.

These words were Himmler at his most pretentious, making "sacrifices" for the good of his people and for their destiny to rule the world for a thousand years.

As the Waffen SS was battling the Soviet army, Himmler sent in his "special" troops, his Einsatzgruppen, to begin clearing the land for his "sublime idea." In this case, of course, clearing the land for Völksdeutsche settlers did not mean removing brush and tree stumps, but removing human beings—or rather, those whom Rosenberg and Himmler considered, in their Lanzian logic, to be *less* than human.

As they had in Poland and Czechoslovakia, the Einsatzgruppen started with the "saboteurs" and intelligentzia, specifically the "Bolshevik commissars," the Communist Party leadership. Because Hitler considered "Bolshevism" to be a crime, there was legal justification in the minds of the SS planners for executing these people. From there, it was a easy roll down the slippery slope to liquidating everyone in the "Jewish-Bolshevik" elite, which included any Jew, anywhere, any time.

The Oberkommando Wehrmacht was not aware that there would be large-scale executions, and when the Einsatzgruppen began their work in the rear areas, the army was taken off guard. Objections were made, but the orders came directly from Himmler and were outside the Wehrmacht chain of command. So nothing could be done. However, the Wehrmacht and Himmler did work out an agreement whereby the Einsatzgruppen would not interfere with ongoing operations on the front lines.

Organized and supervised by Reinhard Heydrich, the roughly 3,000 men of the Einsatzgruppen were assigned to each of the Operation Barbarossa fronts. Einsatzgruppe A was assigned to Heeresgruppe Nord (Army Group North), and Einsatzgruppe B went to Heeresgruppe Mitte (Army Group Center). Einsatzgruppe C and Einsatzgruppe D followed Heeresgruppe Sud (Army Group South) into Ukraine and the Crimea. Each Einsatzgruppe was nominally under the direction of a regional Höher SS und Polizeiführer. Obergruppenführer Erich Julius Eberhard von dem Bach was the HSSPF for the Heeresgruppe Mitte sector.

A report that later wound up in Allied hands calmly states that through September 6, 1941, one Einsatzgruppe C Sonderkommando unit had "dealt with 11,328 Jews." Einsatzgruppe D Report Number 153 recounted that 79,276 people had been eliminated, including "122 Communist functionaries and 3,176 Jews." The balance were apparently mere Slavs.

Einsatzgruppe C was in Kiev on September 19, the same day that the city surrendered to the Wehrmacht. A summary report states, "The Jewish population was invited by poster to present themselves for resettlement. Although initially we had only counted on 5,000 to 6,000 Jews reporting, more than 30,000 Jews appeared; by a remarkably efficient piece of organization they were led to believe in the resettlement story until shortly before their execution."

Another Einsatzgruppe C report from the late summer of 1941 explains that the "Jews of the town were invited to present themselves at a certain spot for registration and subsequent accommodation in a camp. Some 34,000 reported, including women and children. After being stripped of their valuables and clothing all were killed, a task which demanded several days."

Meanwhile, there are Wehrmacht reports that tell another side of the cold Einsatzgruppen efficiency. A certain Major Rosler, who commanded the 528th Infantry Regiment, later wrote that in late July 1941 while his unit was at Zhytomyr in Ukraine, he heard a fusillade of gunfire across a hill. Climbing out to investigate, he witnessed "a picture of such barbaric horror that the effect upon anyone coming upon it unawares was both shattering and repellent."

He went on to describe a huge pit containing countless bodies of Jews and that "in this grave lay, among others, an old man with a white beard clutching a cane in his left hand. Since this man, judging by his sporadic breathing, showed signs of life, I ordered one of the [SS Einsatzgruppen] policemen to kill him. He smilingly replied: 'I have already shot him seven times in the stomach. He can die on his own now.'"

The SS Einsatzgruppen kept meticulous, if grisly, records. From the opening of Operation Barbarossa through the ensuing winter, Einsatzgruppe A eliminated 249,420 untermenschen, Einsatzgruppe B eliminated 45,467, Einsatzgruppe C around 95,000, and Einsatzgruppe D an estimated 92,000 from the utopian homeland that Himmler envisioned for his Völkisch German pioneers.

Of course, not all the Wehrmacht troops had clean hands when it came to the killing of Jews. Wehrmacht documents indicate that Jews suspected of sabotage were to be shot. A December 1941 report from Einsatzgruppe A stated that the regular army troops in Heersegruppe Mitte had killed 19,000 partisans and criminals, many of them Jews.

Initially, the bodies of those murdered by the Einsatzgruppen were buried in mass graves. However, through later 1942 and into 1943, a massive effort known variously as *Enterdungsaktion* or *Sonderaktion* 1005 was made to exhume, crush, and burn these hundreds of thousands of human remains.

In February 1942, Bach was hospitalized in the SS rest-and-recuperation facility at Hohenlychen, claiming a nervous breakdown. His doctor reported, "He is suffering particularly from hallucinations connected with the shootings of Jews which he himself carried out and with other grievous experiences in the East." Reportedly, he "would pass his nights screaming, a prey to hallucinations."

"Thank God, I'm through with it," Bach claims to have told the doctor. "Don't you know what's happening in Russia? The entire Jewish people . . . is being exterminated there."

He claims that Himmler told him personally that the executions were pursuant to "a Führer order. The Jews are the disseminators of Bolshevism. . . . [I]f you don't keep your nose out of the Jewish business, you'll see what'll happen to you!"

Bach painted himself as a victim of the Reichsführer's threats, but his record shows that when he got out of the hospital, his own brutality toward the untermenschen was undiminished until the end of World War II.

As the victorious German armies pressed through the once and future Soviet Union, the vast and sprawling lands were opened up for Völksdeutsche settlement. The Byelorussian Soviet Socialist Republic was renamed Weiss Ruthenien (White Ruthenia), formally freed from its "Jewish-Bolshevik" masters, and handed over for resettlement.

The Reich was supposed to last a thousand years, so as autumn of 1941 arrived, Himmler confidently began drafting five-year plans and twenty-year plans for his Völkisch utopia. However, there were snowflakes in the air out there on the Russian steppes. Soon the rapid progress of the Wehrmacht would slow. Rains would come, and tires would slip, slide, spin, and stick in the thick black mud. The mud would freeze. The snow would come, and with it a barely perceptible shift in the fortunes of the invincible Wehrmacht.

On the eve of Christmas in 1941, a holiday that both Soviet commissars and SS Oberführers forbade their troops to celebrate, the forward march of Barbarossa's children stopped. Adolf Hitler's heretofore victorious legions sputtered to a halt in the primeval ice and snow of Mother Russia's secret weapon—winter. The Aryan warriors, whose lineage was believed by some to have stretched back in time and space to the ice fields of Thule, had reached the end of the road in a snowbank.

It would be a very long walk back.

CHAPTER 15

Bloody Hell

———

T STARTED OUT AS A VAGUE IDEA, a gut reaction to a perverted and paranoid intolerance. It turned into the crime of the century. The idea was called *Die Endlösund* (the Final Solution), a term born within a bureaucracy to describe an apparently benign resolution of an issue that was, in reality, homicide on a heretofore unimaginable scale. It was absolutely a holocaust in the most extreme parameters of this term, and since the 1970s, it has become almost universally referred to as *the* Holocaust.

The plan was simple: kill every Jew in Europe.

Whereas the Einsatzgruppen operations in the Soviet Union, which began in June 1941, functioned to clear both Slavs and Jews from land so that the conquered land could be occupied by Völksdeutsche or German settlers, the aspects of the Final Solution that would be carried out within the Third Reich itself in subsequent years were aimed at clearing Jews and other "undesirables" from the places where Aryan Germans already lived.

The Final Solution was created within the bowels of the SS as the definitive resolution of what the Nazis had called the "Jewish Problem." What exactly was this problem? The problem was that Hitler wished to make Germany and the growing Third Reich into a wonderland, a paradise for Aryans. But there were Jews inside the Third Reich. To him and to those around him, the presence of Jews in the Reich was likened to a viral infection in an otherwise healthy body.

To understand how the neo-pagan minds of the Reich worked, it is important understand that there had been a series of proposed official solutions discussed *before* Heinrich Himmler and Reinhard Heydrich concocted the *Final Solution* to the Führer's dilemma.

Angry racial dogmas had bubbled around the fringes of Austro-German society long before List and Lanz codified them into a neo-pagan pseudoreligion, and long before they flooded into the political and legal mainstream with the Nazis. However, nationalist thugs, especially those of the SA, now took the Nazi rise to power as a license to intimidate. Ernst Röhm, who was openly gay and, therefore, a member of another group that would later suffer from official Nazi persecution, organized boycotts of Jewish businesses and turned his goons loose to harass people and vandalize Jewish property.

At first, even Hitler tried to distance himself from the thuggery. Having come to power through the ballot box, he was still cautious about public opinion. He ordered the SA to cool it, and his interior minister, Wilhelm Frick, even suggested penalties for SA men who attacked people. However, Hitler was moving toward a "legal" method to accomplish the same goal.

Hitler's first "solution" on the road to the Final Solution was to legally isolate the Jews. This he promulgated with legislation known as the *Nürnberger Gesetze* (Nuremberg Laws) because the Führer announced them at an NSDAP rally in Nuremberg in 1935. The hand of the diehard Blut-und-Boden crowd, from Ricardo Walther Darré to Alfred Rosenberg, was evident in the fact that the concept of "German blood" was the cornerstone of this legislation. (Neither of these blood zealots had been born with German citizenship. Darré was born in Argentina, and Rosenberg in Estonia, when it was still part of the Russian Empire. Of course, Hitler had been born in Austria.)

Passed by the Reichstag in September 1935, the Nuremberg Laws took effect at the beginning of 1936. The Reich Citizenship Law restricted citizenship to people with German blood. People who had Jewish ancestors could not be included among citizens. The Law for the Protection of German Blood and German Honor outlawed marriages between Jews and people with "German blood."

The chilling thing about the march from the Nuremberg Laws to the Final Solution was that the frothing hatred of Jews was no longer merely the realm of the neo-pagans and Social Darwinists. German public opinion had swung

Adolf Hitler, emoting dramatically during a speech. The charisma of this man was uncanny. The French writer Maximine Julia Portaz once said that he was the reincarnation of the Hindu god Vishnu, while Heinrich Himmler defined him as a creator, saying that "over the Germanic Reich, over it our Führer, who created this Reich and who still creates." It was his spellbinding power that convinced a nation to embark on a terrible road. However, while it may have been Hitler who turned Jörg Lanz von Liebenfels's Ariosophic nightmare into the rallying cry of a nation, it was Heinrich Himmler's SS that coldly planned, constructed, maintained, and used the industrial-strength gas chambers and crematoria of almost unimaginable capacity, in order to make that nightmare come true. *U.S. National Archives*

firmly in favor of the persecution that was taking place. This shift was most frighteningly demonstrated on the night of November 9–10, 1938.

It all started when a German-born Jew named Herschel Grünspan (Grynzspan) shot a German bureaucrat named Ernst vom Rath at the German embassy in Paris. When Rath died, on the fifteenth anniversary of the 1923 Munich putsch, the Nazi holy day, propaganda minister Joseph Goebbels announced that demonstrations of anti-Jewish outrage would not be interfered with. Tantamount to legalizing mayhem, this declaration set in motion an orgy of violence and vandalism that was called *Kristallnacht* (Night of Broken Glass) because of all the Jewish windows that were smashed all across Germany. The absence of a serious public outcry from non-Jews in response was an ominous turn.

After isolation came exclusion. Jewish doctors, lawyers, and professors were soon drubbed out of their professions. Formerly there had been boycotts of Jewish businesses by non-Jews. Now, Jews were forbidden to enter non-Jewish businesses and even public facilities such as swimming pools. (It should be noted that, at that same time, there were still racial restrictions on some American swimming pools.)

After exclusion came expulsion. It became the responsibility of Heinrich Himmler, as the head of the Gestapo and SS and as the Reich's enforcer-in-chief, to kick the Jews out of Germany. He drew up plans to expel 200,000 Jews annually, although only 40,000 left in 1938 and 78,000 in 1939. Many moved elsewhere in Europe, including 30,000 to Czechoslovakia. Those who had adequate funds, or who met necessary income requirements, could find refuge in France, Britain, and the United States.

The place considered as best candidate for absorbing the lion's share of Jewish evictees was Palestine. Since 1917, when British foreign secretary Lord Arthur Balfour first floated the idea, a plan had been on the international table to set aside Palestine as a permanent sovereign homeland for the world's Jews. This area, part of which later became the state of Israel, had been captured by the British from the Turkish Ottoman Empire in 1917 as part of the action in World War I. In the 1930s, Palestine was managed as a mandate by the British under the League of Nations.

Within the SS, the idea was now proposed to officially relocate all of Germany's Jews to Palestine. This idea of a government-sponsored relocation gained surprising support from the Zionists, the most politically extreme among German Jews. The SD even opened a dialog with Zionist elements and with the Haganah, the Jewish paramilitary force in Palestine that favored the establishment of a Jewish homeland. Untersturmführer Adolf Eichmann of the SD traveled to the Middle East in 1937 for secret talks in Cairo with the Haganah to facilitate the relocation. However, the British refused to let Eichmann enter Palestine and threatened a naval blockade to keep out boatloads of European Jews.

The idea of a government-sponsored relocation of Germans—even German Jews—in response to a British mandate got an icy reception from Britain. There was no love lost between the British and the Haganah, who the British perceived as a terrorist group. Though it had been Balfour who first suggested the idea two decades earlier, the British were fearful of incurring the rath of the Arabs in

Palestine, who also hated the Jews. They pictured themselves walking a tightrope stretched across the ongoing feud between the Jews and Arabs within Palestine, and the last thing they wanted was for the Germans to upset the balance by adding more Jews. (This apprehension of offending Arabs who hold animosity toward Jews is obviously still a recurring theme in Middle East politics.)

For a time, the Nazis actively sought out another place to which the German Jews could be exiled. If plans to move them to Palestine were stymied by His Majesty's government, then where else could the Jews go? Surprisingly, the leading alternative candidate, discussed at length inside Number 8 Prinz Albrechtstrasse, was the Indian Ocean island of Madagascar, which would be made a German colony. Amazingly, Adolf Eichmann later testified that he had imagined himself as the German governor-general of Jewish Madagascar. However, this project was shelved by the SS as impractical after the start of World War II.

For Hitler, the theoretician, and Himmler, the man who would have to carry out the eventual solution, the so-called Jewish problem got much worse in September 1939. When the Reich swallowed Poland, it swallowed a much larger number of Jews than had lived within Germany's prewar borders. The interim solution in Poland was to consolidate the Polish Jews into a "ghetto," a term that had originated in sixteenth-century Venice when Jews were compelled by decree to live in a specific area of the city. In Poland, the Germans now concentrated Jews into ghettos in Warsaw and other major cities, in the same way that Himmler had already concentrated his enemies into his prototype "concentration camp" at Dachau.

The Final Solution as an articulated policy was not mapped out until 1941 and not implemented until 1942, although Hitler had provided the world with a clear preview three years earlier. "I have very often been a prophet, and have usually been ridiculed for it," Hitler said in a speech on January 30, 1939. He continued:

> During the time of my struggle for power it was in the first instance the
> Jewish race which only received my prophecies with laughter when I said
> that I would one day take over the leadership of the State, and with it that

of the whole nation, and that I would then among many other things settle the Jewish problem. Their laughter was uproarious, but I think that for some time now they have been laughing on the other side of their face. Today I will once more be a prophet: If the international Jewish financiers in and outside Europe should succeed in plunging the nations once more into a world war, then the result will not be the Bolshevization of the earth, and thus the victory of Jewry, but the annihilation of the Jewish race in Europe!

Hitler's words, though more conceptual than a precise directive, are nevertheless straightforward. If Hitler ever issued a direct order authorizing the Final Solution, it has never been found. However, it is evident in the documents that have survived that those around him had a clear understanding of what was expected.

Perhaps the first known mention of the Final Solution is in a July 31, 1941, memo from Hermann Göring to Reinhard Heydrich requesting "details of the preliminary measures taken in the organizational, technical and material fields for the achievement of the final solution which we seek."

In a January 9, 1998, article in the Hamburg-based national German newspaper *Die Zeit,* German historian Christian Gerlach quotes a recently discovered diary entry in which Joseph Goebbels writes that "with respect of the Jewish Question, the Führer has decided to make a clean sweep. He prophesied to the Jews that if they again brought about a world war, they would live to see their annihilation in it. That wasn't just a catch-word. The world war is here, and the annihilation of the Jews must be the necessary consequence."

This entry was written on December 12, 1941, the day after the Third Reich declared war on the United States and the same day that Goebbels met with Hitler at his office in the Reich Chancellory. Heinrich Himmler was present at this meeting, as were Hitler's personal assistant, Martin Bormann, and Hans Frank, a longtime NSDAP attorney who was now governor-general of occupied Poland. Hermann Göring and Reinhard Heydrich were, apparently, not present. According to Gerlach, just six days later, Himmler met with Hitler at the

SS Obergruppenführer und General der Polizei Reinhard Heydrich, with his chiseled face and cold serpentine eyes was Director of the Reich Main Security Office Reichssicherheitshauptamt (RSHA) and one of the most feared men in Europe.
National Archives

Führer's field headquarters in East Prussia. That evening, he penned a marginal note in his diary that read *"Judenfrage—als Partisanen auszurotten"* ("Jewish question—like partisans to be exterminated").

In other words, Himmler and Hitler had discussed the SS Einsatzgruppen operations in the Soviet Union, which had by that time killed around a half million "partisans." Furthermore, if he hadn't already, the Führer gave the Reichsführer the green light to apply the Final Solution of mass murder to the Jews within Germany itself.

The direct order had already been given at some time earlier, as Goebbels and Himmler certainly understood the parameters of the Final Solution. In fact, Himmler's sinister dark prince, Reinhard Heydrich, had already gotten the ball rolling on implementing the scheme. In November, he had planned a meeting of senior midlevel management within the SS, Gestapo, and Reich government to discuss details. Some have suggested that he did so under the authority of Göring's July 31 memo directing him to take "preliminary measures . . . in the organizational, technical and material fields." However, Heydrich was under Himmler's chain of command, not in Göring's.

This meeting, known to history as the Wannsee Conference, as it was held in the Berlin suburb of Wannsee, took place on January 20, 1942. While no record exists of the December 12 meeting in Hitler's office—aside from Goebbels's recollection—the minutes of the Wannsee Conference survived the war. They were translated by the International Military Tribunal and are the "smoking gun" of the Final Solution. The minutes say the meeting's participants calmly discussed the practical details of the mass murder of millions. In his opening remarks, Heydrich explained that the Third Reich had expelled 530,000 Jews from the Third Reich since taking power. He went on to say that there were then 11 million Jews left in Europe and the European parts of the Soviet Union, adding that 95.5 percent of these "untermenschen" were living within areas then controlled by the Third Reich or its allies.

"Under proper guidance, in the course of the final solution the Jews are to be allocated for appropriate labor in the East," Heydrich said, continuing:

> Able-bodied Jews, separated according to sex, will be taken in large work columns to these areas for work on roads, in the course of which action doubtless a large portion will be eliminated by natural causes. The possible final remnant will, since it will undoubtedly consist of the most resistant portion, have to be treated accordingly, because it is the product of natural selection and would, if released, act as the seed of a new Jewish revival. In the course of the practical execution of the final solution, Europe will be combed through from west to east. Germany proper, including the Protectorate of Bohemia and Moravia, will have to be handled first due to the housing problem and additional social and political necessities.

How could a roomful of well-educated professionals discuss such things in such a composed, detached manner?

The blind obedience to a party that had morphed into a state was a symptom of how Nazism was not so much an ideology as it was a mesmerizing religion. As Christopher Browning observed in *The Origins of the Final Solution,* published in 2004, this scheme was being planned by those who seem to have had no conscience whatsoever. Browning wrote that among this group "no less than eight of the fifteen participants held the doctorate. Thus it was not a dimwitted crowd unable to grasp what was going to be said to them. Nor were they going to be overcome with surprise or shock, for Heydrich was not talking to the uninitiated or squeamish."

The key word is "initiated." After nearly a decade in power, the government of the Third Reich had almost completely initiated its population, and certainly its bureaucracy, into a pious acceptance of a pagan state religion whose belief system was truly beyond belief.

Beginning with Dachau in Bavaria, the SS already had established a number of concentration camps and forced-labor camps in Germany and all across occupied Europe. Hundreds of thousands of people were shoved into these camps and forced to work in slave-labor conditions on starvation-level rations. To this expanding network of camps were added a half dozen facilities in Poland called *Vernichtungslager* (destruction camps), whose only purpose was to exterminate men, women, and children. The largest of these—actually a complex of three major separate camps and numerous subcamps—was located near the town of Oswiecim, which had been renamed with its former German name, Auschwitz. The original camp had been set up in June 1940 as a concentration camp to house 100,000 slave laborers for nearby factories. A second such labor camp was added in 1942. Also opened in 1942 was the Auschwitz extermination camp at nearby Birkenau (Brzezinka in Polish), which was expanded throughout World War II. It is estimated that at least 1.4 million people were murdered at Auschwitz-Birkenau alone, although the former camp commandant bragged that three million were killed. The second largest of the Vernichtungslager, Treblinka, near Warsaw, saw the murder of around 850,000 people.

The total number of people killed in the extermination camps numbers around 4.5 million. In addition, others died of disease, starvation, or outright murder at other concentration and labor camps, or as they were being transported to the camps in forced marches or squeezed into cattle cars.

An estimated six million Jews died. The calculations are based on SS records that were pieced together after the war and on correlations of prewar and postwar censuses. The estimates vary, based on accounting methods and which countries are included. In the 1988 *Atlas of the Holocaust,* Martin Gilbert puts the number at about 5.7 million, or 78 percent of the 7.3 million Jews that lived in occupied Europe. Yisrael Gutman and Robert Rozett, in the *Encyclopedia of the Holocaust,* estimate up to 5.86 million, and Wolfgang Benz of the Technical University of Berlin suggests that there were as many as 6.2 million.

In her 1986 book, *The War Against the Jews,* Lucy Dawidowicz includes more of the Soviet Union in her prewar totals, estimating that 5,933,900 out of a Jewish population of 8,861,800 were killed, or 67 percent of that total. Going into detail, she notes that 90 percent of Poland's 3.3 million Jews died, along with 90 percent of the 253,000 Jews in the Baltic countries and 90 percent of the 240,000 Jews who were left in Germany and Austria by 1942. The percentage in Ukraine was just 60 percent, but the number killed was 900,000 by her calculation, a total second only to the number of Jews killed Poland.

In the *Columbia Guide to the Holocaust,* published in 2000, Donald Niewyk and Francis Nicosia add that between five million and 11 million non-Jewish civilians were also murdered, mainly outside the camps. In addition to the Soviet Slavs killed by the Einsatzgruppen after June 1941, these included non-Jewish Poles, as well as the Romani people (called Gypsies), another group targeted by the Nazis for eradication. Sizable numbers of others, from Catholics to Jehovah's Witnesses, were murdered because of their religion.

Those who ran the camps were members of the SS Totenkopfverbände, which had been formed in 1935 to staff Dachau and other concentration camps in Germany, such as Buchenwald, Ravensbrück, and Sachsenhausen. The Totenkopfverbände remained as an independent component within the SS until 1942, although personnel rotated between it and the Waffen SS. After 1942, the Totenkopfverbände was placed under the Waffen SS chain of command.

The man Himmler installed to run the Totenkopfverbände during its formative years was SS Brigadeführer Theodor Eicke. As directed by Himmler, Eicke's method of training produced men with blind loyalty to the SS, while at the same time erasing their ability to perceive the suffering of others. Himmler recognized that desensitizing the Totenkopfverbände men was essential. They had to be hard, tough, and unsympathetic to the screams and the horrible pain endured by the untermenschen.

In evidence gathered at the International Military Tribunal, Heinrich Himmler is quoted as having told his Black Knights:

> Most of you will know what it means to see a hundred corpses, five hundred, a thousand, lying there. But seeing this thing through and nevertheless apart from certain exceptions due to human infirmity remaining decent, that is

what has made us hard. This is a never-recorded and never-to-be-recorded page of glory in our history. . . . I can tell you that it is hideous and frightful for a German to have to see such things. It is so, and if we had not felt it to be hideous and frightful, we should not have been Germans. However hideous it may be, it has been necessary for us to do it and it will be necessary in many other cases.

While the emotionless Totenkopfverbände may have been able to accept what they saw, Himmler was obviously nervous about public opinion outside the wire. Most Germans were unaware of exactly what was happening in the concentration camps. The stench of bodies being burned by the ton hung not over Germany itself, but over Polish towns far from the prewar borders of the Reich. They knew that Jews had been rounded up and put into labor camps, but for the most part, the gruesome details of camp life, now so painfully clear, went unseen.

As we have seen in films such as *Schindler's List,* there were numerous Germans—perhaps not a majority, but nevertheless numerous—who helped or tried to help Jews from being rounded up. Often, they whispered their concerns to someone in power whom they could trust, occasionally even someone with the SS runes on his collar. A few times, these pleas even reached the Reichsführer himself.

"Remember," Himmler complained to Felix Kersten, "how many people, Party members included, send their precious plea for clemency to me or some other authority; they invariably say that all Jews are, of course, swine, but that Mr. So-and-so is the exception, a decent Jew who should not be touched. I have no hesitation in saying that the number of these requests and the number of differing opinions in Germany, leads one to conclude that there are more decent Jews than all the rest put together."

It was a job that just had to be done, Himmler felt. He was, after all, doing it for the good of the German people and the purity of their Völkisch blood. As he told Kersten, "You oughtn't to look at things from such a limited and egotistical point of view; you have to consider the Germanic world as a whole. . . . [A] man has to sacrifice himself."

He considered the task of murdering millions to be a daunting task, but not because it was emotionally hard to kill. The difficulty was only in the massive logistics effort involved.   Repeatedly, we get the sense that Himmler sincerely believed that it was *he* who was making a sacrifice.

In the nineteenth century, Social Darwinist cranks had sat around their comfortable drawing rooms, not just in Germany, but also in many "advanced" Western nations, discussing their racial hierarchies. Madame Helena Blavatsky was among those who had turned such hierarchies into a religion. There were many who had contributed to making the doctrine of a racial hierarchy into a pseudoscience, but it was Jörg Lanz von Liebenfels who created Theozoology and proposed the sterilization of lesser, *anthropozoa,* races, especially the Jews. Could Jörg Lanz von Liebenfels ever have conceived, even in his most Ariosophistically passionate moment, of vast factories of death—not one such factory, but many?

It was Adolf Hitler, the down-and-out art student, who read Lanz's magazine, *Ostara,* visited him, and drew from his words the idea that these "apelings" whom Lanz so pseudoscientifically despised could be eliminated. Hitler was not alone in theorizing that the apelings, the untermenschen, should simply be cleansed from German society. It was Heinrich Himmler and his Thule-cold understudy, Reinhard Heydrich, who heard their Führer speak of the "should" and methodically and meticulously craft the "would."

Hitler had turned Lanz's bizarre dreams into the rallying cry of a nation, but it was Heinrich Himmler's SS that coldly planned, constructed, maintained, and *used* industrial-strength gas chambers and crematoria of almost unimaginable capacity to make these dreams—or, for the millions who died and the millions more who survived with firsthand knowledge that such things existed, *nightmares*—come true.

Even Satan himself might cringe at the sight of the places where the SS Totenkopfverbände labored so tirelessly to kill every untermenschen west of the Urals. The camps of Heinrich Himmler's SS were nothing short of a bloody hell.

CHAPTER 16

The Most Feared Address in Europe

———

T HE NEXUS OF FEAR in the Third Reich and in occupied Europe was at Number 8 Prinz Albrechtstrasse, Berlin, SW 11. Merely the mention of the street name, "Prinz Albrechtstrasse," was enough to make a person break into a cold sweat. Number 8 was the *Geheime Staatspolizeihauptamt* (Secret State Police Principal Office) headquarters. Within it was the man whose letterhead bore the title *Reichsführer SS und Chef der Deutschen Polizei*. The Reichsführer SS was also chief of Germany's secret police, the Geheime Staatspolizei, or the Gestapo.

Heinrich Himmler was the most feared man in not just in Germany, but in all of Europe, holding forth from the most feared address in Europe.

Even Alfred Rosenberg, who had Adolf Hitler's ear and had framed the philosophical grounding of the Third Reich, felt beads of sweat forming in Himmler's presence.

"I had never been able to look Heinrich Himmler straight in the eye," Rosenberg admitted. "His eyes were always hooded, blinking behind his pince-nez. Now, however, when I could see them gazing at me from the photograph and I thought I could detect one thing in them—malice."

During the years from 1941 through most of 1944, Heinrich Himmler was at the apogee of his power. Between the initial successes of Operation Barbarossa and the Wehrmacht's overall reversal of fortune after losing over a million men in the Battle of Stalingrad less than two years later, Himmler was the master of the universe of his dreams.

As he was happily anticipating the tide of Völksdeutsche settlement in the East, Himmler sent in the archaeologists from his Ahnenerbe. He wanted them to unearth the artifacts that proved a Germanic link with the East, especially the Völkisch Ukraine. As the German legions swept through Ukraine and into the Crimean peninsula north of the Black Sea in July 1942, the Ahnenerbe's Dr. Herbert Jankuhn led a team to locate those artifacts the fast and easy way: supported by Einsatzgruppe thugs and Waffen SS panzers, they started hitting the museums. The Ahnenerbe team also explored the ancient cliff dwellings and monasteries in the vicinity of Chufut-Kale, Eski-Kermen, Manhup-Kale, and Tepe-Kermen that date back to around the eighth century (and remain favorites of twenty-first century backpackers). Jankuhn was reportedly unable to find any Germanic artifacts, but many Greek and older items were gathered up and shipped to Germany.

Despite his preoccupation with his schemes that involved the future of Lebensraum in the East, Himmler was apparently quite excited about his Ahnenerbe expeditions deep into the Soviet Union and into the mountains of the Caucuses. Was it possible that the Mountain of Tongues was indeed out there in the Caucasus, as medieval Arabic geographers hypothesized? Was it possible that the Ahnenerbe might find such a place? Then, too, there were the "Secret Masters of the Caucasus," whom anthropologist and folklorist C. Scott Littleton mentioned in connection with alleged human sacrifices at Schloss Wewelsburg. Perhaps Himmler hoped to make contact with these individuals.

Himmler ordered Walther Wüst of the Ahnenerbe to organize a Caucasus expedition, and in turn, he turned to SS Obersturmbannführer Ernst Schäfer, the hardy young mountaineer who had led the Ahnenerbe's 1938–1939 expedition to Tibet. Bruno Beger, also late of the Tibet trip, wanted to come along to measure skulls of "mountain Jews." Who better for this job than Schäfer and Beger, together again at last?

The Schäfer expedition into the Caucasus was the subject of intense planning, but the complexity of the plans and the realities of war eventually strangled

Heinrich Himmler held court at Number 8 Prinz Albrechtstrasse in Berlin. Though this wartime magazine picture belies an affable demeanor on the part of the Reichsführer SS, his office came to be regarded as the most feared address in Europe.
Author's collection

the ambitious scheme. Schäfer never made it, but a group of Wehrmacht mountain troops climbed 18,510-foot Mount Elbrus, the highest mountain in the Caucuses. Counterintuitively, Adolf Hitler angrily condemned this feat by his young Aryan troopers as a waste of time.

As for Himmler, nothing could interrupt his enjoyment of his new domain. Through his Einsatzgruppe enforcers, Heinrich Himmler was the lord not merely of both a real and conceptual Prinz-Albrechtstrasse, but also of the vast, wide-open spaces of the East, an area larger than the prewar Reich. It was the Lebensraum of *Mein Kampf.* Even if he didn't care about conquering Elbrus, these vast steppes were Hitler's at last, and Hitler had given it over to Himmler to depopulate and repopulate, to destroy and rebuild as the long awaited Völkisch paradise. It was the "sublime idea" Himmler had once described to Felix Kersten, the bulwark against the evil tides from the East about which Karl Maria Wiligut had warned him. It was, according to Kersten's recollection, Himmler's idea of the "greatest piece of colonization the world will ever have seen."

Himmler took a personal and zealous interest in the newly conquered lands. He established a field headquarters, an "Eastern Prinz-Albrechtstrasse," called Hegewald, outside the town of Zhytomyr, eighty miles west of Kiev, the capital of Ukraine. It was here that Himmler had the idea of beginning his "great piece of colonization" with a sort of human experimental farm. The idea was to create a model Völksdeutsche settlement to serve as a prototype of what he planned for Ukraine and for that 100,000-square-mile swath of western Russia between Bryansk and Leningrad. After finally getting the authorization from Hitler for this experiment in July 1942, Himmler ordered the SS to sweep 10,000 Slavic and Jewish men, women, and children from the best farmland in the Zhytomyr/Hegewald area, load them in rail cars, and ship them somewhere else. Having done this, the SS uprooted Ukrainian Völksdeutsche from the north of the country and brought them in to the Hegewald colony. Here they were given tracts of farmland—and production quotas—as Himmler's own Blut und Boden pioneers.

Through 1941, and into 1942 and 1943, Himmler would travel the endless eastern miles in his armored train, his mobile Prinz-Albrechtstrasse. As he rambled through Russia and Ukraine, he would frequently order the train to stop so that he could get out and gaze at what may have seemed to him as limitless horizons. Hanns Johst, the poet and playwright who became the darling of the Nazis and the defacto poet laureate of the Third Reich, accompanied Himmler on at least one of his many inspection tours of the eastern territories. He observed that Himmler would often bend down, snatch a fistful of earth, and sniff it. He would then sigh dramatically and wax about how wonderful it was to look out at all this land, which was now German soil.

Parenthetically, it was Johst who penned the famous line, often credited to Joseph Goebbels, *"Wenn ich Kultur höre . . . entsichere ich meinen Browning!"* ("Whenever I hear of culture . . . I release the safety catch of my Browning!"). It appeared in Johst's 1933 play *Schlageter*, about Albert Leo Schlageter, who became a Nazi martyr when he was executed for sabotage in the French-occupied Rhineland.

Back in Berlin, at the real Prinz-Albrechtstrasse, Heinrich Himmler's power was absolute. He was the lord of the castle at the only castle that really mattered within wartime Germany. He was the head of the *Reichssicherheitshauptamt* (RSHA, or Reich Main Security Office or Reich Security Main Office). The

RSHA was the umbrella organization for both the Gestapo and the Kriminal-polizei (or Kripo), the criminal-investigation police, as well as the much feared Sicherheitsdienst (SD), which was integrated with the Sicherheitspolizei (or Sipo), the security police, in 1939.

After January 1944, even the Abwehr, the German military-intelligence apparatus, was taken out of Wehrmacht control and brought under the SS as a component of the RSHA. Through the Abwehr, Himmler had control of a vast network of human intel operatives outside the Reich and German-occupied territories. Under its former director, Admiral Wilhelm Canaris, the Abwehr had even run agents within the United States, although with minimal success.

Himmler's full title as Third Reich police chief was *Chef der Deutschen Polizei im Reichsministerium des Innern* (Chief of German Police in the Interior Ministry), meaning that in addition to the SS and the Gestapo, he also headed the regular police, the Ordnungspolizei (or Orpo). Though they were part of Wilhelm Frick's Interior Ministry, they had long since answered only to Himmler's chain of command.

Though police professionals grumbled about it when they knew that no one was listening, they were well aware that Himmler's postwar plan was to consolidate all of the RSHA and Orpo personnel and functions into the SS. Just as the police forces of the individual lander had been consolidated and then finally incorporated into the single national Ordnungspolizei in 1936, Himmler imagined the SS being the super police force for the entire Third Reich and beyond.

The Orpo were also nicknamed the *Grüne Polizei* because of their green uniforms. It was to the Orpo that Himmler's old rival from the early 1930s, Kurt Daluege, had been exiled. While Himmler was the unrivalled master of the Black Knights of the SS, Daluege was his subordinate, an assistant police chief of the regular cops in their green jackets. Within the Orpo, Himmler, through Daluege, controlled every facet of the day-to-day lives of the German people. There was the *Schutzpolizei,* the regular municipal police, which included the *Schutzpolizei des Reiches,* regular cops on the beat in major cities, as well as the *Schutzpolizei der Gemeinden* in small towns and the *Gendarmerie* in rural areas and along the borders. There were also the riot squads, the *Kasernierte Polizei.* The Orpo's

Verkehrspolizei were the equivalent of the highway patrol, and the *Wasserschutzpolizei,* or water police, were like a highway patrol on rivers and in harbors. The *Bahnschutzpolizei* worked the passenger trains of the national railroad, the *Reichsbahn,* and the *Postschutz* guarded the mail and the phone lines. Meanwhile, the *Funkschutz* guarded radio stations and attempted to jam Allied radio stations. (It was illegal for German citizens to listen to Allied broadcasts, but that didn't stop them.) Factory guards and night watchmen were given uniforms and called *Werkschutzpolizei,* but they remained civilians with Orpo bosses.

As individual police departments were absorbed into the Orpo, so too were fire departments. They became the *Feuerschutzpolizei,* a national "fire police" who "policed" fires, not people. When the Allied bombing campaigns against major German cities ramped up in 1943 and 1944 to a near daily regularity, the Orpo's Feuerschutzpolizei and its *Luftschutzpolizei,* or air-raid wardens, had plenty to do.

While the Orpo had Daluege, the components of Third Reich state security within the ever-expanding power of the RSHA were the bailiwick of SS Obergruppenführer und General der Polizei Reinhard Heydrich, Himmler's evil understudy.

Himmler and Heydrich were an odd couple. Both were manic in their attention to detail, and they could not have been more alike in their ruthless visions of an omnipotent SS and of a Europe devoid of Jewry. At that point, however,

These two men, Adolf Hitler and Heinrich Himmler, seen shaking hands circa 1943, became the two most hated and most feared men in Europe. Because of his direct and iron-fisted control of both the SS and the Gestapo, Himmler was perhaps the most dangerous to the lives of most average individual Europeans—especially those who were candidates for his hellish interment camps.

U.S. National Archives

their similarities diverged. Though both had been born Catholic, Heydrich's only religion was now the Führerprinzip of the Third Reich, while Himmler dabbled incessantly in mystic creeds, scampering through the Irminist pagan grottos of the Externsteine, dreaming of the conquests of the Ahnenerbe, or pouring over ancient runic manuscripts—all of which Heydrich considered to be a waste of time. Himmler and Heydrich disliked and distrusted one another, although their professional relationship was highly symbiotic. Each needed the other.

Himmler was shrewd and cunning. He was the magus.

Heydrich was cruel and arrogant. He was the enforcer.

Himmler was the brain behind the pince nez. He was the thinker.

Heydrich was the former fencing champ who earned an Iron Cross while flying missions with the Luftwaffe. He even flew a strike mission on the first day of Operation Barbarossa, during which he was injured. He was the athlete, the man of action.

Heydrich was the *second* most feared man in the Third Reich. He knew the secrets of every man in the German government, every authority figure in the Third Reich. Whatever humiliating document or evidence he didn't have, he could easily forge. He had the tape recordings of embarrassing secrets and confidential admissions whispered by the elite at Salon Kitty.

However, *somehow* word reached Adolf Hitler's ears that Reinhard Heydrich, the Aryan's Aryan, was tainted with Jewish blood. Could this accusation have come from the whisper of the "born criminal" who had once spied on fellow students for his father, the malevolent schoolmaster? Though there was never any evidence that Heydrich actually had a Jewish ancestor, Hitler and Himmler kept it over Heydrich's head. They helped to bury this malicious rumor, but they always remembered where it was buried. Heydrich himself was devastated by the accusation. He would reportedly stare into the mirror and sob at the sight of what he feared might be construed as "Jewish" facial features. His wife, Lina von Osten Heydrich, quoted by Heinz Höhne in his *The Order of the Death's Head: The Story of Hitler's SS,* said that the king of the SD would scream at his reflection, "Just look at his face, his nose—typically Jewish. A real Jewish lout!"

Dr. Paul Joseph Goebbels (1897–1945), the Reich propaganda minister, accepts a bouquet at a Kulturtagens (cultural meeting) in March 1941. His silly expression belies the sinister inner workings of a master manipulator. While Himmler crafted the mythic image of the heroic German people, Goebbels crafted the mythic image—and the personality cult—of the Führer. *U.S. National Archives*

If there was ever any doubt during the Third Reich as to which facial features might constitute "typically Jewish" characteristics, one did not have to look far. Countless illustrated posters and pamphlets—many of which still crop up in memorabilia shops—were published under the auspices of the men at Prinz-Albrechtstrasse. These contained pictures that could best be described as caricatures of ugliness. The people depicted were labeled "Juden," "untermenschen," or less kind appellations. The idea was that these notices were a public service, so that people could recognize Jews or Slavs in their midst and turn them in to the appropriate authorities.

It has been theorized that the rumor made Heydrich even more savagely prone to untermensch persecution than he might otherwise have been. He was a man on a mission, a man with something to prove.

Hitler ranted about "the annihilation of the Jewish race in Europe!"

Himmler dutifully scribbled "Jewish Question—like partisans to be exterminated" in his notebook.

Heydrich called the meeting at Wannsee that began planning for industrial-strength gas chambers. It was as though by eradicating the Jews in

Reichsführer Heinrich Himmler gets some work done while on the road. While the Germans occupied vast tracts of the Soviet Union from 1941 to 1943, Himmler traveled far and wide by air and rail, inspecting this great empire that he intended to become a Völkisch utopia ruled by the SS.

U.S. National Archives

Europe, he could eradicate the Jew within himself.

Since September 1941, Heydrich had been dividing his time between his RSHA desk in Berlin and his office at the castle in Prague where he was serving as the Reichsprotektor of Bohemia and Moravia. Having brutally crushed dissent in the former Czech states, Heydrich had backed off on the violence and began "protecting" his "subjects" with a light touch. This fragment of the former Czechoslovakia was an important industrial center, and Heydrich's mandate from Hitler when he was given the job was to increase production. This he succeeded in doing by first showing the Czechs how harsh he could be and then by showing how benevolent he could be. He increased rations and wages as industrial output increased. He had brought peace to a troubled corner of Hitler's empire by wielding first a stick and then a bunch of carrots.

Meanwhile, members of the Czech government in exile, sitting in London and waiting one day to return, were troubled. They had been prepared for more upon more Nazi sticks—but not Nazi carrots. It was decided that Reinhard Heydrich must go.

Britain's Special Operations Executive (SOE) was one of many forerunners to modern covert special-operations organizations that had its roots in World War II. (The American Office of Strategic Services [OSS] was the operational predecessor to the postwar Central Intelligence Agency [CIA]. The U.S. Army's Rangers were the predecessors of modern U.S. Special Forces, just as the U.S.

Navy's Underwater Demolition Teams [UDT] preceded today's Sea-Air-Land [SEAL] forces.) The SOE was formed in 1940 to train for and facilitate covert actions behind enemy lines. During World War II, it was active throughout occupied Europe, either sending in its own personnel or training indigenous nationals to carry out actions inside their own countries. The latter was the case with regard to a covert mission designed to remove Reinhard Heydrich.

To make a long story short, the SOE trained two members of the Czech army in exile to be assassins and had them infiltrate back into occupied Bohemia. After several planned attacks that they were not able to effect, Jan Kubiš and Josef Gabčík struck on the morning of May 27, 1942. Intercepting Heydrich's convertible as it slowed to make a hairpin turn on a suburban Prague street, Gabčík attempted to open fire with his Sten submachine gun, but the weapon jammed. As Heydrich stood up to return fire, Kubiš tossed a grenade. Heydrich appeared to be uninjured as he continued firing at the two men with his pistol. However, his body had been pierced by shrapnel.

The operation to remove the shrapnel seemed to go well, and Himmler sent Dr. Karl Gebhardt, his own personal doctor, to look after Heydrich's convalescence. The Reichsführer SS even came to Heydrich's bedside himself. Just as it seemed that the patient was about to recover, he went into shock. He died on June 4, ironically from infection, although the conspiracy theory that Himmler had him killed has lived on.

Adolf Hitler's brutality toward the Czechs in response to the assassination is legendary. After a quick, incomplete investigation, he fixated on the town of Lidice, a short distance from Prague, though neither of the assassins had a connection to it. He ordered that the town should be destroyed. It was leveled, and every male citizen over the age of sixteen was killed. Himmler, meanwhile, ordered more than 12,000 people arrested in retaliation. They were in turn jailed or executed. Cornered in a Prague church, the actual assassins committed suicide to avoid what they knew would be meted out at the hands of the SS.

Himmler's prewar nemesis for control of the SS, Kurt Daluege, was named to succeed Heydrich as Reichsprotektor of Bohemia and Moravia. He served only until May 1943, when he suffered a heart attack. Himmler himself wryly told his SS officers a few months later, "Our old friend Daluege has such serious heart disease that he must go through cures and probably will be gone from active service for a year and a half or two years. We have hope that Daluege is again restored to health, and then take his place at the table." But Daluege never returned to duty.

Meanwhile, Ernst Kaltenbrunner was brought in to succeed Heydrich as head of the RSHA. An Austrian lawyer, he was a longtime SS member and a member of the Reichstag after Austria was absorbed into the Third Reich in 1938. Walther Schellenberg became head of the SD.

Kaltenbrunner never wielded power on anywhere the same scale as Heydrich. Heinz Höhne in *The Order of the Death's Head: The Story of Hitler's SS* writes that Kaltenbrunner was "a second-rater selected by Himmler to head the Prinz Albrechtstrasse solely in order to ensure that there should not be another Heydrich. . . . When he was appointed in January 1943 after Heydrich's death, hardly anyone knew him; he had been in charge of SS Oberabschnitt Danube and gossip had it that he owed his career to the fact that by 1938 the semi-Fascist Austrian police had eliminated all his predecessors. In addition Himmler ensured that Kaltenbrunner did not possess the power of his predecessor, Heydrich."

Höhne adds that "when Kaltenbrunner took over the RSHA he found that his Heads of Division had more authority than their new master."

Kaltenbrunner often complained to his old classmate, SS Sturmbannführer Otto Skorzeny, that he was bypassed by the SS division heads, who felt autonomous in the absence of Heydrich. Kaltenbrunner told Skorzeny that he was out of the loop and "learnt many things only when they were over."

No mention of special operations in the same chapter with the SS is complete without a nod to Skorzeny, who was Heinrich Himmler's own special-operations genius. Like Kaltenbrunner, he was born in Austria, but unlike Kaltenbrunner, who got the "dueling scars" on his face in an automobile accident, Skorzeny had actually been a champion fencer. In 1931, at age twenty-three, he joined the Deutsche Nationalsozialistische Arbeiterpartei (DNSAP), the Austrian Nazi party, but it was not until after the start of World War II that he joined the Waffen

SS, specifically the Leibstandarte Adolf Hitler. As an officer with the Waffen SS, he fought in the invasions of the Netherlands, France, Yugoslavia, and the Soviet Union. While recovering from injuries in 1943, he became a student of unconventional warfare, and in April of that year, he pitched his idea for an SS special-operations component to Ernst Kaltenbrunner and Walther Schellenberg. They like what they heard and put Skorzeny in command of a unit that would be known as SS *Jagdverbände* 502.

Heinrich Himmler and his daughter, Gudrun, whom he affectionately called "Puppi." Though she lived with her mother in Bavaria, Himmler would occasionally have her flown up to Berlin for well-orchestrated photo opportunities. "The Reichsführer is a family man," read the resulting photo captions.
U.S. National Archives

Skorzeny's commando group, which would eventually grow to five battalions, was involved in a number of daring operations, most of them at the personal direction of Adolf Hitler. The most spectacular was the successful rescue in July 1943 of Italian dictator Benito Mussolini, who had been overthrown and imprisoned when the Italian government surrendered to the Allies. The least publicized Skorzeny operation was a supersecret infiltration of Iran in 1943, which might have put him in a position to assassinate the Allied "Big Three"—Winston Churchill, Franklin Roosevelt, and Joseph Stalin—at the Tehran Conference. Only an intelligence failure prevented Skorzeny from attempting this brazen coup.

The mission with the biggest stakes came in October 1944, when Skorzeny's relatively small team, supported by a few tanks, overthrew the government of Hungary, a German Axis partner that was on the verge of surrendering to the Soviets. Operation Panzerfaust, as it was called, removed Admiral Miklós Horthy, the regent of Hungary. Four years earlier, he had begged to join the Axis, but now Soviet forces were on his doorstep, and he wanted out. Skorzeny kidnapped Horthy's son, forced the admiral to resign as regent, and installed Ferenc Szálasi of the fascist Arrow Cross Party to run the country as Hitler's puppet. It was the last great international coup staged by the Third Reich.

The most controversial thing that Skorzeny did was in the Battle of the Bulge in December 1944, when his men infiltrated American lines while wearing American uniforms—itself a violation of the Hague Convention of 1907—and some of his men may have been involved in the infamous Malmedy Massacre, gunning down American prisoners.

Sturmbannführer Otto Skorzeny was an SS warrior that matched the type of man whom Heinrich Himmler craved. He was audacious and fearless, he thought outside the box, and he operated with ruthless efficiency. As he demonstrated in Budapest, he was a man who could get done things, with a small team, that most officers would consider impossible. He was, however, much more at home in a fight or on a mission impossible than he was attending a seance at Wewelsburg.

In the Paderborn hills, the SS Schule Haus Wewelsburg, Himmler's Black Camelot, continued to serve as he had intended, as a pagan seminary for the study of Germanic mysticism and as an SS ritual clubhouse. If Number 8 Prinz Albrechtstrasse in Berlin was the most feared address in Europe, Schloss Wewelsburg was one of the strangest. Wewelsburg continued to be one of the most secret of the important sites in Himmler's pagan fantasy world. Taking photographs inside the walls was forbidden, but Himmler's favorite photographer, Friedrich Franz Bauer of Munich, took some of the exterior, including one that shows the Reichsführer appearing to be handing out summer-solstice gifts to children with the castle in the background. Summer solstice and other rituals continued to be held at Schloss Wewelsburg, even as World War II raged. Indeed, a conference of all senior SS leadership was scheduled there each year. Because of the cloak of secrecy, documentation of these mysterious ceremonies is scarce, except for some paperwork left over from a meeting held here in June 1941.

Through the late 1930s and the early years of World War II, prehistoric and medieval artifacts collected by the Ahnenerbe expeditions were housed

An August 1942 inter-SS memo to Rudolf Brandt, chief of Heinrich Himmler's personal staff, from Wolfram Sievers. Note that the Ahenenerbe business manager typed it on the letterhead of the Burghauptmann (commandant) of Wewelsburg, the SS Camelot. Note also that the SS runic logo was one key of the typewriter. *Author's collection*

and displayed at Wewelsburg, as was Heinrich Himmler's personal collection of weaponry.

While Siegfried Taubert officially remained as commandant, or Burghauptmann, at Wewelsburg, as World War II dragged on, he was spending most of his time at Prinz-Albrechtstrasse, attending to other tasks. It is interesting to find in Heinrich Himmler's own files memoranda written in 1942 on "Der Burghauptmann von Wewelsburg" letterhead and signed by SS Gruppenführer Wolfram Sievers, the business manager of the Ahenenerbe. Indeed, it is probably appropriate that the pseudoscientists of the SS "mystic side" were running the SS clubhouse.

Meanwhile, work continued on the renovation project at the Wewelsburg castle under the direction of the bombastic architect Hermann Bartels. Himmler still imagined this activity as only just the first step in the immense undertaking that would involve construction of his vast Zentrum der Neuen Welt (Center of the New World) after the war. However, in 1938, the Reichsarbeitsdienst (RAD) crews were taken off the job, moved to what were considered more important tasks, specifically construction of the Siegfried Line, or West Wall, the fortifications on Germany's western border. Undaunted, Himmler turned to his slaves. If there was one thing that Himmler had in growing abundance, it was very inexpensive labor. Beginning in 1939, he began importing inmates from the Sachsenhausen concentration camp to continue the work at Wewelsburg.

In June 1940, a small concentration camp was completed in the Niederhagen Forest, a short distance from Wewelsburg. In the beginning, the camp housed fewer than 500 persons, mainly Jehovah's Witnesses previously imprisoned at Sachsenhausen. It must have been particularly bizarre for workers from one small religious minority to be helping to build a shrine for another religious minority, the pagans of the SS. Over the next four years, the small Niederhagen concentration camp grew to a population of around 1,200 with the addition of Soviet prisoners of war and Polish civilians. Through the years, close to 4,000 people passed through the camp.

Work on the castle came to a halt in January 1943, when construction projects across the Reich not directly related to the war effort were officially put on hold—until final victory. The Niederhagen camp was closed, and its prisoners transferred to other facilities—for the Final Solution. Thereafter, the SS leaders who gathered at their Schule Haus Wewelsburg did so without the sounds of hammering in the background.

By this time, Karl Maria Wiligut had ceased to be seen around Wewelsburg and at Himmler's elbow as he moved about the halls of Prinz-Albrechtstrasse. The old mystic, who had been promoted to SS Brigadeführer and assigned to Himmler's personal staff, had faded away as World War II had begun. The tide had begun to turn for Wiligut as early as 1937, when Himmler—who, through Heydrich, heard everything—heard something embarrassing. The Reichsführer SS had learned a secret about the old master of secrets whose pseudonym, Weisthor, can be translated as "Thor knows." He learned about Wiligut's wife beating and about his three years in the rubber room back in the 1920s.

In November 1938, Obergruppenführer Karl Wolff, the chief of Himmler's personal staff, under whom Wiligut was assigned at Prinz-Albrechtstrasse, was sent to the Austrian Tyrol to personally check out the allegations. He spoke to Wiligut's estranged wife, Malwine, and heard the stories of the god-king gone crazy. Presumably, he also made inquiries at the hospital where Wiligut had been held.

On August 28, 1939, as Himmler was preparing for the opening salvos of World War II, which would be fired just four days later, he ordered Wolff to take care of some old business. It was announced that effective on that date, the "request for retirement" submitted by seventy-two-year-old Brigadeführer Karl Maria Wiligut was approved. The reasons given were age and poor health. If he hadn't been sick before his retirement, the former center of Himmler's attention certainly was increasingly ill after he sank into the oblivion of retirement. In fact, his retirement was like the hospital years of 1924 to 1927 all over again. Wiligut was exiled from Prinz-Albrechtstrasse and essentially put under house arrest. He had no choice. He had run out of options, there was nowhere else to go other than the Irminsul inside his own head.

Elsa Baltrusch, from the Reichsführer SS's personal staff, was detailed by Himmler and Wolff to function as Wiligut's chaperon and jailer. She took him into exile in the remote village of Aufkirchen, located in the South Tyrol, not far from where he had lived before his earlier hospitalization. In May 1940, however, as his health continued its decline, Baltrusch moved her charge to Goslar in Lower Saxony, near where Wiligut had long believed there had once been an Irminen holy city.

Meanwhile, Heinrich Himmler's own personal life was growing complicated. His only daughter, whom her father had lovingly nicknamed "Puppi," turned thirteen on August 8, 1942, as the Wehrmacht closed in for the milestone fight at Stalingrad and as her father roamed his eastern dominions, watching the Völksdeutsche settlers flow in to replace the untermensch Slavs. Occasionally, she would join her father on his inspection tours, even tours of his concentration camps. As time would tell, she believed in him and his mission to rid the world of the undesirables and to manufacture a heroic place for Germans to live as Wotan had wanted. Most of the time, however, Puppi bided her time with her mother, in peaceful isolation.

Marga Himmler still remained in her chateau overlooking the Tegernsee. As he had done with Wiligut, Himmler had exiled her to the shadows. Though they apparently never seriously took steps toward a divorce, they both understood that their marriage existed in name only. As the story goes, Himmler had good reason to keep his wife at arm's length. Described as shrewish and bitter, Marga had a tendency to be domineering toward the little man seven years her junior, whom she still thought of as a clerk, even after he became the Third Reich's top cop.

According to Heinz Höhne in his *The Order of the Death's Head: The Story of Hitler's SS,* Lina von Osten Heydrich once described Margarete by saying, "Size 50 knickers. . . . That's all there was to her . . . that narrow-minded, humorless blonde female, always worrying about protocol; she ruled her husband and could twist him round her little finger—at least until 1936."

After 1936, Himmler had kept this woman, whom Lina Heydrich cynically called "Madame Reichsführer," out of Berlin. Himmler, who had once wanted to be a chicken farmer, now rubbed shoulders with the beautiful people of the Berlin social scene. Though most of his evenings were spent beneath a desk lamp at Prinz-Albrechtstrasse, no party in Berlin was given without his name on the guest list. The unglamorous Marga would not have fit in, even if given the opportunity.

Like so many lonely politicians and captains of industry with wives whom they perceive as being as shrewish and bitter, Heinrich Himmler found physical love in the only place he could—at his office. Hedwig Potthast was twenty-five when she went to work as a secretary at Prinz-Albrechtstrasse in 1937. She is described as having been an attractive young woman from Cologne, the daughter of a businessman. She learned her secretarial skills at the Industrial College in Mannheim before moving to Berlin to get a job in the mushrooming bureaucracy of the Third Reich. She was hired by the SS and wound up on the personal staff of the Reichsführer SS. Himmler's affair with Potthast began in 1940, during the year of German ascendancy, when the Wehrmacht was blitzkrieging from success to success and as it looked as though all Himmler's dreams would come true. In Potthast, apparently, many of his dreams did come true.

Heinz Höhne writes that she had "a humanizing and relaxing influence on the stiff prim Himmler." Reportedly, she convinced him to trade in his pince-nez for less pretentious glasses. As often occurs between a married man and his mistress, there was talk of Himmler getting a divorce from Marga, but he never went through with it. Nevertheless, as often occurs between a married man and his mistress, there would be complications. By the end of 1941, as Himmler was admiring his new territories in the East, Potthas let him know that she was pregnant.

"For your parents sake I would wish to see you married as soon as possible," Potthast's war-widow sister-in-law, Hilde, wrote in a letter obtained by Heinz Höhne. She continued:

> I fear, Hedwig, that there can never be a reconciliation with [your] parents. They would forgive everything at any time if you would give him up or if he would make himself a free man for your sake. What they cannot swallow is that you should go on living with him. . . . He is after all married and your parents regard your relationship as dishonest towards his wife and disrespectful towards you. Your mother asked me whether his wife knew about it and unfortunately I had to tell her that as far as I knew this was not yet the case. She regarded this as proof of cold feet. Your parents are quite terribly distressed about it all.

As gentlemen did in those days, Himmler needed to build a home for his pregnant mistress, whom, like his estranged wife, couldn't actually *live* with him. Unfortunately for the Reichsführer SS, however, he found himself a bit short. He found himself having to borrow 80,000 reichsmarks from the NSDAP coffers, where the gatekeeper was Martin Bormann, Adolf Hitler's personal assistant and Himmler's biggest rival for access to the Führer. Bormann generously facilitated the loan, and a home that Himmler bought for Hedwig was an Alpine lodge-looking house called Haus Schneewinkellehen in the Obersalzburg in Bavaria. It was close to Schönau and to snowy Berchtesgaden, where Adolf Hitler's famous Berghof retreat was. The building still exists, and a wing has been added with a three-car garage. According to Geoff Walden, who has been there, Haus Schneewinkellehen had belonged to the erotic psychologist Sigmund Freud in the nineteenth century.

Perhaps the reason that Borman steered Himmler to this home was that he had a place nearby. As Potthast took up residence in the Obersalzburg, she and Bormann's wife, Gerda, became friends.

Potthast and Himmler had their first child, Helge Himmler, early in 1942, and Helge's sister, Nanette Dorothea Himmler, was born in 1944. Neither would ever see much of their father.

However, as Himmler roamed his Völkisch playground in the East, he thought often of Potthast and his children. On August 9, 1942, when he was at Hegewald, he scrounged a few small gifts, picked up his black fountain pen, and dashed off a quick missive.

"My dear little bunny!" Himmler wrote. "I'm about to drive over [to a place with a field telephone] and will call you and hear your dear voice. Quickly just a few lines regarding the parcel, they are all without value but chosen with love; perhaps you can use them! An illustrated magazine is also enclosed and I'll be with you in spirit when you look at it. Say hello to our sweet one. . . . The barometer is for you. Thank you for your dear letter! Write again soon! I love you forever." He signed the note with his typical runic "HH."

Potthast kept the letter close to her heart and still had it when she was grabbed by the U.S. Army in the summer of 1945. It recently showed up at auction.

CHAPTER 17

Burdens Borne by Black Knighthood

T HE WARMTH OF HIMMLER'S sweet note to his mistress, Hedwig Potthast, sharply contrasts the words of most of the memoranda that originated from his desk at Number 8 Prinz-Albrechtstrasse and his words to his Black Knights.

His words to the SS, both in written memoranda or telegrams and in chilling sound recordings, show a man who was single-minded about the burden borne by the SS to defeat the enemies, both military and ethnic, of the Aryan. This burden, which he regarded as a sacred burden, was to destroy Bolshevism, carry out the Final Solution, and forge the type of German and European purity that would fulfill the Ariosophist dreams of Guido von List and Jörg Lanz von Liebenfels.

While much of the SS paper trail was destroyed—both purposely and through the fires of war—much still remains. Having been captured by Allied forces at the end of World War II, it is now in the public domain. In the United States National Archives at College Park, Maryland, this author poured through overwhelming numbers of records from the Third Reich. At the Hoover Institution Archives, I leafed though documents from the personal staff of the Reichsführer SS and saw documents bearing the signature of Reinhard Heydrich and that runic "HH" mark with which Heinrich Himmler signed his correspondence.

Many of Himmler's speeches made it to magnetic tape. Germany was, after all, a world leader in recording technology. In addition to the paper trail, there is Himmler's audio trail, consisting of more than one hundred speeches, recorded either on acetate discs or "red oxide" magnetic tape. While nothing he said in the secret ceremonies at Wewelsburg is believed to have been recorded, there is no shortage of other recordings of his shrill voice.

Historians often cite the speech that he delivered on October 4, 1943, at Posen, in eastern Germany, as his definitive policy statement on the "sacred" burden off the SS. The tone was candid, direct, and visionary. The speech was important for its lack of ambiguity and the sorts of metaphors that usually clouded Himmler's references in his orations.

Most historians regard the venue as incidental. However, quite to the contrary, we can see in Posen a significant locale, highly charged with meaning. It possesses a schizophrenic identity; Poles see the city they call Poznan as important to their national identity, while for Germans, the same city, known in German as Posen, is emblematic of traditional Prussian and German hegemony across eastern Europe.

The first Polish king, Boleslaus the Brave, was crowned here in 1025 at the Basilica of St. Peter and St. Paul, the oldest Polish church of its size. As the location of this crowning, it is seen by Poles as the birthplace of the earliest Polish kingdom. Both Boleslaus and his father, Mieszko, are buried here. In 1848, after centuries with a Polish identity, the city and its surrounding region were absorbed into Prussia and the German Confederation as *Grenzmark*

Heinrich Himmler inspects one of his Black Knights. As he told them, "We will instill the laws of the SS Order in [our children]. . . . It must be natural that from [our SS] Order, from this racially superior upper strata of the Germanic people . . . to impose a Fürungsschict [guidance layer] over all of Europe. . . . [I]t is [our noble destiny]. . . . [T]he black uniform will be naturally very attractive in peacetime."
Author's collection

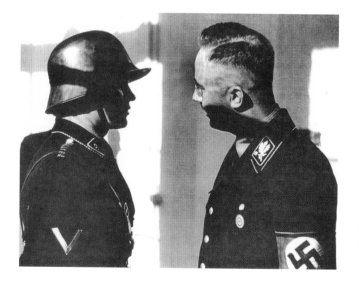

Posen-Westpreussen (Posen-West Prussia). Even after Poland was recreated as an independent state at the end of World War I, Posen remained German.

It was to this city that Himmler came in October 1943, World War II's turning point year. It was in 1943 that the great expansion of Adolf Hitler's empire sputtered and began to falter. It was not, as Britain's prime minister Winston Churchill cautioned at the Allied Casablanca Conference in January 1943, the beginning of the end, but it *was* the end of the beginning.

In North Africa, the German drive toward the Suez Canal had been halted. In the Soviet Union, at Stalingrad, German armies had suffered a defeat of immense proportions. However, Hitler's legions still occupied much of the Soviet territory that they had conquered in Operation Barbarossa. The Allies had landed troops in Italy, but German defenders still appeared to have turned most of the former Axis partner's territory into an impregnable fortress. The greater Germany of the Third Reich remained intact. The cross-channel invasion of German-occupied France had yet to materialize.

When Himmler ascended to the stage at Posen's old Rathaus (city hall), there was a sense that the Third Reich was at a portentous crossroads. His audience in the Rathaus on October 4 included nearly 100 SS officers, mainly from units operating in eastern Europe and the Soviet Union. They were the cream of the dark corps. His words that day were for them and them only. An audiotape was recorded, then transcribed and typed by SS Untersturmführer Werner Alfred Wenn. Both the tape and transcription were locked away in secret for safekeeping, but discovered by American forces after World War II. They are now in the U.S. National Archives.

"In the months which have flowed past since we together were in June 1942, many comrades have given their lives for Germany and for the Führer," Himmler began, asking them to rise for a moment "in the honor of all of our dead SS men and dead German soldiers, men and women."

With that, he "soberly" and "truthfully" began his candid overview of the way World War II was going for the Reich. With regard to the German underestimation of Soviet capabilities, he admitted, "We were mistaken in this evaluation of the situation absolutely."

The Reichsführer SS at the podium. In October 1943, Heinrich Himmler told his Black Knights, "I would like to inoculate the SS . . . [with] one of the holiest laws of the future: Our concern, our obligation, is our people and our blood; but we have to ensure and think to work and fight. . . . Everything else is soap lather, it is fraud on our own people, and is an obstacle to an early end to the war." *U.S. National Archives*

It was a tough challenge for Himmler to spin the losses that the Aryans of the Wehrmacht had taken at the hands of the subhuman Slavs. The only way was to talk of the unlimited "masses" that the Red Army threw into the battle from 1941 and into 1942. In speaking of that winter of decision when the Wehrmacht had been irrevocably turned back from the gates of Moscow, he blamed the Soviet commissars, whose "hardness and unyieldingness, whose fanatical, brutal will drove . . . the raw material of the Slavic and Mongolian masses [*Mongolischen menschenmassen*] to the front."

He goes on to explain that in 1942, "Russia would have been cut off from its sources of main oil, and hunger would have crippled the civilian population," if Germany's Hungarian and Romanian allies not allowed themselves to be beaten by the Red Army. He then complains that the Romanians retreated like the "valueless Italian army."

In his speech, Himmler was scathing in his assessment of Germany's former Axis partner. The Italians had surrendered to the Allies only a month earlier, forcing Hitler to send German armies into the country to face the Allies. It was Himmler's opinion that "the weakness of this people lie in its blood, in its race. . . . Italy was a weak confederate to begin with, [losing major campaigns from] Greece and Africa to Russia. There is no people, who did not lambaste the Italians . . . because as soldiers, they were cowardly men everywhere. . . . [T]he Italians failed everywhere."

To the delight of his audience, the Reichsführer went on to highlight the heroic role that had been played by Waffen SS units, especially the II SS Panzerkorps, during 1943. This unit had been formed as an umbrella corps for the 2nd Das Reich SS Panzer Division and the 9th Hohenstaufen SS Panzer Division. In early February 1943, the corps was under the command of

SS Gruppenführer Paul Hausser, the man Himmler had personally selected to head the SS Verfügungstruppe, the Waffen SS precursor, back in 1934. As Himmler pointed out, the II SS Panzerkorps had stopped the Soviet momentum that began with their Stalingrad victory and helped to stabilize the German front.

Himmler then proceeded to relish the success of the Waffen SS during 1943, recalling, "In the hard fights in this year, the Waffen SS is fused from the most diverse divisions, in the bitterest hours, from which it is formed: Leib-standarte, Verfügungstruppe, Totenkopfverbände, and then the Allgemeine SS. Now, our divisions Reich, Totenkopf, Kavallerie, and Wiking were there. In the past weeks, everyone [in the Wehrmacht took heart, knowing that] beside me is the Wiking Division, beside me is the Reich Division, beside me is the Totenkopf Division. Thank God, nothing can happen to us now. So it is within the Waffen SS."

No doubt thinking of his conversations with Karl Maria Wiligut as they motored around the Paderborn hills, Himmler turned to the romantic notion of titanic clashes between East and West. "With the exception of few high points, which Asia brings out again and again every few centuries . . . of an Attila, or, unfortunately for us Europeans, a Ghengis Khan, a Tamerlane, a Lenin, a Stalin . . . this mixture people of the Slavs developed a unterrasse [lesser race] [inbred] with drops of our blood, a prominent race."

"You know that what I'm about to say about Russians is absolutely true," Himmler snarled wryly. "It is true that the Volga boat operators sing wonderful, it is true that the Russian is today in the modern time a good improviser and a good technician. It is true that to a large extent that he holds his children dear. It is true that he can work very industriously. It is just as true that he is stinking lazy. It is just as true that he is an unrestrained beast, which can torture and tor-ment other humans."

He justified the inhumane treatment of Soviet prisoners, underscoring that an SS man's loyalty is to the black corps, "a basic principle that must be the absolute rule":

Heinrich Himmler (center, engrossed in conversation) enjoys a beer with a table of SS and Wehrmacht officers. Himmler later insisted that "criminal offenses, which occur under the influence of the consumption of alcohol, [should be] twice as highly punished," but he apparently saw no harm in having a few himself.

Author's collection

We must be honest, decent, loyal and comradely to members of our own blood and to nobody else. What happens to a Russian, to a Czech, does not interest me in the slightest. What other nations can offer in the way of good blood of our type, we will take, if necessary, by kidnapping their children and raising them here with us. Whether nations live in prosperity or starve to death interests me only so far as we need them as slaves for our culture; otherwise, it is of no interest to me. Whether 10,000 Russian females weaken and fall down while digging an antitank ditch [for German forces] interests me only insofar as the antitank ditch for Germany is finished.

Pausing for applause, he continued:

We Germans, who have, as alone in the world, a decent attitude to the animal [and we] will take a decent attitude also toward these "people animals," but it is a crime against our own blood to make and bring them the same ideals of concern, with which we approach our own sons and grandsons. If [a German] comes to me and says: "I cannot build the tank ditch with the children or the women, because it is inhumane, because they might die," then I must say: "You are a murderer of your own blood, because, if the tank ditch is not built, then German soldiers die, and those are sons of German mothers. That is *our* blood."

Himmler's view of the sacredness of the SS is perhaps best summarized in this entreaty: "I would like to inoculate the SS . . . [with] one of the holiest laws of the future: Our concern, our obligation, is our people and our blood; but we have to ensure and think to work and fight, for nothing else. We can be indifferent to everything else. My wish is that the SS, with this attitude sidesteps the problem of all foreign, non-Germanic peoples, above all the Russians. Everything else is soap lather, it is fraud on our own people, and is an obstacle to an early end to the war."

With this, Himmler gave the assembled Black Knights his take on what he expected from the opposition:

In my judgement, if the next large offensive is like past ones, Russia is at the end of its manpower potential. One can naturally draw in sixteen-year-olds, one can even anticipate [drafting] fifteen-year-olds. . . . If the fate of the nation demands it, better a fifteen-year-old dies than the nation dies. However, one cannot continue endlessly, because with thirteen-year-old and twelve-year-old boys, one can no longer fight a war to its conclusion.

In my judgement, the manpower potential is one of the weakest points of the Russians, although it was once their greatest strength. Secondly, I am convinced that we have not yet recognized the potential for an outrageous famine to prevail in Russia. Those at the front are still better nourished than are the people behind the front. Nevertheless, it is already very bad at the front in many cases. The Russians also have large transport difficulties that have not yet been overcome.

Having given his views on the imminent collapse of the Red Army and the Soviet Union, the Reichsführer SS turned to their Allies, the two nations that he considered the Soviet Union's softer partners.

In four years of war, England has not yet had very many bloody losses. In England, fear constantly prevails, and when our submarine war begins in full strength again, as I am convinced it will, British equilibrium [will be at risk]. All military operations which England and America want, stand and fall with the [materiel] tonnage. The landing operations in Italy with Salerno [a month earlier in September] certainly cost one half million tons. I doubt very strongly whether England is strong enough itself to carry out many such landing operations. . . . I believe, that the war for England—and this is valid still more for America—really goes to the blood of its sons. The war will become still more unpopular in England and America than it already is.

America leads, more than England, a two-front war, the Pacific war against Japan, our stronger and more martial confederate, and the war in Europe and in the Atlantic. I do not believe that the best conditions prevail in America. America has always had a very large number of Jews and a brutal plutocracy. It is probably inconceivable, how hard pressed the American are. . . . Large political difficulties are coming. England and America are not united. England says to America, "You must help me more in Europe." America wants England to help it with the defeat of Japan. England tries to use the Americans [in the war against] Germany. England is in an ever more difficult situation. Mr. Churchill cannot spare his English soldiers.

Thinking of England, Himmler complained of Germany having not yet ful-filled its destiny to rule all of the Völksdeutsche of the world. He compared the Reich to the British Empire, saying, "We in the old Reich—I mean now small Germany—who are only a nation for 70 years; we did not yet have the oppor-tunity to control [Europe] with a German minority. . . . To control hundreds of millions of humans with a minority as England has for 300 years. . . . If we could wake up in 100 years, we would see that our grandchildren and great-grandchildren could do it better. . . . I believe that we [the SS], are protected against errors in accordance with our . . . self-assured racial attitude."

Himmler predicted then that if a day came when Russia was exhausted or "ruled out," and if the suffering of England or America became too much for them, then the Third Reich would prevail as a *Weltreich*, a world realm. He added that since 1938, "the large Germanic Reich remains with us. . . . [T]he way is free to the east. . . . [T]hat Germany is a Weltreich is justified. That will be the reason for this war, may take it now five, perhaps six, perhaps even seven years."

The idea of the immense struggle between East and West, which Himmler and Wiligut had discussed in an abstract way on their prewar rambles through the Teutoburgerwald, was now looming large in Himmler's conception of those coming five to seven years. He was excited by the notion of his SS knights being such an integral part of this struggle. They and their successors were ready, he hoped, to lay down their lives for this great apocalyptic battle—whenever it materialized. The SS men were indoctrinated to lay down their lives for the cause of Führer and Reichsführer, but in remarks that he made later in the speech, Himmler seemed as though he just wanted to make sure.

"Everyone will know that if he goes into the SS, then there exists the possibility that he will be shot dead," the Reichsführer said, in unambiguously graphic terms. He then ridiculed civilians and others who were not up to the standards of elite SS discipline, saying:

> It is confirmed by a covenant that gambols . . . not in Berlin or celebrating the Munich carnival, but rather placed into an ice-cold winter against the eastern border. . . . [W]e will have a healthy selection [of recruits] for all the future. We will create thereby the conditions for the fact that the entire Germanic people, and that the entire of us, who rule and lead Europe can exist as Germanic people, leading in [future] generations its certain fate in fights erupting in Asia. We do not know when it will be. If, on the other side, the *menschenmassen* with 1 to 1.5 billion begin, then the Germanic people with, as I hope, 250 to 300 million, together with the other European

peoples in a total number from 600 to 700 million . . . will fight the fight of our lives . . . against Asia, beyond the Urals.

The alternative, he proposed, was unacceptable. "If the Germanic people cease to exist, it would be the end of beauty and culture, of the creative strength of this earth." To avoid such an alternative was the sacred duty of the SS to the German people: "For those, we are obligated to pass on the inheritance of our ancestors."

Though he spoke only briefly about the Final Solution at Posen, Himmler's words ring with more chilling candor that just about anything else he ever wrote or said:

> I also want to mention before you in all openness here, a very grave subject. Among us it is to be completely openly expressed, but nevertheless we will never talk about it in public. We barely hesitated on 30 June 1934 [the Night of the Long Knives] to render our obligation as we were ordered, and put our comrades against the wall and shoot them, and we have never spoken and never will speak of this. We all understood clearly that we would do it again, if it is ordered and if it is necessary.
>
> I mean now the Jew evacuation, the extermination of the Jewish people. It is one of the things, which one expresses easily. "The Jewish people are to be exterminated," says each party comrade, "Perfectly clear it is within our program, elimination of the Jews, extermination."

At this point, as he had earlier, Himmler complained that so many Germans had mentioned that there were good people among the Jews.

"And then they all arrive, the good 80 million Germans, and everyone has his decent Jew. It is clear, the others are pigs, but this one is a very good Jew," Himmler said, mocking the Aryans who defended Jewish friends.

> From all who talk in such a way, none watched, none have seen it through [as you have]. Most of you know what it means if 100 corpses lie together,

if 500 lie there, or if 1,000 lie there. To have carried this out, and—apart from exceptions of human weakness—to have remained decent, has made us hard. This is a glorious page of our history that has never been written and which can never be written. Because we know how difficult things would be, if today in every city during the bomb attacks, amid the burdens of war and privations, if we still had Jews as clandestine saboteurs, agitators, and instigators. We would probably be at the same stage as in the years of 1916 and 1917, if the Jews still resided within the body of the German people.

The wealth, which [the Jews had], we have removed from them. I gave a strict instruction, which SS Obergruppenführer [Oswald] Pohl [who managed construction crews comprised of concentration-camp inmates] accomplished, that this wealth was disseminated completely into the Reich. We took nothing of it for ourselves. Those who ignore these orders are punished in accordance with my instructions as I gave at the beginning. He who takes for himself only one Mark of this [wealth] is a dead man. A number of SS men—there is not a great many—disobeyed my order, and for them a graceless death it is.

We had the moral right, we had the obligation to our people to kill the [Jews] who wanted to kill us. We do not have, however, the right to enrich ourselves with even one fur coat, with a clock, with a Mark, or with a cigarette, or with anything else. We do not want to become ill and die from a bacillus at the end, just because we exterminated a bacillus.

I will never see it happen, that even one small bit of rot develops or settles within us. Where it might try to take root, we will burn it out together. Altogether, however, we can say that we fulfilled this heaviest of tasks for the love of our people. And we have taken on no blemish within us, in our soul, or in our character.

With these words, Himmler absolved the SS men of blame in the murders that comprised the Final Solution—so long as nobody stole a fur coat. They were doing it, he assured them, for the good of the German people.

The Virtues of the SS Man
by Heinrich Himmler, October 1943

1. *Die Treue* (Loyalty)

We have had no case so far, in which a distinguished SS man in our ranks has become unfaithful. The one guideline is that if he should ever be unfaithful, even only in his thoughts about the Führer or the Reich, then you must ensure that this man [loses his] life. . . . Everything can be forgiven in this world, but [one quality] cannot be forgiven among us Teutons: that is the unfaithfulness. It would be inexcusable and is inexcusable.

2. *Der Gehorsam* (Obedience)

Military life demands that obedience be carried out in the morning, at noon, and in the evening. The small man also always, or mostly, obeys. If he does not obey, then he is locked up. More difficult is the question of the obedience with the higher dignitaries in state, the party, and the armed forces—also in the SS. I would like to express here clearly: The fact that the small man must obey is natural. It is still more natural that all [SS leadership be the] model of the unconditional obedience.

Instructions must be sacred. If the generals obey, then the armies obey automatically. This sacredness of the instruction is valid all the more, the more our territory becomes larger. An order that applies in our small Germany was not difficult. To push through instruction, [now that we have] garrisons at the Urals, is more difficult. Here, one will not always be able to control all instruction. Control may be with us, not and never—as in Russia—with the [Communist political] commissar. However, [you will be unable] to require obedience of your men, if you do not carry the same obedience for the authority over you, unconditionally and without restriction.

He then complimented his Black Knights and elucidated further burdens that must be borne, because of the special responsibilities of the SS men.

The attitude of our noble leaders and men was honorable in desperate situations at the front, where they exceeded in the dark hours, in the darkest hours . . . in grand heroic death. The attitude was good with our men in the fight, and in the rear areas. The attitude [toward the SS man] was also in the Fatherland. . . . The people see how the small man reacts to an emergency with fear in his heart. . . . How does he perceive how the SS man stands or the face he makes? Has he also a gloomy expression,

3. *Tapferkeit* (Bravery)

Of bravery, few of us need to be counseled, because our leaders and our men are courageous.

To express my thoughts to you, I would like to submit a counter example, an example of how it is with the Russians. I heard of the following event [from a captured Soviet officer]: A unit of the Red Army had been making an attack, which had been stopped by German lead. Thereupon the [Communist political] commissar of this unit ordered the officers to come to him for discussion. The officers had to [stand at attention] and announce themselves in the shelter with prescribed bearing. The commissar continued working calmly and let the officers stand still further. When one began to become jerky and agitated, the commissar looked up and asked: "You seem to be probably tired?"

Then the question came: "Does one of the gentlemen have something to say of the attack?" The answer of an officer came that the resistance of the Germans had been too strong and the attack was impossible [at this point in the line].

The commissar pulled the pistol, shot the officer down and then asked: "Has one of you gentlemen something to say about the attack?"

See, this is an example [of something] which we do not want to have, which we do not need. The commissar, who instructs us to attack, must be our own, possessing our own bravery, our own loyalty, our own obedience. In our ranks we live by our Germanic laws, from which [we say] honor is obligation enough.

Opposite us are the strange peoples who want to bring Asian laws into application. We want never to be mixed up with that. If we have [people of] our blood, a Norwegian or Dutchman, before us, then we can win his heart after ours (i.e., by his and our total Germanic laws). If we have a Russian or a Slav before us, then we want to use the opposite with him—never our holy laws, but the established Russian commissar laws.

leaving his lower jaw to hang? Or how does the SS battalion march to the front? Or how is the post of the Gendarmerie in the Balkans or in Russia? Or how is the SS man with the air raid? Does he remain there, or does he run away?

Is it that which prevents the panic and which encourages the people? Or in reverse, is there an SS leader or an SS man who takes for himself special rights, who aspires to a better life for his wife, over the requirements of others . . . and each Sunday freely takes a drive with his car when [driving of personal vehicles is forbidden], or who says distorted things in the bomb shelter?

A part of bravery is also faith, and here, my gruppenführer, we want to be exceeded by nobody in the world. Faith wins the battles, and faith creates the victories. Men who are pessimistic, or who lose faith, we do not want to have in our ranks.

4. *Die Wahrhaftigkeit* (Truthfulness)

I come now to a fourth virtue, truthfulness, which is very rare in Germany. One of the largest evils, which spread in wars, is the Unwahrhaftigkeit [lack of truthfulness] within messages, reports, and data, which [are given by subordinates] in civilian life, in the state, in the party, and in the armed forces to superior ranks. The message, the report, is the basis for each decision.

It is true that one can in wars, as in many segments, accept that 95 of 100 messages [are] a lie or half truth. That begins with the [Wehrmacht personnel] strength report. I take an everyday example here. . . . [One might receive a report that says,] "I have only 200 men, sadly, only 200 men." [To which one might reply] smartly, "Times your ration strength indicates the regiment concerned has 1,300 men." I must say, "Strange conditions. Strangely, with your 200 men in combat, the other 1,100 men are thus the tail of a small head."

With the topic of truthfulness, I come now to another chapter. It must be true in the war and in peacetime . . . that we no longer bind SS men to written contracts, but that with us, like that which was customary years ago, a given word and a handshake meant the same as a contract. The handshake of an SS man—if it must be—is security for one million or more. It must become that the handshake or the given word of an SS man is probably safer than another's mortgage in the largest bank. So it must be!

On the whole, our attitude was good. Some are still to be improved in our ranks. This is with the sense of the appeal of the commanders and the gruppenfuher. I would like to overwrite this chapter with the heading, "wir selbst" ["we ourselves"]. I'd like to tell you today, in the moment in which the war ends, only then will we truly begin to forge our Order. Into this Order, which we developed ten long years before the war, we instilled the first important principles. . . . In twenty work-rich years after the end of war . . . in thirty, thirty-five, forty years, in a generation still ahead, this Order will march young and strong, in a revolutionary manner, and effectively into the future. In order to fulfill the task, the German people submit to the Oberschicht [higher class], which ties and holds the Germanic people together and

If we conclude contracts, then we must hold to them. If I secure a contract with an agent, even with a bad subject, then I hold the contract. I unconditionally enter this view. . . . If we give our word, it must be held. If the Reichsführer SS assures someone of his protection—as in the Balkans [where the Germans intervened in 1941 to aid Mussolini's misadventures], the case can be often made—so this promise must be upheld. We must make such a call, which gets contractual loyalty in the whole world . . . . We in the SS, and thereby Germany have acquired the highest values (i.e., faith by confidence) . . . . If we assure our protection . . . then it must be impossible that a member of the SS or the police . . . breaks his given word. This word must be holy.

5. *Die Ehrlichkeit* (Honesty)

I come to a fifth point: Sacredness of the property, honesty, probity. . . . If I may say—in the closed hall now, intended only for this small circle—we Germans have become a very corrupt people . . . [although] gradually the people are becoming honest due to [drastic] measures and education. My gentlemen, we must realize that we must always begin first with ourselves [the SS, so that] we would not bring this plague of corruption into our ranks.

Beyond this, however, ambiguity develops over these questions from the state of emergency in which we have lived since the years 1936 and 1937. Since that time we [have had shortages of] the commodities that the human heart demands . . . whether it is now silk, socks, chocolate, or coffee. . . . One can buy that, or perhaps one can not. Can one buy it in France, in Belgium or at an excess price otherwise?

Until we have normal conditions in Germany after the war, these things [will be measured by] sharpest yardstick available to the SS. In the future, if we then get through twenty years of peace, we will achieve a perfect view in all these questions.

thus Europe together. In addition this Oberschicht [who Himmler understood to be the SS itself] must be so strong and vital that each generation can unconditionally sacrifice two and three sons on the battleground from each family, and that the future of the blood line is nevertheless secured.

Part of the burden of the SS, Himmler believed, was that Germany *needed* the Black Knights, as though they were something that Germany had been missing since the days of the Teutonic Knights.

This Germanic Reich needs the Order of the SS. It needs it at least for the next century. Then . . . for one thousand or two thousand years. . . . From

6. *Die Kameradschaft* (Comradeship)

The word "comradeship" is very often expressed. It is generally very favorable with us [in the SS], particularly among the front-line troops. Since I speak of comradeship, however, I would like to tell each of you what to avoid. Controversy is unfruitful. Differences of opinion are fruitful . . . . Controversy and quarrelling . . . are unfruitful and immobilize the worker. They sap strength that we must use for other things (i.e., for the fulfillment of our obligation).

7. *Die Verantwortungsfreudigkeit* (Readiness for Responsibility)

In this war, situations will come, where we must be ready to take on tremendous responsibilities. . . . It must be clear that the individual person takes responsibility not in anonymity, but . . . in the joyfulness of taking responsibility.

The main thing is, it [some decision] is reached. [It matters not] when determining that an objective is to be taken by the 995th Division or whether the 998th Division is responsible. The main thing is that the decision is made . . . so that we do not have to conquer [the objective] again. [The SS] has to be ready to take responsibilities, up to the ultimate one.

this, something new will develop, exactly the same, as from the time of the Teutonic Knights, from which Prussian army took over the torch.

I put everything to all of you, to the heart, my hauptamtchefs, my higher SS and polizeiführers, and the whole gruppenführer corps. The highest stage of this hierarchy is the Order of the SS. Always see the whole, always see the total Order, never see only your section, never see only your upper section, but always see the SS. Over it, see the Germanic Reich, over it our Führer, who created this Reich and who still creates.

Having likened Adolf Hitler to a mystical, godlike creator, Himmler grew more somber, telling his Black Knights that they still had an uphill climb. He went on to predict the course of the war on the Eastern Front as 1943 melded into 1944. The German armies, both black and field gray, were, he warned, looking into the darkness before the dawn.

8. *Der Fleiss* (Diligence)

Of diligence, I would like to speak yet another word. We all teach our men today in the war, and later in peacetime, dass Arbeit nicht schändet [that work that does not violate], that work [brings virtue].

To get through the war, to win it, we must make no errors. . . . At the end of the war we will not be impoverished, but Völkisch [German people], who create much, who work very hard, must see [prosperity]. I hope that then we are not so rich that we eat only meat until our teeth fail us, or that we commit similar foolishness.

9. Alkohol Vermeiden (Alcohol Avoidance)

On the topic of alcohol, we need to spare no word. With the hundred thousands of people whom we lose by the war, we cannot also morally lose still more people as a result of alcohol.

The largest and most merciless severity here is [the loss of] comradeship, which you can confirm [by looking at your own] subordinates. Criminal offenses, which occur under the influence of the consumption of alcohol, are twice as highly punished. I will punish leaders who permit alcohol abuse by the subordinates in their company. I ask that this will be carried out in the same way everywhere.

"The near future will, I believe, bring us heavy burdens," the Reichsführer cautioned. "We will have a hard winter and have a hard spring before us. The attack in the east will be outrageously bitter. The guerrilla warfare will increase. As soon as the weather permits, landings and air strikes will increase likewise on the part of the Englishmen and Americans."

With these words, he correctly predicted that the aerial assaults on the Reich by the U.S. Army Air Forces (USAAF) Eighth Air Force and the Royal Air Force Bomber Command would increase exponentially, and that the Anglo-American Allies would at last make their cross-channel invasion of northern France in 1944.

"In this winter," he ordered, "stand, believe, strike back, fight, never give way—whereupon [victory] will come." He continued:

Regarding the completion and a winning of the war, we must take up altogether the realization that a war must be won mentally, then physically. . . .

Only he who capitulates says, "I do not have the faith and the will to resist any more," which loses and lays down his weapons. Stubbornly to last, [we stand] until we stand after the peace treaty is won.

We want to show the Englishmen, Americans, and Russian untermenschen that we are harder, we, the unswerving we, we who become SS, we who will always be. We will be those who will remain in good spirits in the fifth and sixth year of the war . . . with humor, with will. . . . If we do that, then many will take us as an example for themselves and will become like us. . . . If we are mentally . . . correct, then we will win this war by the laws of history and nature, because we possess the human values, which embody naturally higher and stronger values.

Himmler concluded his remarks at Posen with words that were appropriately mystical and visionary. It was as though he had stirred himself into an Ariosophist trance.

"Into the distance we see them, because we know them," he exclaimed. "Therefore, we are more fanatical than ever . . . more courageous, more obedient, and more decent devoted to our obligation. We want to be worthy of der Führer, Adolf Hitler. [We are the] first SS men in the long history of the Germanic people standing before us. Now we think of der Führer, our Führer, Adolf Hitler, who will lead the Germanic Reich to [take] us into the Germanic future."

As the words were shouted, Himmler was met with the usual choruses of *"Unser Führer Adolf Hitler, Sieg Heil! Sieg Heil! Sieg Heil!"*

CHAPTER 18

The Witches of the Schutzstaffel

———

A S WE PICTURE Heinrich Himmler speaking to the assembled leadership of the Schutzstaffel, we imagine an all-male fraternity of Black Knights. Little has been said about the women of the SS, and much of what has been said can be filed under the heading of misinformation.

One popular conspiracy theory tells of Himmler having created an autonomous, secret women's unit, known as *Sonderkommando* H,—the H standing for *hexen*, meaning witches. However, this special corps seems to exist only in the fantasy world of modern gamers. Indeed, through the years, the SS Hexen seem to have inhabited mainly sensationalist and fetish films and fiction, where seductive images of beautiful blonde women in tight black leather flourish.

Nevertheless, the precedent for women existing among a corps of knights goes back into the medieval history that Himmler so loved. Though very little has been written about them, female knights, known as *chevalière* in French or *ritterin* in German, did exist. These terms did not apply to the wives of men who held the title of knight—chevalier or ritter—but to the female equivalent of the man under arms.

The first knightly order to admit women under arms was probably the Italian *Frati della Beata Gloriosa Vergine Maria* (Order of the Blessed Virgin Mary), better known as the Knights of the Mother of God, founded in 1233. Said to have been approved by Pope Alexander IV in 1261, and by Urban IV, who succeeded him that same year, these women warriors were granted the rank of *militissa*.

A young member of the prewar Bund Deutscher Mädel (League for German Maidens), the girls' component of the Hitlerjugend (Hitler Youth), as depicted in an oil painting by E. Schmitt. Heinrich Himmler observed, "We must achieve, by the selection of these girls, something truly valuable to all of us, through evoking their feeling of honor." *U.S. Army art collection*

Another such order is said to have been the Spanish Order of Calatrava, where women warriors were admitted under the name *Chevalières de Calatrava.*

While SS Hexen did not exist, a female SS corps *did*, and it did begin with *H*. The SS *Helferinnenkorps,* which literally means "corps of aides" or "helpers," was an SS auxiliary unit consisting of uniformed women who were assigned to the SS, though they were not technically members of the SS. Most of the Helferinnen came into the corps having grown up in the *Bund Deutscher Mädel* (League for German Maidens), the girls' component of the Hitlerjugend (Hitler Youth Organization), the Nazi Party's youth movement. Founded in 1930 as an outgrowth of the earlier *Mädchenschaften* organization, the Bund Deutscher Mädel grew in popularity after 1933. It was a sort of Völkisch and nationalist analog of the Girl Scouts. Like the Girl Scouts, it was organized by age, with the *Jungmädel* (young maidens) for girls aged ten to fourteen, and the *Deutscher Mädel* for teenagers. For young women who were indoctrinated to the ideals of Völkisch ethic purity in the Deutscher Mädel, it was an easy step to the Helferinnen. During World War II, the younger members of the Deutscher Mädel were pressed into service in hospitals and as civilian administrative aides on the home front, while their older sisters were enlisted into uniform for similar tasks by the SS and the Wehrmacht.

Both the Wehrmacht and SS Helferinnenkorps were analogous to women's uniformed auxiliary units that existed in many nations during World War II. These included the *Lotta Svärd* organization in Finland, the U.S. Navy's Women Accepted for Volunteer Emergency Service (WAVES), the U.S. Army's Women's Army Corps (WAC), the USAAF Women Air Service Pilots (WASP), or the British Women's Royal Naval Service, known as WREN. Only in the Soviet Union did women carry arms and engage in routine front-line combat duty on a large scale during World War II. There were numerous Soviet women infantry soldiers, and at least two female combat pilots achieved ace status. Katya Budanova and Lilya Litvak each shot down more than a dozen Luftwaffe aircraft.

Himmler mentioned the SS Helferinnenkorps in his Posen speech, noting that a school had been established for them at Oberehnheim (now Obernai) on the eastern slopes of the Vosges mountain range in Alsace.

While it would be interesting to imagine that Himmler had taken an interest, for history's sake, in creating an SS Ritterinkorps, such as we see in B movies, he was reluctant at first even to consider the Helferinnenkorps. However, as he said at Posen, he was pleased with the results, and he took seriously the contributions that the women might make.

"We have already seriously thinned our ranks. Where we can still spare a man, we want to send him out," Himmler said. "I have agreed after long hesitation . . . [that the SS] should create a school for SS Helferinnen. I must say, also this recent institution of the SS is off to pleasing start. Here I made it the duty of the school to be neither an institution for clerks, nor one for amusements."

It was clear that Himmler imagined as lofty an ideal for the helpers as he did for his Black Knights.

"The German people, with all our values, must nevertheless succeed in bringing about an institution similar to the Finnish Lottas," he said, insisting that the Germans could do as well as their fellow anti-Soviet Nordics, the Finns. "We must to achieve, by the selection of these girls, something truly valuable to all of us, through evoking their feeling of honor, that which cannot be achieved through compulsion."

Having himself become a convert to the idea of a women's auxiliary in the SS, he insisted that his officers fall into line, both in utilizing the capabilities of the women and in recruiting even more.

"Here, Mein Herr Obergruppenführer and Gruppenführer," he lectured. "It is your task that every one of you endeavors himself to send this or that valuable young girl from his acquaintance or from among his relatives to us, just as we used to recruit men for the Waffen SS and Junkerschule for SS officers. Our comrade and friend Waldeck has behaved ideally in this regard and has sent us his daughter. He is now going to send us his second daughter."

Having put Obergruppenführer Josias Waldeck—the hereditary prince of Waldeck and Pyrmont—up as an example, Himmler turned to address his officers complaints that the SS Helferinnen usurped male jobs.

Said the Reichsführer, "With each girl, we can replace a man. Yet soldiers and SS men are stubbornly resistant. . . . There was the commander who said, 'I use these girls to train SS men in the intelligence service or as message aides, and then I send the girls away. I want to have no girls in my unit.' This is not completely the sense of purpose of the institution. The sense lies in reverse, to use these girls in order that the men return to other duties."

The Reichsführer then asked—indeed, ordered—his officers to extend to the women "your whole chivalry, your whole sense of justice and nobility, which, in other respects, really exists in our ranks. . . . [T]ake care that this institution remains sacred. I don't want any service jokes here. These are our daughters, the sisters of SS men, and potential brides of young SS men and leaders."

Speaking from his own experience, Himmler said, "When I was with [the Helferinnen] once, I told one girl that a man whom a girl wants to marry might hesitate when he learns that she was a Helferin, saying 'Over God's will, this is out of the question.' But that man, when he experiences that the girl who wants to marry him was an SS aide, must reply 'I *can* marry her, she is suitable.' This must be so. The girls must hold themselves in high regard, and so must it be for you commanders to reinforce this view with your subordinates."

Himmler mentions the Helferinnen serving in the intelligence service, or as message aides, but the women served throughout the SS, especially in the Waffen SS, as logistical and administrative support personnel.

Another, much more nefarious cadre of SS women were the SS *Aufseherinnen,* the roughly 3,000 female guards assigned to the concentration camps. While ranks in Helferinnenkorps used the root word "Helfer," meaning "helper," those in the Aufseherinnen used the root word "Aufseher," meaning "overseer." For example, a Helferinnenkorps SS Oberhelfer was the equivalent to an SS Oberaufseherin Aufseherinnen. Neither had an SS equivalent, because in the sexist Nazi hierarchy, all men, theoretically, outranked all women. There were, nevertheless, a number of high-ranking Aufseherinnen, notably SS Chef Oberaufseherin Luise Brunner at Aushwitz, who wielded considerable power at the camps. Because of their SS rank, the women are erroneously considered to have been actual members of the SS. However, the fact that they weren't is a matter of mere semantics. The harsh brutality meted out at the camps by male SS Totenkopfverbände guards pales by comparison to what many of their female auxiliaries inflicted at the same camps.

One of the most notorious of the "SS women" was Irma Ilse Ida Grese, a high school dropout who worked at an SS rest camp before signing on for Aufseherinnen training. She graduated from training in 1943 at age nineteen and was assigned to Aushwitz. By the time she was twenty, she had been pro-moted to the rank of Oberaufseherin. She also served at Bergen-Belsen and at Ravensbrück, the camp devoted specifically to women prisoners. Grese became infamous for her unbridled sadism, which included torture and sexual abuse, as well as beating women to death or shooting people on the spot. Her trade-mark, however, was attacking prisoners with a pack of half-starved dogs.

The worst of the worst, however, was almost certainly Oberaufseherin Ilse Köhler Koch. She was the archetype for blatant savagery among the women at the camps. Born in 1906, she joined the NSDAP shortly before Adolf Hitler came to power. In 1934, she was working as secretary at Sachsenhausen, an early concentration camp near Berlin, when she met her future husband, the camp commandant, SS Standartenführer Karl Otto Koch. After they married in 1936, she followed him to into infamy at Buchenwald—he as commandant and she, after 1941, as Chief Oberaufseherin. A sexual sadist, she also used the women's unit at the camp as her personal voyeuristic playground, staging rapes as specta-tor sports. It is saying a great deal that her peculiar tastes in spectator sex went so far as to earn her a cautionary notice from the SS.

Koch's most outrageous hobby, however, was her well-documented collec-tion of household items, especially lamp shades, that were made from the tat-tooed skin of inmates. As she prowled the camp, she would look for tattoos that interested her, then order the person stripped of his or her skin—usually post mortem. This skin, in turn, would be tanned, like an animal hide, and made into whatever household accessory that the Oberaufseherin wished for her home. She is recalled as having been especially proud of a handbag with the tattoo of a tropi-cal scene. Even the Germans called her *Die Hexe von Buchenwald* (the Witch of Buchenwald), but she is best known to history as the "the Bitch of Buchenwald."

As for women being recruited as patriotic sex slaves for German troops, such practices were not institutionalized on such a massive scale, as was the case with Germany's Axis partner. The well-organized Japanese "comfort women" program saw upwards of 200,000 young women rounded up from Korea and the Philippines, as well as China and even Japan itself, to service troops at gov-ernment-owned and -operated whorehouses across the Far East.

Adolf Hitler chats with a pair of young female admirers as Heinrich Himmler looks on eagerly. Such women, who had earlier been members of the League for German Maidens, made the transition to various military auxiliary units, including the SS Helferinnen, during World War II. *U.S. National Archives*

When one looks at the number of women who were part of the SS, one must look also at the women who joined the SS *Sippengemeinschaft*, or "Kinship Clan" through marriage to SS members, often through the pagan SS Eheweihen wedding consecrations that Himmler and his black priests had crafted. As Gudrun Schwarz points out in her 1997 book, *Eine Frau an seiner Seite: Ehefrauen in der SS Sippengemeinschaft (A Wife at his Side: Wives in the SS Clan Community),* there were around a quarter million women who "joined" the SS through marriage.

There was no doubt as to the role of the SS wives in the SS marriage: to produce a generation of meticulously pedigreed Aryan children.

Naturally, marriage was a topic that was covered occasionally in the SS in-house publication, *Das Schwarze Corps.* Issue number 33 of the magazine for 1942 carried an article that clearly explained "the concept of what the SS wives are to accomplish in the Sippengemeinschaft, and what place they are to occupy is established tradition. They are to be subordinated to the patriarchy of the man as protector of clan honor and blood."

We are here reminded of that 1939 article in the magazine in which a woman describes the role of the husband and father as "the spiritual direction of the family. . . . [H]e founds it, he leads it, he fights for it, he defends it," while the wife and mother "gives the family the inner attitude, she gives it soul . . . and builds the quiet motive in the family relationship"

These women writing in *Das Schwarze Corps* paint a picture that seems to depict a belief in the strength of traditional family. However, Himmler was already gravitating strongly toward a marriage doctrine that would embrace, and legalize, polygamy. The catalyst for such a thought was the realization that so many young, perfectly selected, Aryan men were dying at the front, their blood being spilled into the dark soil of the East, rather than into the bloodline of future Aryan generations. Then too, Himmler was probably thinking of a rational—or rationalized—justification for his relationship with Hedwig Potthast. As he had told Felix Kersten, "My personal opinion is that it would be a natural development for us to break with monogamy. Marriage in its existing form is the Catholic Church's satanic achievement. Marriage laws are in themselves immoral. . . . With bigamy, each wife would act as a stimulus to the other so that both would try to be their husband's dream woman—no more untidy hair, no more slovenliness. Their models, which will intensify these reflections, will be the ideals of beauty projected by art and the cinema."

Himmler, speaking man-to-man to Kersten, the man whose hands took away the tense pain of knotted muscles and constricted nerves, went on to complain:

> The fact that a man has to spend his entire existence with one wife drives him first of all to deceive her and then makes him a hypocrite as he tries to cover it up. The result is indifference between the partners. They avoid each other's embraces, and the final consequence is that they don't produce children. This is the reason why millions of children are never born, children whom the state urgently requires. On the other hand, the husband never dares to have children by the woman with whom he is carrying on an affair, much though he would like to, simply because middle-class morality forbids it. Again it's the state which loses, for it gets no children from the second woman either.

The man's place was with his wife—unless he is with his *other* wife.

CHAPTER 19

Aryans Beyond Nationality

T HE BLACK KNIGHTS of the SS were carefully screened, carefully crafted, to represent the most genetically Aryan of Aryans, men who would have been right at home among the Armanen god-kings in Asgard or Thule or in the Irminen holy city of Karl Maria Wiligut's imagination. Their ancestry had to be Germanic back to the eighteenth century, but one of the biggest ironies of the SS in the 1941–1943 period was that not all of the Black Knights were German. Like Alexander the Great, who deliberately staffed his undefeated army with men from all nations under his rule, Heinrich Himmler saw the SS as Germanic rather than German. Adolf Hitler had imagined a Third Reich whose borders would embrace all Völksdeutsche, as well as the prewar citizens of the Reich, but Himmler imagined that the Order of Schutzstaffel, the Sippengemeinschaft of the sacred blood, should transcend mortal boundaries.

To begin with, the Scandinavians were perceived as being as purely Aryan as Germans. Indeed, the Nordic literature that formed the pagan scriptures upon which everyone from List to Himmler based his dogma originated in Iceland and the frigid northern reaches of Scandinavia. Places such as Norway, Denmark, and neutral Sweden existed on maps, but if one drew the map based on Aryan racial characteristics, the borders were meaningless in Himmler's mind, like the prewar border between Austria and Germany that Hitler did not recognize.

As Himmler, Walther Darré, and all the racial demographers knew, the Aryans were also to be found in Finland, the Netherlands, and in Flanders, that Nordic sliver of the North Sea coast that had been grafted onto Francophone Wallonia to create the hybrid kingdom of Belgium. There were even Aryans in Wallonia, as well. Himmler also saw them in the Baltic republics—after all, even Alfred Rosenberg, the arbiter of the line between "us" and "them," was Estonian. Himmler saw Völksdeutsche Ukrainians and Russians as Aryan stock—after all, Rosenberg's own original passport was issued by the Russian tsar.

Himmler imagined his multiethnic SS to be the enforcer and ruling class in a united Europe, an authoritarian precursor to the modern European Union. As with that modern institution, Himmler conceived of a continent of individual states using a single currency, united by a trade and a unified legal system, and having a central authority emanating from a centralized location—not Brussels, as in the twenty-first century, but Berlin. He once told Felix Kersten:

> [This] European empire would form a confederation of free states, among which would be Greater Germany, Hungary, Croatia, Slovakia, Holland, Flanders, Wallonia, Luxembourg, Norway, Denmark, Estonia, Latvia, Lithuania. These countries were to govern themselves. They would have in common a European currency, certain areas of the administration, including the police, foreign policy, and the army, in which the various nations would be represented by national formations. Trade relations would be governed by special treaties, a sphere in which Germany as the economically strongest country would hold back in order to favor the development of the weaker ones. Free towns were also envisaged, having special functions of their own, among them the task of representing a nation's culture.

What form postwar Europe would have taken if Germany had won is uncertain. Beyond the fact that it would have been ruled with an iron hand from Berlin, Hitler himself had probably not worked out all the nuances. Himmler's vision, as articulated to Kersten, was more fully defined.

Hitler and Himmler did not agree on the idea of Aryan purity. Hitler's view was from a nationalistic perspective and was, therefore, a much narrower take on German citizenship than that of the Reichsführer. Himmler's view was broader and more purely racial. Like Guido von List and all of the Ariosophists who had come in the intervening doctrinal generations, he looked beyond the Reich to the purity of the greater Aryan race. Heinz Höhne writes in *The Order of the Death's Head: The Story of Hitler's SS*:

> Hitler's ideas and those of the SS were not invariably identical. The next area in which differences began to appear was the treatment of the so-called "Germanic" peoples; though both Hitler and the SS used the phraseology of Nazi dogma, the two were in fact working on different principles. In spite of all the Germanic claptrap, Hitler was still the German nationalist of the Imperial era, who regarded any supra-national institution as a betrayal of Germany; the SS leaders, on the other hand, were genuinely striving for a Great German Reich which, in a vague sort of way, they hoped and believed would produce a new epoch of international brotherhood transcending national boundaries—though under German leadership, of course.

Hitler looked at the political geography of Europe and saw a Greater Reich, with Lebensraum on the steppes to the east. Heinrich Himmler looked at the racial map and saw a pan-European Aryan oligarchy ruled by an aristocracy of racially homogenous, though transnational, Black Knights.

Paul Kluke, a prewar agricultural theorist and professor at the Institut für Agrarwesen und Agrarpolitik der Berliner Universität, and who later helped Himmler plan the mass evacuation of Slavic people from the Soviet Union, said that in contrast to Hitler's nationalistic scheme, Himmler favored "a policy conceived in quite different terms: one of greater autonomy." Kluke called Himmler "far more prepared to remove the Nordic elements from the non-German races, in other words, to carry out those biological fishing expeditions [searching for Aryans] among other peoples which Hitler himself found so dubious."

Himmler had no qualms about recruiting non-Germans into the Waffen SS. Indeed, the idea *excited* him, as though it supported the theory, dating back to the early twentieth century, that Aryan blood was transcendent. He looked for what he called "Nordic-Germanic" blood, not prewar German passports.

Having interviewed Obergruppenführer Felix Steiner in 1966, Heinz Höhne reported, "In one of his moments of enthusiasm, Himmler said that he could quite well imagine that the next Reichsführer SS might not be a German; Hitler, on the other hand, would ridicule Himmler's passion for Germanic experimentation; in his view, unless he had been ideologically brainwashed, every non-German SS volunteer must 'feel himself a traitor to his people.'"

Though Hitler may have ridiculed Himmler, he acquiesced to the Reichsführer's scheme for non-German volunteer, or *Freiwilligen,* units. However, for the most part, the non-German divisions would be designated as "Division der SS," instead of "SS Division." Not all of these new units were permitted to wear the lightning-bolt SS insignia on their uniforms.

The most famous of the "foreign" Waffen SS units was the Wiking (pronounced "Viking," as W in German is pronounced as V in English) Division. The name implies embracing a pan-Nordic warrior theme. Officially known as the Number 5 SS Panzer Division Wiking, it originated as a mechanized infantry division, but soon progressed to a panzer unit. It was created at the end of 1940, after the remarkable success of the German forces during the year resulted in a tide of volunteers who wanted to be part of the victorious German juggernaut. Initially designated as Number 5 Nordische Division, it was composed of a cadre of Waffen SS veterans mixed with a few Danish, Norwegian, Swedish, Dutch, and Flemish volunteers. As the division was forming during early 1941, it gradually transitioned into a multinational unit, although the officer corps was predominantly German. Given the name "Wiking," the division went into combat during Operation Barbarossa, under the command of then-Brigadeführer Felix Steiner, and remained in combat throughout World War II.

As the Wiking Division was proving itself on the eastern front in 1941 and 1942, Hitler agreed to Himmler's desire to create even more multinational Waffen SS units to absorb the continuing influx of Scandinavian, Finnish, and Dutch volunteers, as well as Latvians and Estonians from the Baltic and Bosnians and Coats from the Balkans—all of whom were keen to fight the communists.

In 1943, a Scandinavian panzergrenadier regiment within the Wiking Division, known as *Nordland,* was detached and used as the basis of a new division designated as the Number 11 SS Panzergrenadier Division Nordland. In addition to its core of Scandinavian troops, Nordland's ranks were also filled by volunteers from such diverse countries as Estonia, France, Hungary, Romania, Spain, Switzerland, and even the United Kingdom.

Sometimes, it was political pressure that led to the formation of some Freiwilligen divisions. The lobbying efforts of the Dutch Nazis of the *Nationaal-Socialistische Beweging* led in 1941 to the creation of an all-Dutch battalion, which evolved over time into the Number 23 Freiwilligen Panzergrenadier Division Nederland. Another Dutch Waffen SS division was the Number 34 SS Freiwilligen Grenadier Division Landstorm Nederland. It had evolved out of the *Landwacht Niederlande,* a paramilitary police force consisting of Nationaal-Socialistische Beweging goons, created under German auspices after the Netherlands were occupied in 1940. Unlike the Number 23 Freiwilligen Panzergrenadier Division Nederland, which fought alongside German forces on the eastern front and in the Balkans, Landstorm Nederland fought at home, ironically, defending the German occupation from the British armies that came at the end of 1944 to liberate the Netherlands. They entered combat at the end of September during the Operation Market Garden airborne operation that sought an Allied bridgehead across the Rhine at Arnhem in the Netherlands. The

Heinrich Himmler in full Reichsführer regalia. He imagined a unified postwar Europe ruled by an SS comprised of Aryans from many nations, unified by Aryan blood that transcended national boundaries.
U.S. National Archive

worst of the irony was that attached to the British army for this operation was a Dutch brigade whose objective was to liberate their country. The Dutchmen of Landstorm Nederland found themselves facing off against their cousins in the *Koninklijke Nederlandse* (Royal Dutch) brigade *Prinses Irene*. After the liberation, those who had remained loyal to their "fellow Aryans" in the SS during the war faced criminal prosecution for treason. They were not treated kindly by their countrymen.

In Flanders, where there had been strong Nazi sympathies before World War II, the Waffen SS found fertile ground for recruits. The Flemings hoped for a postwar Flanders independent of French-dominated Belgium. The Number 27 SS Freiwilligen Division Langemarck, consisting of Flemish volunteers, evolved out of the SS Freiwilligen Verband Flandern (later SS Freiwilligen Sturmbrigade Langemarck) and served widely on the eastern front.

Meanwhile, however, the French-speaking Belgians in the Wallonia region also rated a Waffen SS division. As in the Netherlands and in Flanders, the back story in Wallonia began with a prewar fascist movement that would align itself closely with the Nazis. *Christus Rex,* also referred to as the *Parti Rexiste* (Rexist Party), was a fundamentalist political party created in Wallonia 1930 by a journalist named Léon Degrelle. In fact, the party actually did well in regional elections during the 1930s. From the Parti Rexiste evolved the paramilitary Légion Wallonie, which liked to think of itself as a Wallonian analog of Himmler's SS. After Germany occupied Belgium in 1940, the SS wannabes of the Légion Wallonie signed up to fight Bolshevism and became the Number 5 SS Freiwilligen Sturmbrigade Wallonien. They saw action on the eastern front, and the unit was enlarged and redesignated as the Number 28 SS Freiwilligen Grenadierdivision Wallonien in September 1944. After the war, the Belgian government convicted Degrelle of treason in absentia and condemned him to death, but he had escaped to Spain, where he lived until his death in 1994.

France also had its Waffen SS division, the Number 33 Waffengrenadierdivision der SS Charlemagne, which evolved out of the French anti-communist *Légion des Volontaires Français contre le Bolchévisme,* which had been incorporated into the Wehrmacht after 1940. Number 33 "Charlemagne" was created in 1944 as an umbrella for fascist French units that had been serving on the eastern front with various German units, both Wehrmacht and SS, as well as volunteers from Vichy France.

Perhaps the most surprising of the Waffen SS Freiwilligen were units comprised of Muslims from Central Asia. The incorporation of the blonde, blue-eyed Nordic men from the Netherlands or Scandinavia fits the paradigm that one would expect from Himmler's strict Sippenbuch. However, among the millions of Soviet prisoners of war captured by the German armies were sizable numbers from the Central Asia republics, now independent, but then part of the Soviet Union. These people, like the French and Scandinavians, wanted to fight the communists. Tens of thousands of mainly Muslim Azeri, Chechen, Kazakh, Kyrgyz, Turkmen, and Uzbek troops switched sides to join the Wehrmacht. These troops were then organized into units such as the *Kaukasisch Mohammedan* (Caucasian Muslim) Legion, or the *Wolgatatarische* (Volga Tatar) Legion, also known as the *Ostturkische Waffenverband*. In 1944, the SS reportedly also formed the its *Ostmuselmanische* (East Muslim) SS Regiment, comprised of Central Asian men.

Himmler's central focus with his multinational SS concept was Europe, although he also often spoke of his concept of a postwar *Weltreich,* or World Reich, encompassing the former Soviet Union. Indeed, defeat of the Soviet Union and communism was always the key prerequisite for all of Himmler's dreams of the future. He often said, usually to Kersten as he was relaxing during a massage, that he imagined his utopian, pan-European Reich coming into being as soon as the communists had been eliminated from the Soviet Union. Then even Russia would have its own day in the glow of a Nazi sun.

"When Bolshevism had been extirpated in Russia, the Western Territories would come under German administration modeled on the Marches which Charlemagne had instituted in the east of his empire," Himmler pontificated, as Kersten rubbed the angst from the Reichsführer's shoulders and eased his chronic stomach pain. "The methods followed would be those by which England had evolved her colonies into dominions. When peace and economic health were fully restored, these territories would be handed back to the Russian people, who would live there in complete freedom, and a 25-year peace and commercial treaty would be concluded with their new government."

CHAPTER 20

Evil Science

——

THE CRUELEST COROLLARY to the villainy institutionalized by Heinrich Himmler and SS Totenkopfverbände during World War II was probably the use of concentration-camp inmates in the furtherance of what the SS and its Ahnenerbe had the audacity to describe as "science."

Again, their line of thinking stretched back into the nineteenth century to the Social Darwinists and their pseudoscientific belief in a racial hierarchy. When the Social Darwinists wrote of natural selection in human society, advocating the sidelining those in society who were considered inferior, they opened the door to those who considered the inferior human races to be not human at all. The same pseudoscience that gave the Nazis their excuse to eradicate the untermenschen like head lice gave the Nazis permission to use the untermenschen as lab rats.

The use of people from concentration camps for gruesome medical experiments was widespread, although it was not centrally directed, as the "ancestral research" conducted under the Ahnenerbe was. The SS functioned as a sort of medical foundation of the dark side, facilitating various projects with infrastructure, personnel, and, of course, human guinea pigs. Much of the funding and encouragement was filtered through the *Institut für Wehrwissenschaftliche Zweckforschung* (Institute for Military Scientific Research), which was set up within the Ahnenerbe and headed directly by Wolfram Sievers.

One of the most notorious of the SS doctors was Dr. Eduard Wirths, the primary physician at Auschwitz. Having become a member of the NSDAP while a medical student at Würzburg, he joined the Waffen SS in 1939. After suffering a heart attack on the Eastern Front in 1942, he was transferred to concentration-camp duty, first at Dachau and then at Auschwitz. It was at the latter that numerous medical experiments were conducted by SS doctors that were under Wirths's direct command. He was particularly interested in experiments around the spread of typhus and in a large-scale project involving the removal of reproductive organs from live women, which were then sent to various institutes in Germany for study. Most of the subjects involved in both projects died as a result.

While Wirths supervised actual doctors, including those providing medical care to the übermensch SS personnel, he also had a number of doctors on his staff whose principal, or only, function at Aushwitz was "research" using human—or rather "subhuman"—subjects.

Conducting experiments on female subjects under Wirths at Auschwitz was Dr. Carl Clauberg, a prewar professor for gynecology at the University of Königsberg turned SS Gruppenführer. When it became established policy under the Final Solution to prevent the untermenschen from breeding, Clauberg approached Himmler personally with a proposal to conduct experiments to find a practical method of mass sterilization. All he needed, implored Clauberg, was experimental subjects. Himmler sent Clauberg to Aushwitz in December 1942. There Clauberg experimented on both Jewish and Gypsy subjects, using drugs, acid, and radiation—almost always without anesthetic.

Also under Wirths at Aushwitz in 1943 and 1944 was Dr. Joseph Mengele, an SS doctor whose name would later become synonymous with savagery conducted by the Nazis in the name of science. Like Wirths, he had started World War II in the Waffen SS, but had been declared unfit for front-line duty for medical reasons. While at the Universität München (University of Munich), Himmler's alma mater, Mengele studied both medicine and anthropology, and he attracted the attention of the Nazis because of his thesis on racial morphology. He was also interested in genetics and the study of human twins. At Auschwitz, he found himself with access to an almost endless supply of human subjects. Indeed, he conducted experiments on well over a thousand sets of twins and perhaps as many as three times that number. They were mainly children, and most of them died as a result of his experiments. His camp nickname, "Angel of Death," was well deserved. His experiments ranged from attempts to change eye color with dyes to sewing children together to create artificial conjoined ("Siamese") twins.

The Eduard Wirths of Dachau was Dr. Sigmund Rascher. Actually, he was Wirths, Clauberg, and Mengele all rolled into one ambitious package. He had joined the NSDAP in around 1933, while still a medical student, and became a member of the SS in 1939. Through his girlfriend (later wife), Karoline "Nini" Diehl, a singer who knew Heinrich Himmler as he frequented the nightclub circuit, Rascher got close to the Reichsführer. Himmler took a liking to the doctor, who was sent to a cancer-research project—using live subjects, of course—at Dachau.

When World War II began, Rascher joined the Luftwaffe. He started out in aviation medicine, but ended up at Dachau again, doing experiments on high-altitude flying, studying the effects of both low temperature and low pressure. The poor subjects, which included Jews, as well as Soviet and Polish prisoners of war, were put into altitude chambers. They were taken up as high as a simulated 70,000 feet, both with and without oxygen. Others were mistreated so that Rascher could study the effects of hypothermia. Some were thrown into icy water, and others were forced to sit naked in freezing conditions for hours.

Ernst Schäfer, in a postwar interrogation, said that he and Ernst Krause, the Tibet expedition filmographer, were asked by Rascher to film some experiments. According to Schäfer, they pretended to have had an equipment malfunction. Nevertheless, film footage does exist of Rascher's terrible sessions.

Rascher also studied ways by which these nearly frozen people could be successfully warmed up. One such method, well known in the popular folklore of Nazi brutality, was to throw the subject into bed with a small group of naked prostitutes. Like Ilsa Koch at Buchenwald, Rascher was a sadist who couldn't resist cruel sexual exploitation in the dreadful final moments in the lives of his subjects—and at the expense of some obviously terrified women. The "lucky" few who survived the cold hand of Dr. Rascher were subsequently executed.

Rascher also designed cyanide capsules that would produce almost instant death if placed in the mouth and bitten.

Another of the SS doctors to "work" with human subjects from Dachau was Dr. August Hirt of the University of Strasbourg in Alsace (which was known as the Reichsuniversität Strassburg under the German occupation between 1940 and 1944). By 1942, one of his principal subordinates was Bruno Beger, the SS Ahnenerbe anthropologist who had, calipers in hand, accompanied Ernst Schäfer to Tibet. By 1942, Beger had turned his rulers and calipers from jovial living Tibetans to the skulls of deceased individuals, mainly individuals that were referred to in the paper trail of documentation as "Jewish Bolshevik commissars." Beginning around 1940, Beger had also been using X-rays to study human body types and to categorize the physical parameters of Aryan perfection versus untermensch imperfection. It was as though he had ripped a page straight from Jörg Lanz von Liebenfels's 1905 book, *Theozoologie oder die Kunde von den Sodoms-Äfflingen und dem Götter-Elektron (Theozoology or the account of the Sodomite Apelings and the Divine Electron),* which linked the concept of Aryan *Gottmenschen* (god-men) with unseen electronic rays. Later, Beger and Hirt took to removing flesh from skulls in order to get more perfect caliper readings.

The prosecution exhibits from the postwar International Military Tribunal tell much of the ghoulish tale of Beger and Hirt's work in the form of correspondence between Sievers, SS Obersturmbannführer Adolf Eichmann, and SS Sturmbannführer Rudolf Brandt, Himmler's personal aide.

On February 9, 1942, Sievers wrote to Brandt complaining of a shortage of specimens for the research at the Reichsuniversität Strassburg:

There exist extensive collections of skulls of almost all races and peoples. Of the Jewish race, however, only so very few specimens of skulls are at the disposal of science that a study of them does not permit precise conclusions. The war in the East now presents us with the opportunity to remedy this shortage. By procuring the skulls of the Jewish-Bolshevik Commissars, who personify a repulsive yet characteristic subhumanity, we have the opportunity of obtaining tangible scientific evidence. The actual obtaining and collecting of these skulls without difficulty could be best accomplished by a directive issued to the Wehrmacht in the future to immediately turn over alive all Jewish-Bolshevik Commissars.

He then calmly added that a "special deputy, commissioned with the collection of the material [a junior physician attached to the Wehrmacht, the police, or a medical student equipped with car and driver], is to take a prescribed series of photographs and anthropological measurements, and is to ascertain, insofar as is possible, the origin, date of birth, and other personal data of the prisoner. Following the subsequently induced death of the Jew, whose head must not be damaged, he will separate the head from the torso and will forward it to its point of destination in a preserving fluid in a well-sealed tin container especially made for this purpose."

On November 2, 1942, Sievers wrote to Brandt reminding him, "As you know, [Himmler personally ordered] that SS Hauptsturmführer Prof. Dr. Hirt should be provided with all necessary material for his research work. I have already reported to the Reichsführer SS that for some anthropological studies 150 skeletons of inmates or Jews are needed and should be provided by the Auschwitz concentration camp."

Four days later, Brandt sent a memo from Himmler's field command post to Eichmann, explaining that Himmler had previously issued "a directive to the effect that SS-Hauptsturmfuehrer Prof. Dr. Hirt, who is the director of the Anatomical Institute at Strassburg and the head of a department of the institute for Military Science Research in the Ahnenerbe Society, be furnished with everything he needs for his research work. By order of the Reichsführer SS, therefore, I ask you to make possible the establishment of the planned collection. SS-Obersturmbannfuehrer Sievers will get in touch with you with regard to straightening out the details."

Apparently the details were straightened out, though it took more time than Hirt may have wished. Indeed, the rampant spread of diseases, including typhus, that propagated in the squalor of Auschwitz made it difficult for the SS men to find inmates healthy enough to murder. Bruno Beger himself would travel to Auschwitz on a skeleton-collecting mission, wrapping up his work on June 15, 1943.

On June 21, Sievers wrote to Eichmann, sending copies of the letter to Beger, Brandt, and Hirt himself. In that letter he said, "A total of 115 persons were worked on, 79 of whom were Jews, 2 Poles, 4 Asiatics, and 30 Jewesses. At present, these prisoners are separated according to sex and each group is accommodated in a hospital building of the Auschwitz concentration camp and are in quarantine. For further processing of the selected persons an immediate transfer to the Natzweiler concentration camp is now imperative; this must be accelerated in view of the danger of infectious diseases in Auschwitz."

The bodies did reach the Reichsuniversität Strassburg and the laboratory of Hirt and Beger. As it turned out, the men moved very slowly in their dissections. After all of the urgency of acquiring the bodies, Hirt got around to relatively few dissections and reduced even fewer of the bodies to skeletons.

Meanwhile, Ernst Schäfer, Beger's old Tibet colleague, was still on the Ahnenerbe payroll, where for a time, he had headed the important-sounding *Ahnenerbe Forschungsstatte für Innersasien und Expeditionen* (Research Institute for Intra-Asia and Expeditions). Despite the appellation, the institute never sent an expedition back to inner Asia. That was all in the past.

Early in 1943, Schäfer was reunited with Sven Hedin, the seventy-eight-year-old geographer and explorer from neutral Sweden, whose numerous expeditions into Central Asia and Tibet between 1894 and 1935 had been groundbreaking scientifically and an inspiration to men such as Schäfer. In his later years, Hedin had become a convert to Nazism and was in regular contact with Adolf Hitler. In fact, Hitler had brought him to Germany to award him the *Verdienstorden vom Deutschen Adler* (Order of the German Eagle) medal. At one point, Schäfer stopped by Strassburg to pay a visit to Hirt and Beger. Hirt proudly showed him a dissected brain. What a strange step into the shadows that had to have been for Schäfer, whose time was then being spent in the details of the release of *Geheimnis Tibet (Secret Tibet),* the film shot only three years earlier on the other side of the world.

CHAPTER 21

Weird Science

——

THE FACT THAT the doctrines used to justify the Final Solution were promulgated so officially, and that they were accepted so broadly, clearly illustrates that under the Third Reich, Germany sank into a moral and scientific dark age.

Paradoxically, these were years of significant technological advancement in Germany. We recall that when Hermann Wirth and Wolfram Sievers sent the Ahnenerbe to remote Finland in search of the obscure northern Völkisch race who lived where the *Kalevala* originated, they took with them state-of-the-art, German-made reel-to-reel tape-recording technology that was among the best in the world. Likewise, it is well known that in aeronautics, jet propulsion, and rocket technology, Germany continued to be a global leader until the final months of World War II. Also well known is that it was Wernher von Braun, the father of Germany's V2 ballistic missile, was also the father of NASA's Saturn 5, which took Americans to the moon a quarter century later.

Indeed, the sophistication of German technology made possible the horrible hardware that killed so many in the death camps. The deaths of those six million would not have been possible without the massive, and massively efficient, killing machines—ovens and gas chambers—that were built for the death camps.

Despite the obsession by Adolf Hitler and Heinrich Himmler with the lines of inquiry pursued by the pseudoscientists of the Ahnenerbe, prewar Germany had not been a scientific backwater—far from it. Between 1901 and 1939, the country's legitimate scientists had won thirty-nine Nobel prizes for chemistry, physics, or medicine. However, many of the laureates were an embarrassment to the Third Reich. Many of these science Nobels, such as Albert Einstein's for physics in 1921, were awarded to Jews.

When the Nazis took power in 1933, a rift naturally formed in the German scientific community. Under the Nuremberg Laws, the Jewish scientists began to lose their jobs. Their theories, including those for which their Nobels were awarded, were first questioned and next discredited.

The man who put a name to the ostracism of Jewish scientists in Germany was Dr. Philipp Eduard Anion von Lenard, a Hungarian-born German physicist. He himself had won the Nobel Prize in Physics in 1905 for his work in the field of cathode rays, which led to the practical development of the cathode-ray tubes that made twentieth-century television sets possible. Strangely, 1905 was the same time that electronic rays were also playing a role in Ariosophic metaphysics. Indeed, it was the same year that Jörg Lanz von Liebenfels published *Theozoologie oder die Kunde von den Sodoms-Äfflingen und dem Götter-Elektron (Theozoology or the Account of the Sodomite Apelings and the Divine Electron)*, in which the subtext to his hatred of apelings was the unrelated supposition that electronic rays were connected with supernatural mysticism.

It was Lenard's own book, published in 1933, the year that the Nazis took power in Germany, which framed the scientific legitimacy of the Third Reich's version of Ariosophy. In his massive, four-volume *Great Men in Science, a History of Scientific Progress,* Lenard coined the term *Deutsche Physik,* which literally means "German Physics," but which was extrapolated by him to mean "Aryan Physics," or science formulated and perpetuated by Germanic or Nordic scientists. He also coined the term *Jüdische Physik,* which translates as "Jewish Physics," but which he used to mean the scientific work done by the inferior beings whom Heinrich Himmler and Alfred Rosenberg were now characterizing as untermenschen. Though the book purports to be about the contributions of "great men in science," Lenard specifically excluded Albert Einstein, still recognized as *the* towering figure in twentieth-century science. Lenard wrote him off as "the Jewish fraud."

Jörg Lanz von Liebenfels was still around in 1933, but there is no record of what he may have thought of the prince of cathode rays agreeing with his characterizations of the "apelings." We do know what Adolf Hitler thought of Lenard and his scientific theories, for he made the Nobel laureate his *chief* of Deutsche Physik. Together with fellow Nazi Johannes Stark, who won the 1919 Nobel Prize in Physics, Lenard reorganized the German scientific community, bringing it into line with the party line of the Third Reich.

As for Albert Einstein, he was one of the lucky ones among his Jewish countrymen; he got out of Germany before the hammer came down. An avowed anti-Nazi, he emigrated to the United States in 1933 as soon as Hitler took power.

The ironic thing about Lenard's Jüdische Physik is that it may have saved the world. Because Einstein was a leader in the field of nuclear physics, Hitler was so skeptical of atomic energy that he denied the necessary support that would have been required for the Third Reich to develop nuclear weapons. Such a program did exist in Germany during World War II, but Hitler refused to allow it to be fast-tracked because the still-unproven theory behind the nuclear chain reaction was "tainted" by the hands of practitioners of Jüdische Physik.

As we know, that same Jüdische Physik *did* help the United States develop nuclear weapons by 1945. It was on August 2, 1939, that Albert Einstein and fellow Jewish physicist, Leó Szilárd, mailed their famous letter to President Franklin Roosevelt, telling him that Nazi Germany was capable of building nuclear weapons and the United States should not allow Germany to be the first to have such terrible weapons. Roosevelt initiated the steps that led the United States becoming the first nuclear power. Many of the scientists on the project were Jewish.

However, Deutsch Physik allowed for theories far stranger than nuclear weapons—indeed, far stranger than fiction—to develop and receive official sanction within the Third Reich. Certainly the Welteislehre or Glazial-Kozmog-onie of Hanns Hörbiger is an example of a very unconventional idea that was taken seriously. In this case, it was a matter of Nazi leaders *wanting* to believe in an improbable idea because of their Völkisch notion of the Aryans originating in the ice.

Some of the oddest theories to receive official interest in Germany during the Third Reich concerned the physical configuration of the earth itself.

During the nineteenth century, many people had read Jules Verne's 1864 novel *Journey to the Center of the Earth.* Just as conventional wisdom once held that the world was flat, during the nineteenth century, many people were convinced that Verne's version of the world's hollow center might just be true. Indeed, such a thing is mentioned in many pre-nineteenth century religious texts; the Greek idea of Hades and the Christian idea of hell, for example, both involved underworlds. Within the scientific community, there were many who thought a hollow earth was possible. Even the seventeenth-century astronomer Edmond Halley, who discovered the famous periodic comet that bears his name, wrote of a hollow earth.

By the twentieth century, scientific theory migrated toward the now-accepted notion of the earth having a molten core. Nevertheless, hollow-earth enthusiasts continue to hold to their belief even in the twenty-first century. For example, various religious sects, such as Elizabeth Clare Prophet's Church Universal and Triumphant, believe that a race of superbeings travels in and out of the hollow earth by way of a portal on California's Mount Shasta.

Among others still clinging to Jules Verne's vision are those who believe that Adolf Hitler himself escaped into the hollow earth after World War II. While this notion is at the far outer limits of the possible (never say never), Hitler did, in fact, have an open mind to the *Hohlweltlehre,* or Hollow Earth Theory. The Hohlweltlehre was mentioned in the literature of the Thule Gesellshaft, whose members were certainly aware of Verne's *Journey to the Center of the Earth.* Indeed, the novel could easily have been written about the Thuleans. As the book begins, the German main character, Professor Otto Lidenbrock, lives in Hamburg. He learns of the secret entrance to the earth's interior while deciphering an ancient runic manuscript of an Icelandic saga. These runes were penned by none other than Snorri Sturluson, the twelfth-century Icelandic historian who wrote down the Younger Edda, the prose version of the ancient Nordic scriptures that were so thoroughly devoured by the Armanen and by Heinrich Himmler.

Verne's fictitious entrance to the inner world is located in Iceland, which had to have delighted members of the Thule Gesellshaft. As they and other Hohlweltlehre devotees contemplated the Hohlweltlehre, which they took to be fact, they studied numerous ancient texts, from Nordic to Buddhist, searching for clues that might lead them to locate the actual entrance. Assuming that it must be located in a place cold and icy, many early twentieth-century counter-culturists picked up on suggestions in various pieces of literature saying it might be located either in Tibet or Antarctica. Perhaps the most well-known of these were by the creator of Tarzan, Edgar Rice Burroughs, who set a series of seven novels in the land of Pellucidar inside a hollow earth with openings at the poles. The first five had been published by 1937. It is interesting to note that the Third Reich sent expeditions to both Tibet and Antarctica in 1938 and 1939.

In the case of Tibet, there is no evidence that Ernst Schäfer, Bruno Beger, and their team ever looked for a doorway to a "middle earth." (As a practical matter, if such a doorway did exist in Tibet, one would have had to descend four miles just to get to sea level, never mind the center of the earth!) Nor is there any widely disclosed evidence that Captain Alfred Ritscher's German Antarctic expedition looked for such an entrance. Within today's online world of conspiracy theory, however, there is still much speculation.

While the belief in a hollow earth is unconventional, perhaps the strangest of all theories concerning the physical configuration of the earth is that the world is not spherical, flat, or hollow, but concave! This idea was advanced, perhaps for the first time, by Dr. Cyrus Reed Teed, a nineteenth-century American physician turned self-styled messiah from upstate New York. Teed reported that he had "confirmed" his concave-world theory, which he called "Cellular Cosmogony" through surveys that he did in Florida in the 1890s.

According to various sources, including Louis Pauwels and Jacques Bergier in their 1960 book *The Morning of the Magicians,* both Hitler and Himmler were convinced by concave-earth theorists active in Germany in the 1930s that the surface of our planet is actually the concave *inside surface* of a spherical bubble surrounded by an infinite mass of solid rock. This theory holds that the sky is actually a cloud of blue gas in the center of the sphere that is illuminated by the sun, which is much smaller than conventional astronomers insist that it is. This strange conviction is discussed further in such books as *In the Name of Science* (1946) by Gerard S. Kuiper and *Pseudo-Sciences Under the Nazi Regime* (1947) by

Willy Ley, which were published close to the time that this idea was alive and well in the Third Reich's halls of power.

As the story goes, Hitler was so convinced of this theory that he sent Dr. Heinz Fisher, supposedly one of Germany's leading experts in radar and infrared radiation, to the Baltic Sea island of Rügen in April 1942. Fisher was told to undertake a long-distance search for the British fleet. Because, under the theory, the universe is inside the bubble, he had only to direct his radar straight *up* to detect China. Thus, using a less than forty-five-degree angle, he ought to have been able to "see" the British fleet in the North Atlantic. A great deal of rare, high-technology equipment is alleged to have been devoted to the

project. Needless to say, Fisher's attempt to locate Hitler's military adversary proved futile. In spite of such "techno-logical setbacks," some members of the Oberkommando Wehrmacht are reported to have continued to believe in the theory of a concave earth. After the war, Fisher came to the United States to work on advanced weapons projects. As late as 1957, according to Pauwels and Bergier, he was working on the American hydrogen bomb program.

Another intersection of the mystic and the scientific in the Third Reich, mentioned by Pauwels and Bergier, among others, is Vril. In modern pop culture, "Vril" is a term closely associated with the most esoteric of theories entertained by both Hitler and Himmler. However, the concept

Hitler and Himmler came under the influence of theorists who believed that the surface of the earth is actually the concave inner surface of a spherical bubble surrounded by solid rock, and the sky is a cloud of blue gas in the center of the sphere. In 1942, Hitler sent radar and infrared radiation experts to the Baltic Sea island of Rügen to scan the skies for the British fleet. *Author's collection* dates back to the nineteenth century. "Vril" is actually a word coined by the British novelist Edward Bulwer-Lytton, the author of *The Last Days of Pompeii*. (He also coined the notorious opening line, "It was a dark and stormy night.") In his 1871 novel *The Coming Race,* Bulwer-Lytton concocted Vril as an energy force. It was possessed by a race of beings who could have readily been concocted by a committee whose members included Guido von List, Jörg Lanz von Liebenfels, Madame Helena Blavatsky, Alfred Rosenberg, Karl Maria Wiligut, and, of course, Heinrich Himmler. These "coming race" beings had it all. Called "Vril-ya," they were a powerful breed of supermen and superwomen, and they lived inside a hollow earth. Not unlike List's Armanen or Wiligut's Irminen, they were the descendants of a primeval superrace.

In the late nineteenth century, many of Madame Blavatsky's Theosophists thought that Bulwer-Lytton was actually revealing a secret truth in his novel. It didn't hurt that the author made reference to the work of many real nineteenth-century scientists—from Charles Darwin's evolution studies to the electromagnetic research of Michael Faraday—using these people in the book as though they are characters.

Indeed, the Vril-ya can be seen as protoypical of many of the concepts of mystical superbeings that were popular in the counterculture of the late nineteenth and early twentieth century. (In the twenty-first century, there are still believers.) In fact, with its mental telepathy, body morphing, great battles, and naughty sex, *The Coming Race* reads like the script of any number of science-fiction fantasies that have emerged from Hollywood.

It was indeed a dark and stormy night when Hitler and Himmler got their hands on the book and seized upon the line that reads, "If they ever emerged from these nether recesses into the light of day, they would, according to their own traditional persuasions of their ultimate destiny, destroy and replace our existent varieties of man."

Far more sinister than any Hollywood tragedy is how the Nazis brought their own, similar concept into reality. Willy Ley, the German aerospace engineer who had emigrated to the United States in 1937, wrote of an organization called the *Wahrheitsgesellschaft* (Society for Truth) that was "literally founded upon the novel. . . . [This organization,] which was more or less localized in Berlin, devoted its spare time looking for Vril."

Jacques Bergier and Louis Pauwels mention a similar "Vril Gesellshaft" that existed in Germany before the Nazis came to power, and they suggest that it may have been a subgroup of the Thule Gesellshaft. It had further been asserted that this society was founded, at least in part, by Rudolf Hess's old boss, the geographer Karl Haushofer.

In recent years, especially since the 1990s, there has been a notion swirling in print and across the world wide web that the Nazis had made contact with a heretofore unknown subterranean race that resembled the Vril-ya of Bulwar-Lytton's fiction, and that these beings introduced the Germans to "flying saucers." A corollary to this theory holds that the subterranean people actually originated on another planet. (Of course, modern popular mythology holds that flying saucers are of extraterrestrial origin, so by conventional esoteric logic, if there are flying saucers, they *cannot* have originated on earth.) The supposition in the modern theory connecting flying saucers and Vril is that the "secret base" where the Nazis interacted with this phenomena was in Antarctica. This interaction, it is theorized, is the reason for Captain Ritscher's visit to the ice continent in 1939.

The term "flying saucer" actually entered the lexicon of pop culture in 1947, the same year as the American expedition to Antarctica led by Admiral Byrd and two years after the fall of the Third Reich. On June 24 of that year, a private pilot named Kenneth Arnold spotted mysterious flying objects near Mount Rainier in Washington State, describing them as appearing like "saucers" being "skipped across water." This "sighting" begat media attention, which begat copycat "sightings," which begat more media attention and a public outcry that the U.S. Air Force should look into the matter. After such a look, the air force shrugged off the sighted objects as "unidentified flying objects," and the acronym "UFO" became a permanent part of the pop-culture lexicon.

Unknown to Arnold or the news media of the late 1940s was that less than three years earlier, disc-shaped aircraft of a much more earthly kind may have been flying in the skies over Europe. An often repeated, but never confirmed, legend holds that a disc-shaped, gyroscopically stabilized German aircraft not only flew, but also exceeded the sound barrier in a test flight near Prague in February 1945. The February 1989 issue of the German periodical *Flugzeug* contains what is alleged to be an eyewitness account from a person who saw disc-shaped aircraft at Praha-Kbely airport (Prag-Gbell in German) near Prague. This is only one of many unsubstantiated stories of German experiments with advanced, disc-shaped aircraft of this type during the war. Today the term "Vril" usually comes up in references to German UFOs, and vice versa.

This brings us around to that recent addition to conspiracy theory that suggests that scientists running one or more of the flying-saucer projects had escaped to Antarctica in the spring of 1945. Here, as the story goes, they continued to operate their aircraft from a secret underground facility in Neuschwabenland at a location surveyed by Captain Ritscher in 1939. Operation Highjump, the well-documented, fifteen-ship U.S. Navy expedition to Antarctica under the command of Admiral Richard Byrd in 1947 is thought by conspiracy theorists to have been a cover for a mission to attack this secret Nazi "flying-saucer base" at the South Pole.

Just as there is no evidence that the Nazis communed with beings from within the hollow earth, there is nothing to establish that they were in touch with beings from other worlds. (Even though General Heinz Guderian did say that Heinrich Himmler "seemed like a man from another planet.")

As with the archeological theories of Gustaf Kossinna, and with scientific theories throughout history, artifacts and data can be manipulated and interpreted to say whatever the scientist or pseudoscientist wants them to say—and there will almost always be true believers of any unfounded theory.

As with the dogma of Adolf Hitler, and with political doctrines throughout history, political doctrines, too, can also be manipulated and interpreted to promise whatever the honey-tongued politicians want them to—and there will almost always be true believers who think they are right.

Germany, the nation that had produced so many Nobel laureates and led the world in many aspects of technology, had slipped into an epoch of scientific and political prevarication. As Edward Bulwer-Lytton might have said, the era of the Third Reich was the darkest of dark and stormy nights.

CHAPTER 22

The Reich and Its Stormy Night

KARL PÄTEL WROTE in his 1955 book *The SS in The Third Reich,* "Ten months before the end, the SS finally had Germany in its grip. In 1944–1945, no agency of the economy, the State or the Party could stand in the way of the SS. The Order had taken possession, sometimes openly, sometimes more discreetly, of all power. All that was not part of it was, in its view, no more than an instrument. At the end of 1944, there were only two men who mattered in Germany: Adolf Hitler and Heinrich Himmler."

As head of both the SS and the Gestapo, Himmler was still the police chief of occupied Europe. He also commanded the reserve army under the direct order of the Führer. He ran both the Abwehr and the Ministry of the Interior, as well as the *Stabshauptamt des Reichskommissars für die Festigung des Deuthscen Volkstums* (High Office of Reich Commissioners for the Strengthening of Germanism).

At Posen in 1943, Heinrich Himmler still had the optimism to look ahead. He was still planning for victory. He told his men that with the war out of the way, "We begin our work. When the war will end, we do not know. The end can come suddenly, or the war may last for a long time: We will see that then. But I forecast to you today, already, if suddenly the armistice and peace come, nobody can believe that he can fall into the sleep of the fair one. Adjust also all your commanders, your SS leaders to it. Only then, my gentlemen, we will *become alive.*"

Hermann Göring (1893–1946) was one of the most imposing figures of the Third Reich, both because of his physical size and his pompous presence. He was as visible in the halls of power as Himmler was a man of the shadows. He commanded the Luftwaffe and held ministerial portfolios from aviation to forestry. He ruled the state of Prussia, and he imagined himself as Hitler's heir apparent.

U.S. National Archives

The idea of the SS "coming alive" certainly thrilled the Reichsführer. Indeed, he was impatient to have the war out of the way so that he could indulge his passion of building his Germanic order into a supranational elite. He promised, "I will wake the whole SS in such a way, I will keep you so fundamentally awake that we can go then immediately to the structure of Germany. In the Allgemeine SS, the Germanic work will begin immediately."

Still on Himmler's mind was the importance of indoctrinating the SS, and future generations of the SS, to the Armanen, Irminen, and Nordic ancestors from which their precious blood had flowed. He believed that only with a firm understanding of this lineage could the SS men fulfill their destiny to be the *Fürungsschict* (Guidance Layer), the superior guiding elite for all of Europe. He told them:

If the peace is final, then we will be able to go to our great future work. We will settle [the occupied lands]. We will instill the laws of the SS Order to [our children]. I regard it as inevitably necessary in the life of our peoples that we not only teach our grandchildren and future generations of our ancestors, but rather teach them how it feels as part of our nature. . . . It must be natural that from [our SS] Order, from this racially superior upper strata of the Germanic people, the most numerous offspring come. The SS must be able in 20 to 30 years, to impose a Fürungsschict over all of Europe. In the east, the SS, as well as the farmers, will work together to operate the settlements. . . . In 20 years, we will push the national boundary of the Reich eastward by 500 kilometers.

In 1943, Himmler could still excitedly picture the SS as the guardians of that eastern frontier—indeed, as the masters of that expansive, 500-kilometer swath.

"I asked the Führer that the SS—if we end the war with our task and our obligation fulfilled—gets the privilege to hold the easternmost German border as a military border," he confided. "I believe that we alone have this privilege, as we do not have a competitor. I believe that nobody will deny us this privilege. . . . [This will] come only to us, because it is [our noble destiny] and because the black uniform will be naturally very attractive in peacetime."

By the end of 1944, however, it was clear that were black uniforms to be attracting attention, it would never be in that 500-kilometer swath of Russia that Himmler had planned to rule as his destiny. This swath was no longer ruled by the Reich.

For Heinrich Himmler and his fellow Nazi leaders, 1944 would develop into a year of worry, a long, hard epoch of bad news. If, as Winston Churchill had pointed out, 1942 had marked the end of World War II's beginning, then there is no doubt that 1944 was the beginning of the end. In a matter of weeks after his October 1943 speech at Posen, Himmler's precious Hegewald was gone, overrun by the Red Army. His "great piece of colonization," his model Völksdeutsche human experimental farm in Ukraine, was no more.

As the year began, the Eastern Front was still deep within the Soviet Union. At the end of the year, the Red Army had rolled the Wehrmacht and the Waffen SS out of the Soviet Union and back into Poland, Hungary, Romania, and Slovakia.

In Italy, the Wehrmacht and the Waffen SS began the year of 1944 bleeding the Allies dry on the apparently invulnerable Gustav Line south of Rome. However, during the year, the Allies had liberated Rome and pushed the Germans into defensive positions along the Gothic Line, far to the north.

In Western Europe, the year had begun with the Third Reich in solid control of all their Blitzkrieg conquests of 1940. The Oberkommando Wehrmacht was certain that their Atlantic Wall fortifications would prevent the "weak-kneed" Americans and British from being able to invade France. However, on June 6 of that "beginning-of-the-end" year, the Allies had indeed invaded France, and they had come to stay. By the end of September, thanks to Gen. George Patton's United States Third Army having conquered more territory in a shorter time than any American army ever, most of France had been cleansed of Nazi hegemony.

It was a bitter paradox that the Reichsführer's ultimate consolidation of internal power finally came as the noose was about to be drawn tight around the perimeter of the Reich. Perhaps nowhere is the irony more evident than in Himmler's own portfolio of power.

For the previous decade, this portfolio had included Walther Darré's Rasse und Siedlungshauptamt (Race and Settlement Office), which guarded Aryan racial purity and proudly settled the limitless Eastern territories with the Völksdeutsche, who were intended to put down roots that would grow for a *thousand years.* However, his portfolio now also contained the Völksdeutsche Mittelstelle (Office for Repatriation of Ethnic Germans), whose mandate was to repatriate all of those hapless settlers who had lasted less than *three years* on the steppes of Russia and Ukraine. His proud Völkisch pioneers were now refugees, either rounded up by the Soviet Bolshevik equivalent of the SS Einsatzgruppen or running for their lives—westward, toward an imploding Reich, where the Völksdeutsche Mittelstelle would endeavor to resettle them for the second time in three years.

Even inside the Aryan paradise of the Reich itself, trouble brewed. Within Germany, the year 1944 was marked by a paradigm shift of discontent, which culminated most dramatically on July 20, 1944, when a bomb went off at Adolf Hitler's *Wolfsschanze* (the Wolf's Lair) in Rastenburg, East Prussia (now Ketrzyn, Poland). One of several field headquarters, or *Führerhauptquartier,* used by Hitler during World War II, the Wolfsschanze was the one from which he had plotted and planned operations on the eastern front since Operation Barbarossa. The detonation of the bomb was the culmination of Operation Valkyrie, a long-running assassination plot aimed at removing Hitler permanently. Valkyrie involved a large number of military officers, who were at the crest of the wave of discontent that had come as the Wehrmacht began suffering an epidemic of serious reversals on the eastern front since the end of 1943. Notable among the conspirators were General Ludwig Beck, former chief of the general stall of the Oberkommando des Heeres (Army High Command), who had been earmarked by the plotters to replace Hitler as head of state.

The assassination failed, but Hitler was badly shaken, both physically and emotionally. The latter was arguably the worst, especially when he saw how many people were involved in the conspiracy. The breadth of the conspiracy, more than the blast itself, illustrated that Hitler's bubble had burst. The cult of Führer worship that had brought him to power a decade earlier had largely evaporated. The roster of conspirators, especially among the Wehrmacht officer corps, was sobering. How deep into the Nazi hierachy the plot went has been the topic of numerous studies, but suffice it to say that by German records, a total of 4,980 people, most of them professional soldiers, were tortured and executed—by Heinrich Himmler's Gestapo. A few, including national hero Erwin Rommel, were allowed to commit suicide. Ludwig Beck failed in his own suicide attempt and was shot.

If Hitler had not seen it coming, he was one of the few in the Reich who hadn't.

Heinrich Himmler had picked up on the discontent. He had only to look at the reports marked *Geheime!* (secret) that crossed his desk periodically from the SD. Brigadeführer Walther Schellenberg's SD snoops throughout Germany's empire were submitting reports that were distilled into "Report from the Reich" intelligence assessments. On April 6, 1944, Himmler had read, "In this uneasy period of waiting for invasion and retribution and also for a change of fortunes in the East, many are wondering what would happen if we could no longer hold out. People are

Heinrich Himmler looks up from his work. "One man at least, believed in this specious story of SS omnipotence—its own Grand Master," wrote Heinz Höhne of the Reichsführer's outlook in 1944. "In a sort of ecstasy he proclaimed in August 1944: 'What we are waging now is a sacred war of the people.'"
U.S. National Archives

asking themselves whether the many severe sacrifices and hardships which the war demands and will continue to demand are worth it. . . . [P]eople are gradually beginning to long for peace."

A few weeks later, on April 20, the SD's Report from the Reich informed the Reichsführer SS, "The continual pressure, alarm at developments in the East and the continually deferred hope of 'a saving miracle' are gradually producing signs of weariness among the people. In general people are 'fed to the back teeth' with the war. Desire for a rapid end to the war is everywhere very great."

As Heinz Höhne later summarized in *The Order of the Death's Head: The Story of Hitler's SS:*

> Those of the SS leaders who read these secret SD reports must inevitably have wondered what would become of the SS on the day when everything in which they had believed collapsed. The SS leaders had long since begun to think about the unthinkable. To many the thought of Germany without Hitler no longer seemed revolutionary. The war had demolished many of their illusions; the daily grind of the regime and above all the Eastern campaign had destroyed the old identity of view between Adolf Hitler and his SS. Even the SS leaders could no longer evade the question with which every person in authority found himself confronted in 1944—whether to allow the country to be completely wrecked for the sake of a criminal regime.

There was already a groundswell of opposition to Hitler growing even within the SS itself. It was growing in small patches, like mold spores on a piece of bread. The senior leadership of the Waffen SS, like that of the Wehrmacht, would have been happy to see Hitler gone, although as SS men, they had sworn a personal oath and would firmly oppose assassination. Gruppenführer Arthur Nebe, a former Kripo officer who had run Einsatzgruppe B in the East, was the centerpiece of the only contingent of SS men involved in the July 20 conspiracy. Nebe was among those arrested and executed.

Himmler had emerged from July 20 more powerful than ever. As Heinz Höhne wrote, "Himmler's power was in fact such that even at the time many

In November 1944, it was Heinrich Himmler, not Hermann Göring, who stood in for the Führer at the annual anniversary commemoration of the Beer Hall Putsch. Each year, Adolf Hitler had made a point of returning to Munich in triumph to gloat about the ultimate success of his revolution. In 1944, he wasn't feeling so triumphant and sent the Reichsführer SS in his stead. Left to right in the row behind Himmler are Field Marshal Wilhelm Keitel, chief of the Oberkommando Wehrmacht (with the baton); Franz Xaver Schwarz, Nazi Party treasurer and Reichsschatzmeister (national treasurer); and Wilhelm Frick, former minister of the Interior, who had been named protector of Bohemia and Moravia. *U.S. National Archives*

succumbed to the belief that, behind the aging and decaying Hitler, he alone was responsible for holding the disintegrating regime together. Late in 1944 the world press from Stockholm to San Francisco carried the headline 'Himmler—Dictator of Germany.' Anyone who did not have personal experience of the gruesome and grotesque realities of National Socialism's final phase may be forgiven for thinking that, in its last months, Hitler's Germany was ruled from the SS barracks."

Within those barracks still reigned the belief in the mystical power of the Black Knights who *could* still snatch victory from the jaws of defeat. Indeed, on December 16, the world got a small taste of how much fight the Wehrmacht and Waffen SS still had left in them. Operation *Wacht am Rhein* (Watch on the Rhine) caught the Americans by surprise, violently punching a hole in their lines and sending them reeling. Four German armies flowed into the famous "bulge" behind the previous American lines. Among these was the Sixth SS Panzer Army, under Obergruppenführer Sepp Dietrich. Created on October 26, it was spearheaded by Kampfgruppe Peiper of the 1st SS Panzer Division under the command of Obersturmbannführer Joachim Peiper and

Gudrun Himmler at the age of fifteen. Interned by the British during her later teens, she emerged from captivity as an angry and unrepentant Nazi. A lifelong disciple of her father and still a follower of his cause in the twenty-first century, she was referred to during the postwar years as a "Schillernde Nazi Prinzessin" ("dazzling Nazi princess").

U.S. National Archives

was comprised of veteran Waffen SS divisions, such as Dietrich's old Leibstandarte Adolf Hitler.

Though the Americans recovered and pushed the Germans back again, the Battle of the Bulge badly mauled the Yanks, cost them close to 100,000 casualties, and delayed their offensive into the Reich by more than a month. For a time, it also frightened the Allies and greatly heartened the German leadership. It gave men such as Hitler and Himmler the optimism they needed to keep on believing that the war would end with a favorable armistice.

How had Heinrich Himmler *really* pictured the way the war might end?

Himmler had always predicted that World War II would end in German victory, but even in 1944, he imagined a fate no worse than the way that World War I had ended—a negotiated armistice with armies in place and with Germany's borders unviolated. Apparently, Himmler could not conceive of what the Allies meant by the doctrine of Unconditional Surrender that had been articulated at the Casablanca Conference in January 1943.

At Posen, Himmler still could not imagine that German forces would ever lose all of the land that they had captured within the Soviet Union during Operation Barbarossa—much less that Allied armies would ever set foot inside Germany. In the Posen speech, he had told his Black Knights that when World War II was over, "we will bring the equipment and the best training of the Waffen SS into all our [SS components]. Then we continue working in the first half year after the war, as though the next large-scale attack may begin the next day. It will be very relevant in the negotiations for an armistice or peace, if Germany has an operational reserve, an operational weight of 20, 25 or 30 intact SS divisions."

He was picturing a powerful Germany—still dictating terms, even if not totally victorious—thanks to the power of the Aryan supermen of his SS. Specially selected and specially endowed with an Aryan blood line stretching back to the Armanen god-kings, they were—or so they believed—an invincible warrior race that *would* snatch victory from the jaws of defeat.

A year later, did they still believe that this was possible?

Himmler did. As Heinz Höhne wrote, "One man at least, believed in this specious story of SS omnipotence—its own Grand Master. To him it seemed that the hour had come when he could purge National Socialist Germany of all 'treachery' and all doubts, of those satanic powers which, in his distorted view, had so far prevented Germany's final victory. In a sort of ecstasy he proclaimed in August 1944: 'What we are waging now is a sacred war of the people.'"

The arrests and executions that followed the July 20 bombing served their purpose. Whatever discontent there had been in the ranks of Wehrmacht or Waffen SS on July 19, it went back in the box as the dust settled at the Wolf's Lair. The arrests and executions succeeded in putting a lid on active dissent within the armed forces, which made operations such as Wacht am Rhein possible.

Elsewhere though, it was a different story.

Himmler's own house was beginning to unravel. The Ahnenerbe, largely forgotten by the Reichsführer amid the exigencies of war and a failed coup, was essentially dissolving. At the Reichsuniversität Strassburg, the Ahnenerbe's Institut für Wehrwissenschaftliche Zweckforschung (Institute for Military Scientific Research) was closing up shop. Two years earlier at the Reichsuniversität, Dr. August Hirt and Bruno Beger had been devoting themselves to medical experiments that had required that around 100 bodies be collected. On Himmler's orders, SS Standartenführer Wolfram Sievers had been personally involved in seeing to it that these bodies were delivered. Now the presence of these bodies at the Reichsuniversität was seen as a growing liability. What would the approaching Americans and Frenchmen say if they found these "specimens"?

Wolfram Sievers, the Ahnenerbe business manager, was nervous and fearful for his own future. On September 5, 1944, as the Allied armies were racing across France and closing in on Alsace, Sievers sent a message to SS Sturmbannführer Rudolf Brandt, Himmler's personal aide:

> According to the proposal of [February 9, 1942] and your approval of [February 23, 1942, referencing Document Number] AR/493/37, Prof. Dr. Hirt has assembled the skeleton collection which was previously non-existent. Because of the vast amount of scientific research connected therewith, the job of reducing the corpses to skeletons has not yet been completed. Since it might require some time, Hirt requested 80 copies of the directives pertaining to the treatment of the collection stored in the morgue of the Anatomical Institute, in case Strassburg should be endangered. The Collection can be defleshed and thereby rendered unidentifiable. This, however, would mean that at least part of the whole work had been done for nothing and that this singular collection would be lost to science, since it would be impossible to make plaster casts afterwards. The skeleton collection as such is inconspicuous. The flesh parts could be declared as having been left by the French at the time we took over the Anatomical Institute and would be turned over for cremating.

Sievers then asked Brandt what the next course of action should be, naming three options: "(1) The collection as a whole is to be preserved; (2) The collection is to be dissolved in part; (3) The collection is to be completely dissolved." Despite his fears, Sievers was torn over the issue of letting all of that "research material" go to waste. Such was the mindset of those within the Ahnenerbe. Even when the difference between right and wrong did finally dawn on him, Sievers could not let go of his arrogant Ariosophy.

Nevertheless, when Brandt visited Sievers at his operational headquarters on October 21, Sievers told him, "The collection in Strassburg had been completely dissolved in the meantime in conformance with the directive given him at the time. He [Sievers] is of the opinion that this arrangement is for the best in view of the whole situation."

Sievers was lying.

According to Frederick Kasten, in his article "Unethical Nazi Medicine in Annexed Alsace Lorraine," which appeared in George Kent's 1991 book *Historians and Archivists: Essays in Modern German History and Archival Policy,* the skeletons, many still with their flesh intact, remained in Strasbourg as the Ahnenerbe researchers scampered away. He also notes that, some years after the war, they were dissected by French medical students, who had no idea how they came to be at the university.

Bruno Beger wound up in the Waffen SS and spent the latter part of 1944 in the Balkans, stamping out partisans even as the Red Army approached. Early in 1945, he was transferred to the Wolgatatarische Legion, then on the collapsing German positions in northern Italy. Perhaps it was fitting that the proud, Ariosophist SS man who had spent the year before the war measuring the skulls of Central Asians should have ended the war surrounded by Central Asians wearing the uniform of the Third Reich.

By now, Ahnenerbe president Walther Wüst had exiled Beger's old Tibet companion, Ernst Schäfer, to the mountains of the Obersalzberg. Wüst had created a new institute, using Sven Hedin, the prestigious old Swedish Central Asia explorer, as a figurehead. He then assigned Schäfer to run the Sven Hedin Institute for Innerasian Research out of Schloss Mittersill, a mountaintop castle overlooking the Obersalzburg's Pinzgau Valley.

Early in 1945, as the Ahnenerbe staff begin abandoning Widmayerstrasse like rats fleeing from a sinking ship, forgetting all about Schloss Mittersill, Ernst Schäfer got in touch with the Academy of Natural Sciences in Philadelphia. He proposed that they might want to take over the Sven Hedin Institute after the war, which Schäfer expected would be very soon. Brooke Dolan II, who had headed Schäfer's first Tibet expedition in 1931 was associated with the academy, and Schäfer thought that he had an in.

He didn't.

Dolan was out of town, doing clandestine work for the United States government in the Far East. After having made a secret visit to Tibet during World War II, Dolan would die in a mysterious plane crash behind Japanese lines in China in August 1945.

In the meantime, Schäfer had been able, at least, to avoid the increasing number of Allied air raids that blasted Munich. And the Alpine Obersalzberg reminded him a little of Tibet and of the good old days before the noose was pulled tight.

CHAPTER 23

Götterdämmerung

I T HAS LONG BEEN a favorite metaphor to describe the end of the Third Reich as "Götterdämmerung," the "Twilight of the Gods," that is epitomized so dramatically in the opera of the same name that concludes Richard Wagner's *Ring of the Nibelungen,* the operatic cycle that had been so inspirational to Heinrich Himmler and his pagan elite.

Wagner had based his opera on the ancient story from the Eddas known as the *Ragnarök,* or *Ragnarökkr,* which is translated into modern German as Götterdämmerung. The Ragnarök tells the tale of a titanic battle in which the gods Thor, Freyr, Heimdall, and even Wotan himself are killed—hence the term "Twilight of the Gods." Snorri Sturluson includes the story in his twelfth-century Prose Edda, and it is a recurring theme wherever Nordic mythology is examined in depth.

In the Wagnerian opera, *Götterdämmerung* is the climactic moment in which the Valkyrie Brünnhilde orders an immense funeral pyre for her deceased heroic lover, Siegfried. Having sent Wotan's ravens home to roost, she rides into the funeral pyre herself. She and Siegfried are consumed by fire. As she immolates herself, the Ring of the Nibelungen, which Brünnhilde is wearing, is cleansed of its curse and is afterward reclaimed by the Rhine Maidens. This completes the cycle, as the Rhine Maidens were present at the beginning of *Das Rheingold,* the first opera of the Ring Cycle.

According to the memoirs of Albert Speer, the Reich's minister of armaments, the final performance by the Berlin Philharmonic Orchestra before they were evacuated from the city in 1945 was of Brünhilde's immolation scene, at the climax of Wagner's *Götterdämmerung*. It was an appropriate choice. If 1944 had been, to paraphrase Winston Churchill again, the "beginning of the end" for the Third Reich, then 1945 was its final descent into a fiery immolation. The most symbolic scene of the real-life immolation of the Reich came in January, when Allied bombers over Berlin scored a hit on Number 8 Prinz-Albrechtstrasse, once the most feared address in Europe, blowing it to rubble.

Within weeks of the beginning of the year, Allied armies had crossed the borders of prewar Germany on all sides. By March, the Americans had reached the Rhine, the mother river of German identity and of the Wagner Ring Cycle. On March 7, the U.S. Army's 9th Infantry Division captured and crossed the Ludendorff Bridge at Remagen, a few miles south of Bonn. Within a couple of days, the better part of three divisions had become the first Allied troops to cross the Rhine with dry feet.

Meanwhile, the Soviet armies on the eastern front, which had been more than 600 miles east of Berlin a year earlier, were now closing in on the German capital. Adolf Hitler was desperately ordering the creation and deployment of new divisions and new armies—both real and imaginary.

One of the real ones would be the source of Heinrich Himmler's last moment of glory as a military commander. On January 24, Hitler put Himmler in command of *Heeresgruppe Weichsel* (Army Group Vistula), an amalgam of German forces that were put in place to try to stop the Red Army at Poland's broad Vistula River, a natural barrier about 200 miles east of Berlin. Army chief of staff Heinz Guderian had originally urged Hitler to put this last-ditch-effort group under Wehrmacht control, but the paranoid Hitler no longer trusted the Wehrmacht. He wanted the Black Knights of the SS to spearhead the final miracle defense of his capital and his Reich.

On February 12, Himmler was on the cover of *Time* magazine, his grim visage above a pair of crossed bones, a totenkopf motif. Calling him "the Man Who Can't Surrender," the magazine said, "Clearly or dimly, most Germans realized that Himmler was the new master of the Third Reich. Last October, Himmler himself had told how Germany would be defended: 'Every village, every house, every farm, every ditch, every forest and every bush.' As Adolf Hitler's longtime

chief butcher, torturer, spy and slavemas-
ter, Heinrich Himmler is the archetype
of the top Nazi who cannot surrender.
Now, while keeping Hitler as the Führer
symbol, Himmler does the dictator's job
of maintaining Germany at war. Around
himself and his henchmen he has formed
the last granite-hard core of German
resistance."

Many diehard German officers,
especially SS officers, were ordering
their troops to fight to the last man,
while elsewhere, the order of the day was
"every man for himself."

On March 31, about 100 miles due
east of the Rhine and 100 miles northeast of the Remagen bridgehead, SS
Sturmbannführer Heinz Macher was
following orders. Heinrich Himmler
had personally ordered Macher to do

the unthinkable: destroy the most sacred shrine of the
Schutzstafel. Macher and his fifteen-man demolition team
had arrived at the SS Schule Haus Wewelsburg that morning with a partial truckload of explosives—as much as they
were able to scrounge on short notice. They had stopped by
the local fire department in Wewelsburg village, and Macher
had told them to expect to see smoke and flames. He then
ordered them to *ignore* the smoke and flames. This immolation scene had been ordered by the Reichsführer himself.

With that, they went to work. The unfinished institute,
which was intended to be the seat of Aryan higher learning
for a thousand years, met an ignoble end. The guardhouse

In 1945, Wilfried Nagal
painted this impression of the
untermenschen from the East
descending upon the Reich,
pushed forward by death himself.
In Nagal's fantasy, and that
of many Nazis, this was the
nightmare struggle between East
and West about which Karl Maria
Wiligut had warned Heinrich
Himmler a decade earlier.
U.S. Army art collection

The SS Ehrenring (SS Honor Ring) was better known as the "Totenkopfring" because of the death's head that was placed at the center. It was conceived by Heinrich Himmler as a means of recognizing the founding members of the SS, but it was eventually awarded to most senior SS leaders. His signature is engraved on the inside.
Photo by Kris Simoens, used by permission

and southeast tower were rocked by explosions. The team ran out of explosives before they could finish the job, so they turned to fire, one of those primal elements that had been celebrated in pagan rites during Wewelsburg's halcyon days. Files were heaped into bonfires, and soon the building itself was engulfed in flames.

Himmler had earlier proclaimed that all the Totenkopfrings of the SS dead be returned to this Aryan Valhalla, where they would be enshrined for a thousand years. Some of the estimated 9,000 rings that were at Wewelsburg that morning had been here for less than a year when Macher went to the place where the rings were kept. He took them into the Niederhagen forest and buried them. As the story goes, they are still where he put them.

Two days later, when elements of the U.S. Army's 3rd Infantry Division reached the site, the smoldering ruins of the gutted Schloss Wewelsburg had been thoroughly looted by local people. Around forty people who were still at the nearby Niederhagen concentratuion camp were set free.

Meanwhile, *Time* magazine had related in its Himmler cover story the fascinating rumor that Himmler was planning a massive guerrilla war after Germany's defeat. The magazine asserted that the Reichsführer SS

spends much time picking obscure but fanatical Nazis for his guerrilla army. Some have been planted in concentration camps, to pose as anti-Nazis when the Allies take over. Others have been given identity cards taken from ordinary Germans killed in air raids, and from 30,000 people associated with the old Weimar Republic who were recently purged. Thus equipped, the chosen Nazis can merge into the general population without detection. Hitler Youth are being trained in underground techniques in three schools known as Ordensburgen, and in a postgraduate institution called the Führer Schule, at Chiem See in

Bavaria. The guerrilla army already numbers more than 500,000; the 'general staff' has been picked.

The rumor was far from the truth.

The SS was filled with men who expected to go down with the ship, but there were also realists. Just as Himmler himself harbored fantasies of a negotiated armistice that would allow the SS to remain intact, Walther Schellenberg of the SD had been acting on similar fantasies. As Heinz Höhne writes:

> As early as autumn 1941 he had begun cautiously and tentatively to probe the possibilities of a separate peace with the Western Allies and for this purpose he used a circle of anti-Nazi resisters, who, using international channels, had been carrying on confidential discussions with the Allies or with pro-Allied foreigners ever since the outbreak of war. There were many curiously fortuitous connections between these anti-Nazis and SS headquarters. Dr. Carl Langbehn, for instance, a Berlin attorney and a member of the [July 20 plotters], was in contact with Himmler via his daughter who was a school friend of Himmler's daughter, Gudrun.

Some months before the noose tightened in the late winter of 1945, Schellenberg had approached Himmler, obliquely asking him about his own thoughts on how the war might be ended, now that total victory was out of the question. Himmler was taken aback at such talk, which SS doctrine considered blasphemy, but he neither arrested nor executed the SD boss. Instead, he listened as Schellenberg suggested that it might be possible to exploit the deep divisions between the Anglo-American Allies and the Soviet Union.

As Höhne writes, Himmler had actually begun

> toying with the alluring thought that, should the war situation worsen, his mission might be to replace Hitler and bring peace to Germany and the world. The idea had flashed through his mind and he had, as quickly, put it behind him—the Reichsführer SS could never be unfaithful to the 'greatest

brain of all time' [as Himmler referred to the Führer]. But the insidious thought returned again and again. . . . That Himmler, the agent of the most gruesome crimes of the century should seriously have believed that the world would be prepared to regard him as a peace negotiator, today seems a fantastic idea. At the time, however, things looked different; people [such as Schellenberg] wished to see Himmler at the conference table precisely because they believed he had the power.

Through Schellenberg and Felix Kersten—who had moved his family out of Germany to neutral Sweden in 1943—Heinrich Himmler began a dialog with Count Folke Bernadotte of Wisborg, a wealthy Swedish nobleman who was no stranger to the Third Reich. In his role as vice president of the Swedish Red Cross, he had made a number of visits to Germany, where he had been successful in negotiating the release of around 30,000 people, mainly Scandinavian nationals, from concentration camps.

They first met on February 18 at the Hohenlychen SS sanatorium near Ravensbrück, about fifty-five miles north of Berlin. Bernadotte's recollections of Himmler provide a portrait of a man still very much in control and very confident of the outcome of World War II. The physical description is of the slight man who had trouble with athletics as a boy. Emotionally, though, he was optimistically cocky and relishing his own sick, off-color jokes. Bernadotte described Himmler as having "small, well-shaped and delicate hands, and they were carefully manicured, although this was forbidden in the SS. He was also, to my great surprise, extremely affable. He gave evidence of a sense of humor, tending rather to the macabre. . . . Certainly there was nothing diabolical in his appearance. Nor did I observe any sign of that icy hardness in his expression of which I had heard so much. Himmler . . . seemed a very vivacious personality, inclined to sentimentality where his relations with the Führer were concerned, and with a great capacity for enthusiasm."

When Bernadotte presented him with a gift, a seventeenth-century treatise on runic inscriptions in Scandinavia, Himmler was "noticeably affected."

Himmler ignored Schellenberg's earlier caution not to go off on any mystical tangents. The book had proven to be the catalyst for Himmler to excitedly lecture for about an hour on runic lore. Instead of discussing the dire state of affairs facing his Reich, Himmler became lost in time and space, as though thrown into a Listian trance at the very sight of these sacred runes.

This was, perhaps, the last lecture on the Armanen Futharkh ever to be delivered in Nazi Germany.

When they finally got down to business, each man had an agenda. Bernadotte wanted to talk Himmler out of as many Jewish Scandinavian camp inmates as possible, and Himmler wanted to talk about Bernadotte's brokering a deal with the Western Allies so that he could divert all the attention of the Reich to fighting the Red Army. Though Schellenberg recalled that Himmler had seemed favorably disposed to Bernadotte personally and hoped to maintain contact with him, no progress was made on either agenda item.

Over the coming weeks, Heeresgruppe Weichsel failed to stop the Red Army at the Vistula, and the Soviets began closing in on the Oder River, only about thirty miles east of Berlin. On March 20, Hitler finally ordered Himmler to relinquish command to the Wehrmacht. General Gotthard Heinrici took over the mission impossible, and Himmler returned to his intrigues.

When Bernadotte met the Reichsführer SS for a second time at Hohenlychen on April 2, the mood was different. Gone was the affable sense of locker-room humor and the happy talk of runes. Himmler was depressed and grew only more morose when Bernadotte told him that the Allies would probably not want to parley with the king of those concentration camps that they were only now starting to discover.

By the time that Himmler traveled to Berlin to toast the haggard and delusional Adolf Hitler on his fifty-sixth birthday on April 20, nearly everyone in the leadership of the Third Reich was talking about surrender. The only ones who still fully subscribed the fight-to-the-finish mentality were Martin Bormann and Josef Goebbels—but neither of them was actually doing any fighting. They were cowering with Führer in his bunker, deep beneath the Chancellory building, listening to Hitler's rants about imaginary armies, to bad news on the shortwave radio, and to the distant rumble of Soviet artillery.

Sipping champagne with Hitler and Himmler in the bunker that day were many of the notables of the Nazi regime. Bormann and Goebbels were there, of course, because they now lived here (Goebbels with his wife and their six children). So too were Hermann Göring, Joachim von Ribbentrop, Albert Speer, and Admiral Karl Dönitz, who now commanded both the largely nonexistent German navy and the armies defending northwest Germany.

Having seen his Führer for the last time, Himmler met with Bernadotte the following day and again on April 23. The count recalled him as now "spent and weary," as well as nervous and irritable. Nevertheless, Himmler did agree to several of Bernadotte's requests for releasing this or that group of prisoners to the Swedish Red Cross. Himmler also reiterated his willingness to surrender to the British and Americans, cautioning the count that he would *never* surrender to the Bolsheviks in the East. Bernadotte again told him that it was way too late for a separate peace deal, closed his briefcase, and departed.

He and Himmler would never again cross paths.

By now, Himmler was essentially a vagabond. Having abandoned Prinz-Albrechtstrasse and Berlin, he had held court for a time in Hohenlychen, but he had smelled the Red Army in the distance and moved on. By the last week of April, he, in his Mercedes, followed by his entourage of SS staff in cars and SS guards in trucks, were roaming northern Germany. They now numbered around 150, including SS bureaucrats and young women from his clerical staff. Among this entourage were SS Sturmbannführer Rudolf Brandt, the Reichsführer's personal aide, and Sturmbannführer Heinz Macher, who made that last official SS visit to Schloss Wewelsburg two months earlier.

By now, the entourage also included the old Ahnenerbe astrologer, Wilhelm Wulff, who was a friend of Felix Kersten. He made an odd addition given that in 1941, Himmler's Gestapo had briefly incarcerated every astrologer in the Reich for fear that they had influenced deputy Führer Rudolf Hess in his mysterious and never explained flight to Scotland that year. Hitler had been further opposed to astrology because it applied equally to all races, untermenschen as well as übermenschen. Himmler's mind, on the other hand, was open to the stars.

The convoy must have been an amazing sight—indeed, straight from a film by Federico Fellini—as they swaggered into this command post or that. Here was the erstwhile "most feared man in Europe," accompanied by his Ahnenerbe astrologer and his masseur, and surrounded by Black Knights in full SS regalia, complete with their silver-trimmed daggers dangling at their waists.

By April 28, Himmler was at Plön in Scheswig Holstein, where Dönitz had his headquarters. Here, the Reichsführer and the admiral sat down to talk about the future, together with Johann Ludwig Schwerin von Krosigk, a former Oxford Rhodes scholar, who had been the German minister of finance since 1932. They agreed that when, not if, Hitler was no more, they would all be willing to serve his successor. They also all agreed that Hitler would probably pass the torch to Himmler.

However, that same day, the news that Himmler had been talking to third parties about surrendering the Third Reich was picked up by the Western media and broadcast on the BBC. When Hitler heard this on his shortwave, he became furious and ordered Himmler arrested. This message did not reach Plön until late on April 30, along with word that Dönitz was designated as the Führer's successor.

By this time, though, a great deal had changed in the Führer's bunker in Berlin. Earlier in the day, Goebbels and his wife had murdered their six children and committed suicide. Meanwhile, Hitler had killed his dog, murdered Eva Braun, his longtime girlfriend and wife of one day, and then had committed suicide himself. Martin Bormann slipped out of the bunker, hoping to escape Berlin. Rumors swirled for decades that he had escaped, all the way to a comfortable retirement in South America. The conventional wisdom today is that he died on the streets in the Soviet shelling.

It has often been pointed out that the night of April 30 has special significance in the calendar of ancient Nordic paganism. It is Walpurgisnacht, the

night on which the witches dance with the gods in an age-old Germanic festi-
val celebrated with immense bonfires. Some say that the deaths in the Führer's
bunker represented a pagan self-sacrifice.

Exactly two decades had passed since April 30, 1925, when Adolf Hitler had
first severed his ties with Ernst Röhm, the man who had controlled his SA. This
break had underscored the Führer's need to develop Heinrich Himmler's SS into
an alternate party security apparatus. It was an eerie anniversary.

On May 1, 1945, the men in Plön finally learned the news from the bunker.
On the morning after Walpurgisnacht, the morning after Götterdämmerung,
as Dönitz pondered what he was to do as the Reich's new Führer, the Reichsführer was once again on the road. By now, the highways and muddy byways of
Germany were clogged with people. There were retreating soldiers and soldiers
racing to surrender to the Americans or British. There were civilians fleeing the
Soviets, and there were people who had lost their homes in bombing raids and
Allied artillery barrages. It seemed as though everyone were on the road, as
though everyone in Germany were a refugee.

At one point, Himmler considered, but rejected, the idea of taking his
convoy to seek refuge at Schloss Arolsen. This nearby castle was the family
home of Waffen SS General Josias Waldeck, the hereditary prince of Waldeck
and Pyrmont and a loyal Black Knight who had two years earlier enlisted two of
his daughters in the SS Helferinnenkorps.

During that same turbulent day, Himmler also learned that Count Schwerin
von Krosigk had now been named as foreign minister, so Himmler got in touch
with him with a scheme. Shortly after their biography of Heinrich Himmler was
published in 1965, Roger Manvell and Heinrich Fränkel were approached by the
count himself, who told them for the first time of his strange conversation with
Himmler on the evening of May 1. They had met on the road between Plön and
Eutin, where Himmler insisted that the new foreign minister ally Germany with
Britain and the United States, whereby Germany, *together* with the Allies, would
have "a splendid chance of expanding their eastern borders as far as the Urals."
They had, Himmler insisted, "never been so near to that most desirable aim of
German foreign policy."

Schwerin von Krosigk took Himmler aside and quietly suggested that he shave off his trademark mustache, lose the black uniform, and just try to slip away.

Himmler ignored him. Manvell and Fränkel wrote, "Himmler seemed utterly unable to grasp realities; he was convinced that his own future as 'the second man in the Dönitz administration' was assured." The Reichsführer told Schwerin von Krosigk, "All I want is a brief chat with Montgomery and Eisenhower. It should be easy enough to convince them that I and my SS are an indispensable Ordnungsfaktor [guarantee of law and order] in the struggle against Bolshevism."

Himmler was, however, totally out of the loop.

The following day, May 2, the German armies in Italy surrendered unconditionally, and General Helmuth Weidling, the commander of the Berlin Defense Area, surrendered the capital to Soviet general Vasily Chuikov. By then, most of what was left in Berlin after the American and British air assault had been blown to bits by Red Army artillery.

DÖNITZ—WITHOUT HIMMLER'S KNOWLEDGE—had already begun putting out peace feelers of his own, trying to contact British field marshal Bernard Montgomery, the commander of the Allied 21st Army Group, which was then closing in on Schleswig Holstein from the west. Two days later, he and Montgomery concluded a deal, whereby Dönitz officially surrendered all the German forces in Denmark, the Netherlands, and northwestern Germany. Having surrendered explicitly to Montgomery, Führer Dönitz was indulging his own unrealistic fantasies about setting up a provisional government at his new command post in Flensberg, near the Danish border.

In the meantime, Himmler and his unwieldy caravan had caught up with Dönitz again. He now fully expected a ministerial role for himself in the so-called Flensburg Government, but on May 6, Dönitz dealt him the final, crushing blow. A man whose role in the government of the Third Reich only a few weeks early had been nonexistent personally handed the Reichsführer SS a memo that read: "In view of the present situation, I have decided to dispense with your further assistance as Reich Minister of the Interior and member of the Reich Government, as Commander-in-Chief of the Reserve Army, and as chief of the Police. I now regard all your offices as abolished. I thank you for the service which you have given to the Reich."

In the space of less than a week, Heinrich Himmler had been fired by *two* Führers; had his astrologer predicted that alignment of dark stars? As Himmler now looked around him, he saw his entourage melting away. It was now every SS bureaucrat for him- or herself.

The wheels of total surrender were already in motion. In the wee hours of the morning of May 7 in Rheims, France, under Dönitz's orders, the Oberkommando Wehrmacht chief of staff, Gen. Alfred Jodl, sat down at the headquarters of the Supreme Allied commander, Gen. Dwight Eisenhower, and signed the unconditional surrender paperwork that surrendered all German forces to the Allies. A similar surrender was inked later in the day in Berlin by Field Marshal Wilhelm Keitel of the Oberkommando Wehrmacht and Soviet marshal Georgi Zhukov. World War II in Europe was officially over.

At last, on May 8, the day that the unconditional surrender took effect, Heinrich Himmler took Schwerin von Krosigk's advice and took a razor to his upper lip.

As it hit the road, the Himmler entourage had dwindled to just a handful, including Brandt and Macher. They no longer swaggered, these SS men, nor did they sport the regalia of Black Knights. Having changed clothes, they were just a few more frightened refugees who had discarded the proud trappings of a sacred order that was supposed to have lasted a thousand years.

Heinrich Himmler, the former "most feared man in Europe," had even discarded his ID and now carried the papers of someone else. Ironically, they were those of a man named Heinrich Hitzinger, whose execution Himmler had once ordered. Himmler even got his hands on an eyepatch to use to disguise his identity.

Heading westward, the men abandoned their Mercedes when they reached the Elbe River and paid a man with a boat to shuttle them across—for 500 reichsmarks a head. For the next two weeks, they roamed the countryside, scrounging for food and sleeping in the dirt.

Nearly three decades earlier, when he was a young man, Heinrich Himmler had spent another postwar summer down on the farm. Flushed with Völkisch enthusiasm, he had gotten the rich dark Germanic soil under his fingernails, and he had loved it. He was, for a brief moment, a city boy overwhelmed with the charm of rural life. He had even joined the brotherhood of the Artamanen Gesellschaft, and he had later owned a chicken farm. Now here he was, back to the rustic countryside of the Völkisch past, with no running water, no electricity, and no polished porcelain Prinz-Albrechtstrasse bathrooms.

On May 23, the day that Führer Dönitz finally surrendered his provisional "Flensberg Government" to the Allies and became just another prisoner himself, Himmler's little band of scruffy men reached a British checkpoint on a bridge near Bremervörde. Such checkpoints had been set up all across Germany for the expressed purpose of checking IDs, issuing Allied paperwork to genuine refugees, and snagging just such persons as the Reichsführer SS. Without Allied papers, refugees couldn't travel far, and to apply for papers at a checkpoint was to place yourself under Allied scrutiny. Himmler and his entourage submitted to the scrutiny, but instead of papers, they got a free ride to the civilian interrogation camp at Lüneburg.

"The first man to enter my office was small, ill-looking and shabbily dressed, but he was immediately followed by two other men, both of whom were tall and soldierly looking, one slim, and one well-built," recalled Captain Tom Selvester, the camp commandant, in his official after-action report, obtained by Manvell and Fränkel in the 1960s. "I sensed something unusual, and ordered one of my sergeants to place the two men in close custody, and not to allow anyone to speak to them without my authority. They were then removed from my office, whereupon the small man, who was wearing a black patch over his left eye, removed the patch and put on a pair of spectacles. His identity was at once obvious, and he said [he was] 'Heinrich Himmler' in a very quiet voice."

At this point, Selvester immediately put his office under armed guard and called in an intelligence officer. They proceeded to get a signature sample from Himmler, who refused at first because he erroneously thought they were asking for his *autograph!*

Next the British officers proceeded to strip-search the Reichsführer, looking for anything that their prisoner might be able to use to commit suicide.

"Himmler was carrying documents bearing the name of Heinrich Hitzinger, who I think was described as a postman," Selvester wrote.

In his jacket I found a small brass case, similar to a cartridge case, which contained a small glass phial [vial]. I recognized it for what it was, but asked Himmler what it contained, and he said, "That is my medicine. It cures stomach cramp." I also found a similar brass case, but without the phial, and came to the conclusion that the phial was hidden somewhere on the prisoner's person. When all Himmler's clothing had been removed and searched, all the orifices of his body were searched, also his hair combed and any likely hiding place examined, but no trace of the phial was found. At this stage he was not asked to open his mouth, as I considered that if the phial was hidden in his mouth and we tried to remove it, it might precipitate some action that would be regretted. I did however send for thick bread and cheese sandwiches and tea, which I offered to Himmler, hoping that I would see if he removed anything from his mouth. I watched him closely, whilst he was eating, but did not notice anything unusual.

When his clothes were taken away, Himmler was offered a British uniform, which was the only thing available, but he refused, claiming he feared being photographed in "enemy uniform." At last, he relented, but for some reason, refused to wear pants. As he sat there in shirt and underwear, someone offered him a blanket. Who wants to have to stare at a Reichsführer in his underwear, especially when you don't want to take your eyes off him because a vial of poison is missing?

Despite Selvester's concerns, Himmler did not appear suicidal.

"During the time Himmler was in my custody he behaved perfectly correctly, and gave me the impression that he realized things had caught up with him," the British captain wrote. "He was quite prepared to talk, and indeed at times appeared almost jovial. He looked ill when I first saw him, but improved tremendously after a meal and a wash (he was not permitted to shave). He was in my custody for approximately eight hours, and during that time, whilst not being interrogated, asked repeatedly about the whereabouts of his 'adjutants,' appearing genuinely worried over their welfare. I found it impossible to believe that he could be the arrogant man portrayed by the press before and during the war."

Colonel Michael Murphy, the chief of intelligence on General Montgomery's staff, arrived around 8 p.m. to escort the prisoner to Second Army Headquarters for interrogation. It was here that Heinrich Himmler bit down on the tiny, blue-glass potassium-cyanide capsule, which had been in his mouth the whole time. It was one of the capsules that had been developed by Dr. Sigmund Rascher, the zealous researcher from the Institut für Wehrwissenschaftliche Zweckforschung whose main stock in trade had been freezing people to death in the name of science.

Attempts to get Himmler to spit or vomit the poison were unsuccessful, as was the stomach pump that was brought in.

Heinrich Himmler himself was the last victim of the mad scientists of his own Ahnenerbe.

A cigarette butt and the body of the Reichsführer grow cold on the floor of the British interrogation room on May 23, 1945. Shortly after 8 p.m., Heinrich Himmler bit down on a tiny, blue-glass potassium cyanide capsule that he had hidden in his mouth. He is seen here wrapped in the blanket that he had been given after he had been strip-searched and then refused to wear pants. *U.S. National Archives*

CHAPTER 24

The Sands of Time

"**O**N THE FLOOR of an unfurnished room in a two-story brick house here there lay today the stark cold body of Heinrich Himmler, one of the arch criminals of Nazi Germany, chief of the SS," wrote correspondent James MacDonald in Heinrich Himmler's *New York Times* obituary, submitted "by wireless" and printed on the front page on May 25, 1945.

Two days later, the Sunday *New York Times* reported his funeral, saying simply, "The body of Heinrich Himmler was returned unceremoniously today to the soil of Germany that he stained with the blood of thousands of victims of his Gestapo."

Heinrich had died on July 2, 936. Heinrich died again, 1,008 years, ten months and twenty-one days later—for the last time.

On June 4, 1945, *Time* magazine, whose cover he had graced in February, wrote that "wherever he had travelled, death followed him like a shadow—and the shadow fell on many, at Maidanek, Oswiecim [Aushwitz], Buchenwald. 'You find people there,' he once said of his concentration camps, 'with hydrocephalus, cross-eyed and deformed ones . . . a lot of cheap trash. . . . [T]he prisoners are made up of slave souls.' On his last trip, from Berlin to Flensburg to the north German moors, his shadow caught up with him. Heinrich Himmler, whom his fellow Nazis had ironically nicknamed 'gentle Heinrich,' had shaved his Hitlerian mustache, replaced his scholarly pince-nez with a black eye patch. He had become Herr Hitzinger. His papers were in perfect order. He loved order."

The only problem with this orderliness was the papers were not his.

The man with the purloined papers was buried in the bloody soil, along with the fearsome hallucination that he had fabricated out of strange dreams of warrior-heroes turned into god-men.

It was reported that British army medical personnel removed his brain and took plaster casts of his skull. What an irony that this was so much like the work that Dr. August Hirt had been doing under Ahnenerbe auspices at the Reichsuniversität Strassburg.

Time went on to relate that "a British Army detail, sworn to secrecy, buried the unembalmed body in a grave on the heath near Lüneburg. There was no coffin, no marking on the grave. The shifting sand would soon obliterate the last sign; there would be no site for a martyr's monument. The only words spoken at the graveside came from a British Tommy: 'Let the worm go to the worms.'"

As her husband was wandering across northern Germany, Marga Himmler and her teenaged daughter, Gudrun, were also on the move. When they abandoned their chateau overlooking the Tegernsee to escape the U.S. Third Army that spring, they had not seen Himmler in months. Mother and daughter headed south, hoping to reach Italy, and made it as far as the former Austrian city of Bozen, which had become the Italian city of Bolzano after the Italians helped win World War I. Here, they were among the civilians processed by the American 88th Infantry Division. As had happened with the family patriarch, they were identified.

Interviewed a few days before her husband committed suicide, Marga was asked how it felt to be married to Europe's most feared man. Her answer was a laconic "Nobody loves a policeman." When she learned of his death, she said simply, "I'm proud of him." She didn't say that she would miss him. She had moved beyond that.

In Berlin, the charred remnants of the feared Number 8 Prinz-Albrechtstrasse were pulled down by the Soviets after the war. In 1951, the street itself was renamed as Niederkirchnerstrasse, after Käthe Niederkirchner, a Third Reich–era communist who was killed by the Nazis in 1944. In 1961, the communists bisected the street with their Berlin Wall. When this wall finally came down three decades later, a small section remained at the site of Number 8.

Marga and Gudrun Himmler, the wife and daughter of the Reichsführer SS, after they were picked up by the American 88th Infantry Division in Bolzano, Italy. When asked how it felt to be married to Europe's most feared man, Marga's answer was a terse "Nobody loves a policeman."
U.S. National Archives

To hold the captured Nazi leadership accountable for war crimes and crimes against humanity, the Allies formed the International Military Tribunal and proceeded with a series of trials known as the Nuremberg War Crimes Trials. These took place over eleven months beginning in November 1945, and were held in the city of Nuremberg, because this was the city where the Nazis had once celebrated themselves with immense torchlit rallies. With Hitler, Goebbels, and Himmler having all sentenced themselves to death before the trials, the biggest fish at Nuremberg was Hermann Göring. Convicted and sentenced to death, he cheated the hangman by committing suicide the night before his scheduled institution.

Among those sentenced to death and executed were Keitel and Jodl, the old generals who surrendered the Reich, as well as Joachim von Ribbentrop and Alfred Rosenberg, the intense Völksdeutscher from Estonia, whose racial theories legally defined the difference between Aryans and untermenschen, paving the way for the Final Solution and the reign of the Einsatzgruppen.

Karl Dönitz, the second Führer, was convicted of war crimes—unrestricted submarine warfare—served ten years in Berlin's Spandau Prison, never repented, and wrote a bestselling autobiography. Albert Speer, whose Reich Armaments

Ministry ran the biggest slave-labor operation in modern history, served twenty years, repented, and wrote his own bestselling autobiography.

Rudolf Hess, the enigmatic deputy Führer, who had been in British custody since his strange 1941 flight to Scotland, was sentenced to life in Spandau, where he was the only prisoner for the final two decades before his death in 1987. He never said a word, much less an entire autobiography, and died without telling anyone why he had gone to Scotland.

Obergruppenführer und General der Polizei und Waffen-SS Ernst Kaltenbrunner, Reinhard Heydrich's successor, was the highest-ranking SS officer tried at Nuremberg. With Rudolf Hess, the commandant of Auschwitz, giving evidence against him, Kaltenbrunner was convicted of crimes against humanity, and he met the hangman on October 16, 1946. When asked for any last words, he said, "I have done my duty by the laws of my people and I am sorry this time my people were led by men who were not soldiers, and that crimes were committed of which I had no knowledge. Germany, good luck."

Kurt Daluege, Himmler's old rival, whom he had marginalized with the posting as Reichsprotektor of Bohemia and Moravia, spent the last two years of the war recovering from a heart attack, only to be arrested by the Czechs whom he had brutalized. Convicted of war crimes, he was executed in Prague on October 26, 1946.

The SS men, especially officers, had reason to be wary. Their infamy had preceded them. Because of the reputation of the SS for being the most fervent of Nazis, and the fact that they ran the concentration camps, the Allied tribunals were especially diligent in rounding up and evaluating everyone who had worn the totenkopf uniform.

SS Brigadeführer Walther Schellenberg, the SD boss who was with Himmler off and on near the end, was in Denmark when he was apprehended by the Allies in June 1945. He turned on his fellow Nazis, one of many who gave evidence at Nuremberg in exchange for leniency. Not sentenced until 1949, he served only two years of a six-year stretch, during which time he penned his memoirs. Released for health reasons, he eventually settled in Italy, where he died of cancer on March 31, 1952.

Master Sergeant Charles Dickey of the 101st Airborne Division smiles after discovering Himmler's "rainy-day fund." Searching a barn near the villa occupied by Himmler's wife in Bavaria, American troops discovered sacks of money hidden by the Reichsführer. Located on May 27, 1945, four days after Hitler's death, the hoard included an estimated $4 million worth of currency from twenty-six nations.
U.S. National Archives

After the principal War Crimes Trials, the United States held a series of additional trials, notably the so-called "Doctor's Trial," in which nearly two dozen Nazis, mainly SS doctors, were tried for crimes against humanity, including the experiments on living humans. Also in this trial were Rudolf Brandt, Himmler's aide, and Wolfram Sievers, the Ahnenerbe's managing director, about whose work a mountain of evidence—mainly their own records and correspondence—was presented. Both were convicted and executed in 1948.

Dr. Sigmund Rascher, who froze people to death for the Luftwaffe and who created Heinrich Himmler's exit strategy, was executed as well, but not by the Allies. He and his wife, Nini Diehl, Himmler's old nightclub-singer friend, had been involved in a bizarre case of fraud. The doctor had cooked up a scheme to fake the results of fertility-enhancing experiments. On the face of it, Rascher's "treatments" had allowed Nini to get pregnant in her forties three times, something that was not always possible with the state-of-the-art science in the 1940s. Instead, it turned out that they had *kidnapped* three babies. The doctor was executed at Dachau, by the SS, on April 26, 1945, less than a month before Himmler bit into one of his blue-glass vials.

Dr. August Hirt, the Ahnenerbe's skeleton collector at Strassburg, who anguished about the destruction of his grisly collection of human bodies, was another good candidate for the Doctor's Trial, but never made it to

Nuremberg. Hirt committed suicide in Schönenbach in the Black Forest on June 2, 1945.

Dr. Josef Mengele, the "Angel of Death" at the Auschwitz-Birkenau concentration camp, was on the list for the trials, but no trace of him could be found. The Allies thought he was dead. In fact, he was one of a number of SS officers who managed to escape to South America after the war. Rumors that he was still alive surfaced in the 1950s, but he was never apprehended. After spending time in Argentina and Paraguay, he was living in Brazil at the time of his death on February 7, 1979. Buried under an assumed name, he was later exhumed, and his identity was confirmed.

Another one that got away was SS Obersturmbannführer Adolf Eichmann, the man who tried to negotiate a prewar homeland in Palestine for Germany's Jews, but who later masterminded the logistical apparatus that took them to the death camps. He escaped to Argentina, but was nabbed by the Israeli Mossad and taken back to Israel to stand trial for crimes against humanity. He was executed on May 31, 1962.

During the 1960s and 1970s, the subject of escaped Nazis was a staple of conspiracy theories and adventure fiction. A widely held belief was that the *Organization der Ehemaligen SS Angehörigen* (Organization of Former SS Members), better known by the acronym ODESSA, had facilitated the escape of many SS personnel. In fact, both Mengele and Eichmann made use not of a secret "underground railroad," but rather of the general chaos of early postwar Europe to make good their exit.

Felix Kersten, Himmler's Estonian-born, Völksdeutsche masseur, who was at the Reichsführer's side more or less constantly, escaped prosecution altogether because documentary evidence showed that he had played an important role in helping Folke Bernadotte evacuate thousands of concentration-camp inmates to neutral Sweden in white buses marked with red crosses. In his own memoirs—first published in 1947—Kersten also claimed credit for foiling an SS scheme to deport the entire population of the Netherlands. He became a Swedish citizen in 1953 and died in Stockholm on April 16, 1960, at the age of sixty-one.

The SS required its officers to prove a purely Aryan pedigree through all generations back to 1750. The resulting genealogical data was kept in an individual's Sippenbuch, a kinship or clan book, not unlike the sort of stud book that owners keep for racehorses. It was also kept by the SS in meticulously detailed files. Here, a group of Allied intelligence officers begin to open the first 450,000 of those files at Fürstenhagen on November 15, 1945.

U.S. National Archives

As for Bernadotte himself, he was appointed as the first United Nations mediator in Palestine in 1948, after the announcement of the unpopular United Nations Partition Plan. He brokered a truce following the 1948 Arab-Israeli War and helped set up a United Nations refugee-relief apparatus for the Middle East. Israelis were upset with Bernadotte's apparent favoritism toward Arabs, and the militant Zionist organization Lehi, also known as the "Stern gang," marked him for assassination. One of those ordering the hit was Yitzhak Shamir, who served as prime minister of Israel in from 1983 to 1984 and 1986 to 1992. The man who had saved thousands of European Jews was gunned down in Jerusalem on September 17, 1948.

Back in Nuremberg, the trials and executions reached deep into the ranks of the SS Totenkopfverbände concentration-camp guards. Among them were many women from the SS Aufseherinnen. Irma Grese, the young sadist with the pack of dogs, was convicted of crimes against humanity and was executed in 1945.

However, Ilse Koch, the Bitch of Buchenwald, escaped the death penalty. Both she and her husband, Buchenwald commandant Karl Otto Koch, had been arrested in 1943 for embezzling SS funds. He was convicted of disgracing the SS and was executed in April 1945, but she was released. Free for two months within the imploding Reich, she was picked up in June 1945 by the Allies and charged with crimes against humanity. Sentenced to life imprisonment in 1947, she had her sentence commuted by General Lucius Clay, the interim military governor of the American zone in Germany. Rearrested by the new government of West Germany in 1949, she was convicted on over a hundred murder counts and sent back inside for life in 1951. Sixteen years later, she hanged herself in prison.

The man who had ordered the execution of Karl Koch was picked up by the Allies on April 13, three weeks before the war's end. He was Waffen SS general Josias Waldeck, the hereditary prince of Waldeck and Pyrmont, at whose castle in Arolsen Himmler had considered making his last stand in May 1945. His highness was convicted on the somewhat ambiguous grounds of the Buchenwald concentration camp having been geographically located within his area of command and, amazingly, for executing Koch. Lucius Clay, the governor who had released Koch's widow, commuted Waldeck's life sentence to twenty years, although Waldeck was released for health reasons from Landsberg (the same prison where Hitler had done time) in 1953. He had been elevated to head of the House of Waldeck and Pyrmont in 1946 while incarcerated, and he exercised this noble office until his death in 1967.

Ricardo Walther Darré, the Argentine Völksdeutscher prophet of the Blut und Boden doctrine, who was Himmler's brother in the back-to-the-land Artamanen Gesellshaft, was arrested in 1945. He was tried several years later for his role in the crimes of the Third Reich while heading the Rasse und Siedlungshauptamt (Race and Settlement Office). Acquitted of the most serious charges, he was sentenced to seven years, but was released in 1950 due to advanced liver cancer exacerbated by decades of heavy boozing. He died on September 5, 1953, at the age of fifty-eight.

Hermann Wirth, the impassioned Ariosphist and amateur rune scholar who was Himmler's first head of the Ahnenerbe, was given a pass because his written work dwelt on the Völkisch *ancient* past of the Germanic people rather that the brutal *recent* past of the Third Reich. He lived out his years in relative obscurity, studying the lore and fate of the ancient city of Atlantis. He died in 1981 at the age of ninety-six.

Walther Wüst was the credentialed university professor whom Himmler named to take over Hermann Wirth's job at the Ahnenerbe in 1937 in order to give it more academic credibility. For him, there was good news and bad news. Unfortunately, his tenure at the think tank coincided with the ghoulish medical experiments of the Ahnenerbe's Institut für Wehrwissenschaftliche Zweckforschung. But fortunately for Wüst, he was finally able to convince the postwar courts that he "knew nothing" of all that. Released in 1950, he melted back into academic life at the Ludwig Maximilians Universität (Ludwig Maximilian University) in Munich. He died in 1993 at the age of ninety-two.

Franz Altheim, the Ahnenerbe's real Indiana Jones, who conducted some of that agency's most ambitious international field trips in the 1930s, was likewise written off by the tribunals as a mere researcher of quaint folklore. Altheim was able to profit academically from his Ahnenerbe years, using the fruits of his prewar field research in many postwar papers and monographs. He joined the faculty of the Frei Universität Berlin in 1950 and went on to publish numerous books on history and religion, including the five volume *Geschichte der Hunnen, (History of the Huns),* published between 1959 and 1962. His published work on runic studies from Italy to the Middle East is still showing up in academic bibliographies. He died in Münster in 1976, eleven days past his seventy-eighth birthday.

Edmund Kiss, the Thulean amateur archeologist and disciple of Hanns Hörbiger's Welteislehre/Glazial-Kozmogonie, was on the threshold of getting Walther Wüst to send him to the Bolivian Andes when the war started. He had joined the Waffen SS during World War II and served at Hitler's Rastenberg command post late in the war. Interned along with other Waffen SS prisoners, he was released in 1947 for health reasons, as seems to have been the case for so many SS men over sixty. He died in 1960 at the age of seventy-four.

Bruno Beger, the anthropologist who measured Heinrich I's skull at Quedlinburg and 376 skulls of living Tibetans, was in Italy when the war ended, serving with the legion of Volga Tatars in German uniform. He surrendered to the U.S. Army and spent time in a series of prisoner-of-war camps from Pisa to Darmstadt. He was kept in custody for four years because he was an SS officer. Though his name came up repeatedly in the paper trail that condemned Wolfram Sievers to the gallows, Beger was finally released in 1948. Having conducted some further anthropological field trips during the 1950s, this time to the Middle East, Beger was later rearrested by German authorities on charges related to the skeleton collection. He was convicted as an accessory to murder in 1971, but did not serve time. When he was interviewed in 2003 by Christopher Hale for the latter's book about the Tibet expedition, Beger was still alive and well at age ninety-two and living in a small town near Frankfurt, surrounded by souvenirs brought back from Tibet.

Ernst Schäfer, the Tibet expedition leader, who had been exiled to the purposeless Sven Hedin Institute at Schloss Mittersill, surrendered to the Allies and hoped for the best. Having spent two years in various interment facilities, he finally reached the tribunal in Nuremberg in 1947. He testified, was fined, and was finally released in 1949. After spending several years establishing and operating a wildlife park in Venezuela, he and his family resettled in Germany in 1954. He lived there until his death in 1992 at the age of eighty-two.

As the war ended, a few men remained from the mystical hard core, those who were active in the Thulean and Ariosophic subcurrents of the Germanic New Age in the early years of the twentieth century.

Rudolf Freiherr von Sebottendorff, formerly Adam Alfred Rudolf Glauer, the prominent Thulean who had embarrassed Hitler by daring to suggest that the Nazi Party predated the Führer, spent World War II in Turkey. That country, which had been a German ally in World War I, remained neutral in the next. As such, Istanbul was a favored meeting place for spies on both sides. Various stories tell of Sebottendorff doing espionage work for the Abwehr or of his being a double or triple agent who was on the payroll of British intelligence. Others have him simply lounging about Istanbul and pontificating about this mystical dogma or that. He is said to have committed suicide on May 8, 1945, the day after Germany surrendered. However, this story also has an alternate ending, which has the old pagan philosopher changing his name once again and living on.

Karl Haushofer, the famous geographer who influenced Hitler's geopolitics, was among those of the Führer's old acquaintances who earned the scrutiny of the Allied tribunals. Even though his son, Albrecht, had been arrested and executed for playing a part in the July 20 plot to assassinate Hitler, the old academic was brought in for questioning. It was eventually determined that Haushofer had committed no crimes against humanity, but nevertheless, the seventy-seven-year-old geographer and his wife poisoned themselves on March 10, 1946.

Karl Maria Wiligut, the man who influenced Himmler's mystical side more than any other, also survived World War II. Having been Himmler's close companion and mystical advisor throughout most of the 1930s, he was abruptly retired on the very eve of World War II. Keeping him on ice to avoid the embarrassment of his three years in the mental institution, Himmler had sent him into seclusion under the care of Elsa Baltrusch from his personal staff.

In 1940, Wiligut and Baltrusch moved to Goslar, where he could live near where he imagined the Irminen to have built their long-vanished holy city. In 1943, she moved the old magus farther from Allied bombing, to the popular resort area around the Wörthersee, a lake near Klagenfurt in Austria. When the war ended, Wiligut, like so many others, was placed in a refugee camp. After suffering a stroke, he was moved again, finally winding up in Arolsen, Josias Waldeck's bailiwick. It was there that he died on January 3, 1946, three weeks past his seventy-ninth birthday. The inscription on his headstone reads *"Unser Leben Geht Dahin wie ein Geschwätz"* ("Our life passes away like idle chatter").

And then there was Jörg Lanz von Liebenfels, the creator of Theozoology and Ariosophy, which had helped provide the basis for the Völkisch racial doctrines of Darré and Himmler. The same Lanz who had been, in print and possibly in person, the muse of Hitler. The same Lanz who was the zealous understudy to Guido von List and the first Aryan-centric prophet to fly a swastika flag from the stone tower of a Germanic castle. Having spent World War II as an ignored spectator to the hellstorm that he had helped create, the mad monk Lanz outlived his philosophical protege, Himmler, by nearly a decade. He died a forgotten man on April 22, 1954, at the age of seventy-nine.

THE SANDS OF TIME

Guido von List had died a few months before Adolf Hitler had even become acquainted with the party that became the Nazis. The godfather of it all, he missed it all. But his spirit lived on. His system of runes, his Armanen Futharkh, survived the war and still survives. Scrubbed clean of Nazi connections and connotations—or as clean as possible—it was revived by the self-styled mystic Karl Spiesberger, a prominent figure in an organization called Fraternitas Saturni (Fraternity of Saturn). Citing what he called "the personal force of List and that of his extensive and influential Armanen Orden," Stephen Flowers wrote in his 1984 book, *Futhark: A Handbook of Rune Magic,* that List's Futharkh "by 1955 had become almost 'traditional' in German circles."

Also not forgotten are many of the doctrines that swirled around the Völkisch New Age in which men such as List and Lanz held court. One can walk into any number of alternative bookstores throughout Europe and America and, amid the smell of incense, have the sense of being back in time a hundred years or more. Astrology, numerology, and like pseudosciences have never faded away. Madame Helena Blavatsky's works are still in print, and one does not have far to look before finding recent tomes on runic lore.

The Bhagavad Gita, the ancient Hindu scripture, which Himmler carried in his briefcase, can be had today in a format to fit any twenty-first-century briefcase or backpack. Topics such as Atlantis and races of ancient god kings are as alive and vibrant on the Internet and in the multiplex as they were in the coffee shops of Munich and Vienna in the years before World War II.

Gudrun Himmler, Heinrich's only legitimate daughter, his beloved "Puppi," was just two months shy of her sixteenth birthday when she got the news that daddy was dead. She spent her teens in British custody. As reported in a 1998 piece in the *Berliner Morgenpost,* "She complained later bitterly that these had been the worst years of their life, and that she paid [with those years] for her father." She was finally released in 1949 as the Federal Republic of Germany (West Germany) was formed out of the British, French, and American occupation zones. She later married Wulf Dieter Burwitz, a journalist and author.

Through the years, she was active in the organization known as *Stille Hilfe für Kriegsgefangene und Internierte* (Silent Assistance for Prisoners of War and

Far beneath Schloss Wewelsburg, an elaborate swastika is centered in the ceiling of the Obergruppenführersaal, the crypt set aside for the worship of glorious SS martyrs.

Photo by Kris Simoens, used by permission

Interned Persons). It was founded in 1951 by Princess Helene Elizabeth of Isenburg to aid former Nazis, especially SS men. According to Oliver Schröm and Andrea Röpke, in their 2001 book *Stille Hilfe für Braune Kameraden,* she had a reputation as a *Schillernde Nazi Prinzessin* (dazzling Nazi princess). Darius Sanai wrote in the February 1, 1999, issue of London's *Independent* that she was still "an unreconstructed Nazi . . . in the news in Germany at the moment, and has been ever since she was revealed to be helping a former Nazi concentration camp commandant fight extradition to be tried for war crimes in the Czech Republic."

Even in the twenty-first century, Puppi would remain a staunch champion of her father and still a popular figure among those with a nostalgia for the Germany of the late 1930s. She was among that dwindling number of diehards for whom the black uniform would be, in her beloved father's words, "naturally very attractive in peacetime."

Along with Bruno Beger and Gudrun Berwitz, another figure from those earlier days who lived to see the twenty-first century was SS Sturmbannführer Heinz Macher, the man who set the demolition charges at Schloss Wewelsburg in the fiery days of Götterdämmerung. He died in Schenefeld on December 21, 2001, ten days before his eighty-second birthday.

As for Wewelsburg itself, Macher's shortage of explosives on that day in 1945 saved the shell of the building, and over the years, the castle has been gradually restored. A youth hostel first opened there in 1950, and in 1973 work began on rebuilding the heavily damaged north tower. Schloss Wewelsburg reopened as a war monument in 1982, and a memorial to the inmates of the Neiderhagen camp

was added later. The *Historisches Museum des Hochstifts Paderborn* (Historical Museum of the Paderborn Bishopric) was unveiled in the south and east wings in 1996. The hostel is still one of the largest in Germany.

The personal safe that Heinrich Himmler installed somewhere beneath the west tower has never been found, nor have the thousands of Totenkopfrings that Macher buried somewhere in the Niederhagen forest.

Today, long after the sands of time have drifted over most of the moldering remains of the Third Reich, one may once again visit the restored crypt at the heart of this SS Valhalla. One may stand in the literal inner sanctum of the SS, at the edge of the stone fire pit around which the Black Knights once gathered.

You will be chilled to the bone in any weather.

A large ceremonial fire pit dominates the center of the floor of the Obergruppenführersaal. It was to have been an SS Valhalla to last a thousand years.
Photo by Kris Simoens, used by permission

Bibliography and Recommended Reading

Andreas-Friedrich, Ruth. *Berlin Underground (1939–1945)*. Oxford: Latimer House, 1948.

Arendt, Hannah. *Eichmann in Jerusalem: A Report on the Banality of Evil*. New York: Viking Press, 1963.

———. *The Origins of Totalitarianism*. London: Allen & Unwin, 1958.

Bartz, Karl. *Downfall of the German Secret Service*. London: William Kimber & Co., 1956.

Bennecke, Heinrich. *Die Reichswehr und der "Röhm-Putsch."* Munich: Günter Olzog Verlag, 1964.

———. *Hitler und die SA*. Munich: Günter Olzog Verlag, 1962.

Bernadotte, Folke. *The Fall of the Curtain*. London: Cassell & Company, 1945.

Best, Werner. *Die Deutsche Polizei*. Darmstadt, Germany: L.C. Wittich Verlag, 1941.

Biss, Andreas. *Der Stopp der Endlüsung. Kampf Gegen Himmler und Eichmann in Budapest*. Stuttgart, Germany: Seewald Verlag, 1966.

Blavatsky, Helena Petrovna. *Isis Unveiled: A Master Key to the Mysteries of Ancient and Modern Science and Theology*. New York: J. W. Bouton, 1877.

———. *The Key to Theosophy*. London: Theosophical Publishing Company, 1889.

———. *The Secret Doctrine*. London: Theosophical Publishing Company, 1888.

Blum, Ralph. *The Book of Runes, A Handbook for the use of Ancient Oracle*. New York: St. Martin's Press, 1932.

Bouhler, Philipp. *Kampf um Deutschland*. Munich: Zentralverlag der NSDAP, 1939.

Bramwell, Anna. *Blood and Soil: Richard Walther Darré and Hitler's "Green Party."* Oxford: Kensal Press, 1985.

Browning, Christopher. *The Origins of the Final Solution*. Lincoln: University of Nebraska Press, 2004.

Buchheim, Hans, Martin Broszat, Helmut Krausnick, and Hans-Adolf Jacobsen. *The Anatomy of the SS State*. Translated R. H. Barry, Marian Jackson, and Dorothy Long. London: Collins, 1968.

Bullock, Alan. *Hitler: A Study in Tyranny*. London: Odhams Press, 1964.

Burckhardt, Carl J. *Meine Danziger Mission (1937–1939)*. Munich: Verlag Georg D. W. Callwey, 1960.

Cooper, John C. *Religion in the Age of Aquarius*. Philadelphia: The Westminster Press, 1971.

Crankshaw, Edward. *The Gestapo, Instrument of Tyranny*. New York: Putnam, 1956.

D'Alquen, Gunter. *Auf Hieb und Stich*. Berlin: Franz Eher II GmbH, 1937.

———. *Die SS. Geschichte, Aufgabe und Organization der Schutzstaffel tier NSDAP*. Berlin: Junker & Dünnhaupt Verlag, 1939.

Däniken, Erich von. *Chariots of the Gods?: Unsolved Mysteries of the Past*. New York: Bantam, 1968.

Darré, Walther. *Neuadel aus Blut und Boden*. Munich: Eher Verlag, 1934.

Dawidowicz, Lucy. *The War Against the Jews*. New York: Bantam, 1986.

Degrelle, Leon. *Die Verlorene Legion*. Linz, Austria: Veritas Verlag, 1955.

Dicks, Henry V. *Licensed Mass Murder*. New York: Basic Books, 1972.

Diels, Rudolf. *Lucifer ante Portas*. Zürich, Switzerland: Interverlag, 1949.

Dornberger, Walther. *V.2* New York: Viking, 1954.

Dulles, Allen. *Germany's Underground*. New York: Macmillan, 1947.

Eisenbach, A. *Operation Reinhard (Mass Extermination in Poland)*. Poznań, Poland: Instytut Zachodni, 1962.

Epstein, Fritz T. "Wartime Activities of the SS Ahnenerbe." In *On the Track of Tyranny: Essays Presented by the Wiener Library to Leonard G. Montefiore, on the Occasion of His Seventieth Birthday*. Manchester, NH: Ayer Publishing, 1971.

Fest, Joachim C. *Hitler*. New York: Harcourt Brace Jovanovich, 1974.

———. *The Face of the Third Reich*. New York: Pantheon Books, 1970.

Flowers, Stephen E. and Michael Moynihan. *The Secret King: Karl Maria Wiligut, Himmler's Lord of the Runes*. Los Angeles: Dominion Feral House, 2007.

Flowers, Stephen E. *Futhark: A Handbook of Rune Magic*. York Beach, ME: Samuel Weiser, 1984.

Frischauer, Willi. *Himmler.* Watford, England: Odhams, 1953.

Gilbert, G. M. *The Psychology of Dictatorship.* New York: Ronald Press Company, 1950.

Gilbert, Martin. *Atlas of the Holocaust.* New York: Routledge, 1988.

Gisevius, H. B. *To the Bitter End.* London: Jonathan Cape, 1948.

Goebbels, Josef. *My Part in Germany's Fight.* London: Paternoster Library, 1938.

———. *The Early Goebbels Diaries.* Edited by Helmut Heiber. London: Weidenfeld and Nicolson, 1962.

———. *The Goebbels Diaries.* Edited and translated Louis P. Lochner. London: Hamish Hamilton, 1948.

Goodrick-Clarke, Nicholas. *Helena Blavatsky, Western Esoteric Masters Series.* Berkeley, CA: North Atlantic Books, 2004.

———. *Hitler's Priestess: Savitri Devi, the Hindu-Aryan Myth, and Neo-Nazism.* New York: NYU Press, 2000.

———. *The Occult Roots of Nazism, Secret Aryan Cults and Their Influence on Nazi Ideology.* New York: NYU Press, 1993.

Graddon, Nigel. *Otto Rahn and the Quest for the Grail: The Amazing Life of the Real Indiana Jones.* Kempton, IL: Adventures Unlimited Press, 2008.

Graf, Arturo. *The Story of the Devil.* New York: Macmillan Company, 1931.

Grunberger, Richard. *Hitler's SS.* New York: Delacorte Press, 1970.

Guderian, Heinz. *Panzer Leader.* Translated Constantine Fitzgibbon. London: Michael Joseph, 1952.

Hale, Christopher. *Himmler's Crusade: The Nazi Expedition to Find the Origins of the Aryan Race.* Castle Books, 2006. Also published as *Himmler's Crusade: The True Story of the 1938 Nazi Expedition into Tibet* New York: Bantam, 2004.

Hanfstaengl, Ernst. *Hitler: The Missing Years.* London: Eyre & Spottiswoode, 1957

Hartshorne, E. Y. *German Youth and the Nazi Dream of Victory.* New York: Farrar & Rinehart, 1941.

Heckethorn, Charles W. *Secret Societies of All Countries.* New York: New Amsterdam Book Company, 1897.

Hitler, Adolf. *Mein Kampf.* Translated by James Murphy. London: Hurst & Blackett, 1939.

———. *Mein Kampf.* Translated by Ralph Manheim. New York: Houghton Mifflin, 1943.

Hoess, Rudolf. *Commandant of Auschwitz.* London: Weidenfeld and Nicolson, 1959.

Hoffer, Eric. *The True Believer.* New York: Harper & Row, 1951.

Höhne, Heinz Zollin. *The Order of the Death's Head: The Story of Hitler's SS.* Translated by Richard Barry. London: Penguin, 2000.

——. *Der Orden Unter dem Totenkopf.* Hamburg, Germany: Verlag der Spigel, 1966.

Hossbach, Friedrich. *Zwischen Wehrmacht und Hitler (1934–1938).* Hannover, Germany: Wolfenbütteler Verlagsanstalt, 1949.

Howe, Ellic. *Astrology: A Recent History Including the Untold Story of Its Role in World War II.* New York: Walker & Company, 1968.

Irving, David. *The Mare's Nest.* London: William Kimber, 1964.

Jackel, Eberhard. *Prankreich in Hitlers Europa.* Stuttgart, Germany: Deutsche Verlagsanstalt, 1958.

Jung, Carl Gustav. *Civilization in Transition.* New York: Pantheon Books, 1964.

——. *Psychology and Religion: West and East.* New York: Pantheon Books, 1958.

Kent, George O. *Historians and Archivists: Essays in Modern German History and Archival Policy.* N.p.: University Publishing Association, 1991.

Kersten, Felix. *The Memoirs of Dr. Felix Kersten.* New York: Doubleday & Company, 1947.

Kessel, Joseph. *The Man with Miraculous Hands.* Translated by Helen Weaver and Leo Raditsa. New York: Farrar, Straus & Cudahy, 1961.

Kimche, Jon and David. *The Secret Roads.* London: Secker & Warburg, 1955.

Koehl, Robert L. *RKFVD: German Resettlement and Population Policy (1939–1945).* Cambridge, MA: Harvard University Press, 1957.

Kogon, Eugen. *The Theory and Practice of Hell.* London: Secker and Warburg, 1951.

Kramarz, Joachim. *Stauffenberg, The Life and Death of an Officer.* London: Andre Deutsch, 1967.

Kubizek, August. *The Young Hitler I Knew.* New York: Houghton Mifflin Company, 1955.

Langer, Walther. *The Mind of Adolf Hitler.* New York: Basic Books, 1972.

Leibenfels, Jörg Lanz von. *Theozoologie oder die Kunde von den Sodoms-Äfflingen und dem Götter-Elektron (Theozoology or the account of the Sodomite Apelings and the Divine Electron).* Vienna: Europa House, 1905.

List, Guido von. *Das Geheimnis der Runen (The Secret of the Runes).* Vienna: Guido von List Verlag, 1908.

——. *Deutsch-Mythologische Landschaftsbilder.* Vienna: Guido von List Verlag, 1891.

——. *Die Religion der Ario-Germanen in ihrer Esoterik und Exoterik.* Vienna: Guido von List Verlag, 1910.

Ludecke, Kurt Georg. *I Knew Hitler.* New York: Charles Scribner's Sons, 1937.

Manvell, Roger, and Heinrich Fränkel. *Doctor Goebbels.* London: Heinemann, 1960.

———. *Heinrich Himmler.* London: Heinemann, 1965.

———. *Heinrich Himmler: The SS, Gestapo, His Life and Career.* New York: Skyhorse Publishing, 2007.

———. *Hermann Göring.* London: Heinemann, 1962.

———. *The July Plot.* London: The Bodley Head, 1964.

Meerloo, Joost A. M. *The Rape of the Mind.* N.p.: World Publishing Company, 1956.

Mitscherlich, A., and F. Mielke. *Doctors of Infamy.* London: Elek, 1962.

Mosse, George L. *Nazi Culture.* New York: Grosset & Dunlap, 1966.

Müller, Dr. Karl Alexander von. *Im Wandel einer Zeit (In the Change of Time).* Munich: Süddeutscher Verlag, 1966.

Nicosia, Francis, and Donald Niewyk. *Columbia Guide to the Holocaust.* New York: Columbia University Press, 2000.

Padfield, Peter. *Himmler: Reichsführer SS.* Revised ed. London: Cassell, 2001.

Pätel, Karl O. *The SS in The Third Reich.* London: Weidenfeld & Nicolson, 1955.

Papen, Franz von. *Memoirs.* London: Andre Deutsch, 1952.

Pauwels, Louis, and Jacques Bergier. *The Dawn of Magic.* Anthony Gibbs & Phillips, 1960. Also published as *The Morning of the Magicians.* New York: Stein & Day, 1963.

Phelps, Reginald H. "Before Hitler Came: Thule Society and Germanen Orden." The *Journal of Modern History* 35, no. 3 (Jan. 1963): 245.

Poliakov, Leon. *The Aryan Myth.* New York: Basic Books, 1974.

Rahn, Otto. *A Heretic's Journey in Search of the Light Bringers.* Rochester, VT: Inner Traditions, 2008.

———. *Crusade Against the Grail: The Struggle between the Cathars, the Templars, and the Church of Rome.* Rochester, VT: Inner Traditions, 2006.

Rauschning, Hermann. *Men of Chaos.* New York: G. P. Putnam's Sons, 1942.

———. *The Voice of Destruction.* New York: G. P. Putnam's Sons. 1940.

Ravenscroft, Trevor. *The Spear of Destiny.* New York: G. P. Putnam's Sons, 1973.

Reitlinger, Gerald. *The Final Solution.* London: Valentine Mitchell, 1953.

———. *The House Built on Sand.* London: Weidenfeld & Nicolson, 1960.

———. *The SS: Alibi of a Nation.* London: Heinemann, 1956.

Reynolds, Quentin. *Minister of Death. The Eichmann Story.* New York: Viking Press, 1960.

Ribbentrop, Joachim von. *The Ribbentrop Memoirs*. Translated by Oliver Watson. London: Weidenfeld & Nicolson, 1954.

Roberts, Stephen H. *The House That Hitler Built*. New York: Harper & Bros., 1938.

Röhm, Ernst. *Die Geschichte Tines Hochverraters*. Munich: Verlag Franz Eher II, 1933.

Rozett, Robert, et. al. *Encyclopedia of the Holocaust*. New York: Facts on File, 2000.

Ryan, Cornelius. *The Last Battle*. New York: Simon & Schuster, 1966.

Sargant, William. *The Mind Possessed*. Philadelphia, PA: J. B. Lippincott Company, 1974.

Schellenberg, Walther. *Hitler's Secret Service*. New York: Pyramid Publications, 1974.

———. *The Schellenberg Memoirs*. Translated by Louis Hagen. London: Andre Deutsch, 1961.

Schlabrendorff, Fabian von. *The Secret War against Hitler*. London: Hodder & Stoughton, 1961.

Schröm, Oliver, and Andrea Röpke. *Stille Hilfe für Braune Kameraden*. Berlin: Christoph Links Verlag, 2001.

Schwarz, Gudrun. *Eine Frau an Seiner Seite: Ehefrauen in der SS-Sippengemeinschaft (A Wife at His Side: Wives in the SS Clan Community)*. Hamburg, Germany: Hamburger Edition, 1997.

Seabury, Paul. *The Wilhelmstrasse*. Berkely, CA: University of California Press, Cambridge University Press, 1954.

Sebottendorff, Rudolf von. *Bevor Hitler Kam: Urkundlich aus der Frühzeit der Nationalsozialistischen Bewegung (Before Hitler Came: Documents from the Early Days of the National Socialist Movement)*. Munich: Deufula Verlag Grassinger & Company, 1933.

Semmler, Rudolf. *Goebbels, the Man Next to Hitler*. London: Westhouse, 1947.

Shirer, William L. *Berlin Diary*. New York: Knopf, 1941.

———. *End of a Berlin Diary*. New York: Knopf, 1947.

———. *The Rise and Fall of the Third Reich*. New York: Simon & Schuster, 1960.

Sklar, Dusty. *The Nazis and the Occult*. New York: Dorset Press, 1977.

Skorzeny, Otto. *Skorzeny's Special Missions*. London: Robert Hale, 1957.

Smith, Bradley F. *Heinrich Himmler: A Nazi in the Making*. Stanford, CA: Hoover Institution Press, 1971.

Speer, Albert. *Inside the Third Reich*. New York: The Macmillan Company, 1970.

Spykman, Nicholas John. *America's Strategy in World Politics*. New York: Harcourt, Brace, 1942.

Standish, David. *Hollow Earth: The Long and Curious History of Imagining Strange Lands, Fantastical Creatures, Advanced Civilizations, and Marvelous Machines Below the Earth's Surface.* Cambridge, MA: Da Capo Press, 2007.

Stein, George H. *The Waffen SS.* Ithaca, NY: Cornell University Press, 1966.

Steiner, Felix. *Die Armee der Geüchteten.* Gottingen, Germany: Plesse Verlag, 1963.

———. *Die Freiwilligen.* Gottingen, Germany: Plesse Verlag, 1958.

Symonds, John. *The Lady with the Magic Eyes: Madame Blavatsky, Medium and Magician.* Whitefish, MT: Kessinger Publishing, 1959.

Taylor, Telford. *Final Report to the Secretary of the Army.* Washington, D.C.: U.S. Department of Army, 1949.

Toland, John. *The Last 100 Days.* New York: Random House, 1965.

Trachtenberg, Joshua. *The Devil and the Jews.* New Haven, CT: Meridian Books, 1970.

Trevor-Roper, H. R. *The Bormann Letters.* London: Weidenfeld & Nicolson, 1954.

———. *The Last Days of Hitler.* New York: Macmillan & Company, 1956.

Vogelsang, Thilo. *Reichswehr, Staat und NSDAP.* Stuttgart, Germany: Deutsche Verlagsanstalt, 1962.

Webb, James. *The Occult Establishment.* Chicago: Open Court Publishing Company, 1976.

———. *The Occult Underground.* Chicago: Open Court Publishing Company, 1974.

Webster, Nesta H. *Secret Societies and Subversive Movements.* London: Boswell Printing & Publishing Company, 1924.

Wheeler-Bennett, John W. *The Nemesis of Power.* New York: St. Martin's Press, 1953.

Wulf, Josef. *Heinrich Himmler.* Berlin: Arani Verlags-GmbH, 1960.

Wulff, Wilhelm. *Zodiac and Swastika.* New York: Coward, McCann & Geoghegan, 1973.

Wykes, Alan. *Himmler.* New York: Ballantine Books, 1972.

Zipfel, Friedrich. *Gestapo und Sicherheitsdienst.* Berlin: Arani Verlags-GmbH, 1960.

———. *Kirchenkampf in Deutschland (1933–1945).* Walther de Gruyter & Company, 1965.

Periodicals and Newspapers Cited

Berliner Morgenpost

Müchener Post

New York Times

Ostara: Briefbücherei der Blonden und Mannesrechtler

Schwarze Corps

Telegraph

Time

Völkisch Beobachter

Die Zeit

Index